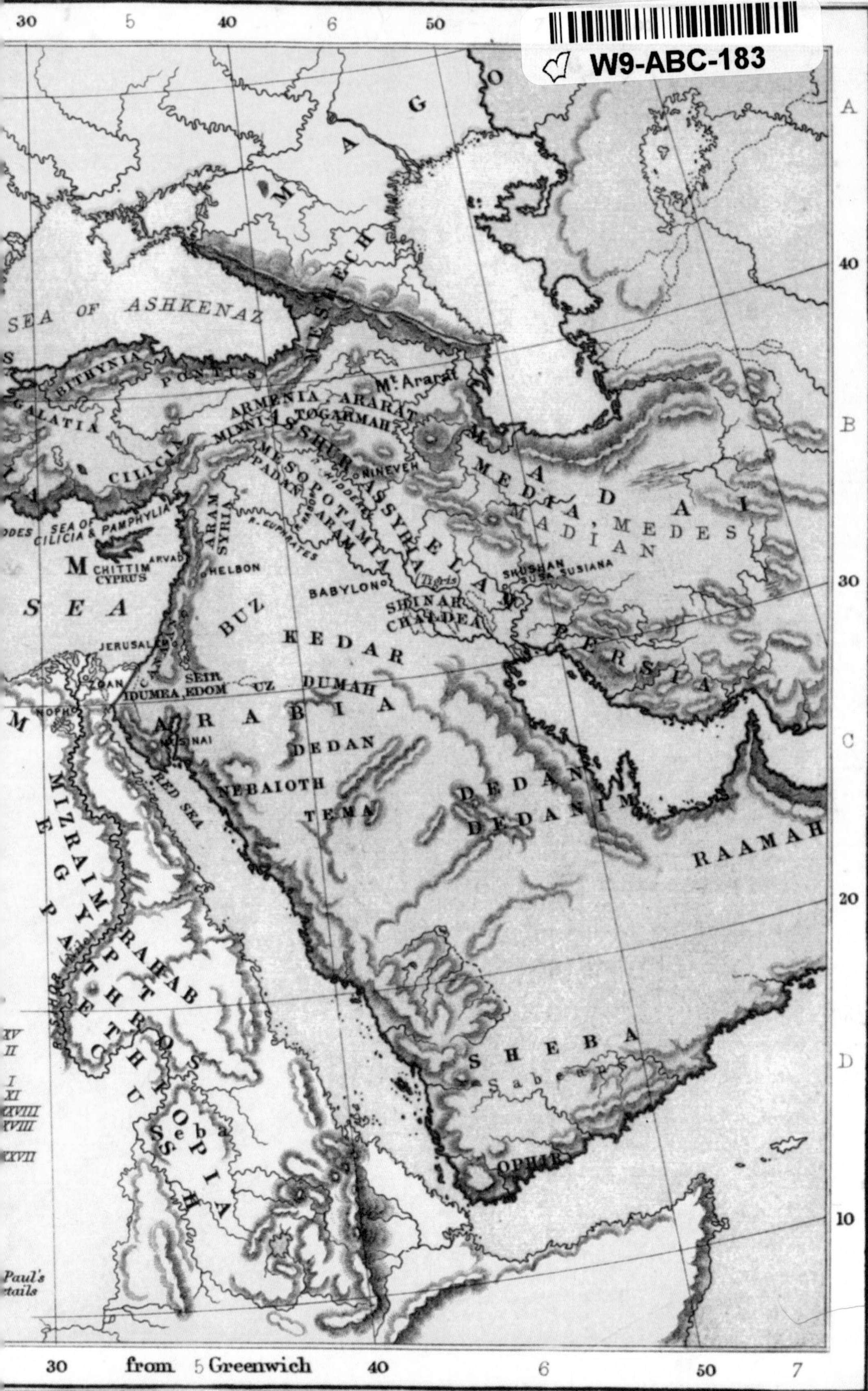
30
5
40
6
50
A
B
C
D
40
30
20
10
SEA OF ASHKENAZ
BITHYNIA
PONTUS
GALATIA
CILICIA
SEA OF CILICIA & PAMPHYLIA
CHITTIM
CYPRUS
ARVAD
ARAM SYRIA
HELBON
SEA
JERUSALEM
ZOAN
NOPH
SEIR
IDUMEA, EDOM
UZ
DUMAH
BUZ
KEDAR
ARABIA
SINAI
RED SEA
DEDAN
NEBAIOTH
TEMA
DEDAN
DEDANIM
RAAMAH
MIZRAIM
EGYPT
PATHROS
RAHAB
ETHIOPIA
CUSH
Seba
SHEBA
Sabeans
OPHIR
Mt. Ararat
ARMENIA
ARARAT
MINNI
TOGARMAH
ASSHUR
ASSYRIA
NINEVEH
MESOPOTAMIA
PADAN ARAM
R. EUPHRATES
BABYLON
Tigris
SHINAR
CHALDEA
ELAM
SHUSHAN
SUSA SUSIANA
MEDIA
MADAI
MADIAN, MEDES
PERSIA
MESHECH
MAGOG
30
from
5
Greenwich
40
6
50
7

THE COMPACT TIMELINE OF THE BIBLE

THE COMPACT TIMELINE OF THE BIBLE

SAMUEL T. JORDAN

METRO BOOKS
NEW YORK

This 2008 edition published by Metro Books,
by arrangement with Third Millennium Press Ltd.
Reprinted 2010

Designed and produced by
DAG Publications Ltd., London.

Metro Books
122 Fifth Avenue, New York, NY 10011

ISBN: 978-1-4351-1154-7

Printed and bound in Thailand.

10 9 8 7 6 5 4 3 2

Title page: *"The day following Jesus would go forth into Galilee, and findeth Philip, and saith unto him, Follow me. Now Philip was of Bethsaida, the city of Andrew and Peter. Philip findeth Nathanael, and saith unto him, We have found him, of whom Moses in the law, and the prophets, did write, Jesus of Nazareth, the son of Joseph." (John 1:43–45)*

CONTENTS

THE BIBLICAL DATING SYSTEM

"The poor world is almost six thousand years old." — Rosalind,
in William Shakespeare's *As You Like It*, Act IV, Scene 1 (1598–1600)

The dating system used in this book takes as its starting-point the traditional chronology of the Bible used and accepted for many hundreds of years. Until the end of the nineteenth century it was generally believed that the Earth was some 6,000 years old, a key sentence in interpreting the days of Creation being that set forth by the apostle Peter, who wrote: "But, beloved, be not ignorant of this one thing, that one day is with the Lord as a thousand years, and a thousand years as one day." *(2 Peter 3:8)* This was seen as 4,000 years before Christ; and a duration of 2,000 after.

The chronology was calculated by Archbishop James Ussher, Bishop of Armagh and Primate of All Ireland, a theologian of great repute in the seventeenth century (his contemporary reputation being evidenced by the fact that he was give a state funeral on the orders of Oliver Cromwell). His famous work, *Annales veteris testamenti, a prima mundi origine deducti* (*Annals of the Old Testament, deduced from the first origins of the world*) was published in two volumes in 1650 and 1654, and presented a chronological interpretation of Biblical events that won general acceptance. The publisher Thomas Guy (1644–1724), founder of the famous Guy's Hospital in London, first began incorporating the Ussher chronology in his Bibles in 1675, and in 1701 the Church of England also adopted Ussher's framework for the Authorized Version (King James). Thus for centuries the Ussher chronology has been the accepted, traditional timeline of the Bible, used in the famous *Schofield Bible* of 1917 and featuring as recently as the 1970s in many *Gideon Bibles*. In the 1890s, Professor Edward Hull, Director of the Geological Survey of Ireland and Professor at the Royal College of Science, Dublin, based his famous graphic *Timechart History of the World* upon Ussher's chronology.

Archbishop James Ussher
(1581–1656)

Ussher's method of calculating the date of Creation and of the other events narrated in the Bible was to begin with known dates in Greek and Roman history, then to work backwards adding together the ages of the patriarchs and kings, back to Adam and Eve. His conclusion, taking account of the seasonal equinoxes (bearing in mind the ripeness of the fruit in the Garden of Eden), was that the Earth was created on the night preceding October 23, 4004 BC. Others had attempted this calculation before – dating back to the medieval English historian Bede, and including the famous seventeenth century scientists Johannes Kepler (1571–1630) and Sir Isaac Newton (1643–1727) – and all identified a date very close to Ussher's. But Ussher's chronology was perceived to be accurate and won general acceptance.

It is a testimony to Ussher's dating that it has withstood so well the claims of geological and other scientific discoveries in the nineteenth and twentieth centuries. Indeed, it is still regarded as a valuable framework, even when considered in relative rather than absolute terms.

The chronology of the New Testament, meanwhile, has been taken from a harmonization of the accounts given in the Gospels of Matthew, Mark, Luke and John.

THE OLD TESTAMENT

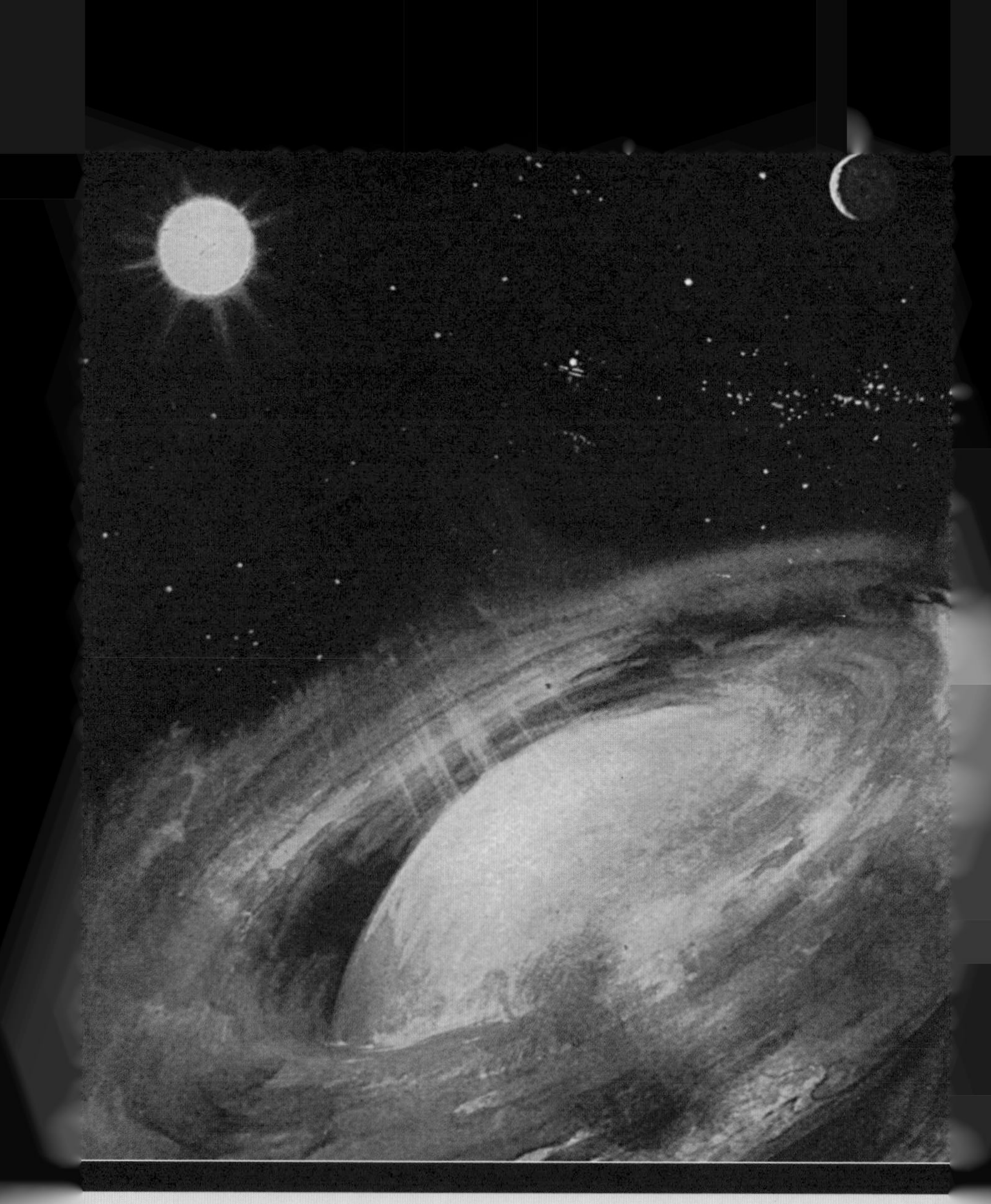

1: In the beginning God created the heaven and the earth. 2: And the earth was without form, and void; and darkness was upon the face of the deep. And the Spirit of God moved upon the face of the waters. 3: And God said, Let there be light: and there was light. 4: And God saw the light, that it was good: and God divided the light from the darkness. 5: And God called the light Day, and the darkness he called Night. And the evening and the morning were the first day. 6: And God said, Let there be a firmament in the midst of the waters, and let it divide the waters from the waters. 7: And God made the firmament, and divided the waters which were under the firmament from the waters which were above the firmament: and it was so. 8: And God called the firmament Heaven. And the evening and the morning were the second day. 9: And God said, Let the waters under the heaven be gathered together unto one place, and let the dry land appear: and it was so. 10: And God called the dry land Earth; and the gathering together of the waters called he Seas: and God saw that it was good. *—Genesis 1:1–10*

4004 God, having in the beginning created the Heaven and the Earth, separated the light from the darkness on the first day.

On the second day, he created the firmament, and divided the waters which were under the firmament from those which were above it.

On the third day, he divided the land from the seas; he also commanded the Earth to bring forth grass, herbs, and trees.

On the fourth day, he created the sun, the moon, and the stars.

Left: God creates all living things.

Right: He creates man in his own image.

On the fifth day, he created fishes and birds.
On the sixth day, he created beasts and reptiles; formed man after his own image and likeness, and blessed all his creatures.
On the seventh day, God rested from all his work, and sanctified that day.

11: And God said, Let the earth bring forth grass, the herb yielding seed, and the fruit tree yielding fruit after his kind, whose seed is in itself, upon the earth: and it was so. 12: And the earth brought forth grass, and herb yielding seed after his kind, and the tree yielding fruit, whose seed was in itself, after his kind: and God saw that it was good. 13: And the evening and the morning were the third day. 14: And God said, Let there be lights in the firmament of the heaven to divide the day from the night; and let them be for signs, and for seasons, and for days, and years: 15: And let them be for lights in the firmament of the heaven to give light upon the earth: and it was so. 16: And God made two great lights; the greater light to rule the day, and the lesser light to rule the night: he made the stars also. 17: And God set them in the firmament of the heaven to give light upon the earth, 18: And to rule over the day and over the night, and to divide the light from the darkness: and God saw that it was good. 19: And the evening and the morning were the fourth day. 20: And God said, Let the waters bring forth abundantly the moving creature that hath life, and fowl that may fly above the earth in the open firmament of heaven. 21: And God created great whales, and every living creature that moveth, which the waters brought forth abundantly, after their kind, and every winged fowl after his kind: and God saw that it was good. 22: And God blessed them, saying, Be fruitful, and multiply, and fill the waters in the seas, and let fowl multiply in the earth. 23: And the evening and the morning were the fifth day. 24: And God said, Let the earth bring forth the living creature after his kind, cattle, and creeping thing, and beast of the earth after his kind: and it was so. 25: And God made the beast of the earth after his kind, and cattle after their kind, and every thing that creepeth upon the earth after his kind: and God saw that it was good. 26: And God said, Let us make man in our image, after our likeness: and let them have dominion over the fish of the sea, and over the fowl of the air, and over the cattle, and over all the earth, and over every creeping thing that creepeth upon the earth. 27: So God created man in his own image, in the image of God created he him; male and female created he them. 28: And God blessed them, and God said unto them, Be fruitful, and multiply, and replenish the earth, and subdue it: and have dominion over the fish of the sea, and over the fowl of the air, and over every living thing that moveth upon the earth. 29: And God said, Behold, I have given you every herb bearing seed, which is upon the face of all the earth, and every tree, in the which is the fruit of a tree yielding seed; to you it shall be for meat. 30: And to every beast of the earth, and to every fowl of the air, and to every thing that creepeth upon the earth, wherein there is life, I have given every green herb for meat: and it was so. 31: And God saw every thing that he had made, and, behold, it was very good. And the evening and the morning were the sixth day. —*Genesis 1:11–31*

1. Thus the heavens and the earth were finished, and all the host of them. 2: And on the seventh day God ended his work which he had made; and he rested on the seventh day from all his work which he had made. 3: And God blessed the seventh day, and sanctified it: because that in it he had rested from all his work which God created and made. —*Genesis 2:1–3*

The Garden of Eden and The Fall

7: And the Lord God formed man of the dust of the ground, and breathed into his nostrils the breath of life; and man became a living soul. 8: And the Lord God planted a garden eastward in Eden; and there he put the man whom he had formed. 9: And out of the ground made the Lord God to grow every tree that is pleasant to the sight, and good for food; the tree of life also in the midst of the garden, and the tree of knowledge of good and evil ... 15: And the Lord God took the man, and put him into the garden of Eden to dress it and to keep it. 16: And the Lord God commanded the man, saying, Of every tree of the garden thou mayest freely eat: 17: But of the tree of the knowledge of good and evil, thou shalt not eat of it: for in the day that thou eatest thereof thou shalt surely die. 18: And the Lord God said, It is not good that the man should be alone; I will make him an help meet for him. 19: And out of the ground the Lord God formed every beast of the field, and every fowl of the air; and brought them unto Adam to see what he would call them: and whatsoever Adam called every living creature, that was the name thereof. 20: And Adam gave names to all cattle, and to the fowl of the air, and to every beast of the field; but for Adam there was not found an help meet for him. 21: And the Lord God caused a deep sleep to fall upon Adam and he slept: and he took one of his ribs, and closed up the flesh instead thereof; 22: And the rib, which the Lord God had taken from man, made he a woman, and brought her unto the man. 23: And Adam said, This is now bone of my bones, and flesh of my flesh: she shall be called Woman, because she was taken out of Man. 24: Therefore shall a man leave his father and his mother, and shall cleave unto his wife: and they shall be one flesh. 25: And they were both naked, the man and his wife, and were not ashamed.

—Genesis 2:7–25

1: Now the serpent was more subtil than any beast of the field which the Lord God had made. And he said unto the woman, Yea, hath God said, Ye shall not eat of every tree of the garden? 2: And the woman said unto the serpent, We may eat of the fruit of the trees of the garden: 3: But of the fruit of the tree which is in the midst of the garden, God hath said, Ye shall not eat of it, neither shall ye touch it, lest ye die. 4: And the serpent said unto the woman, Ye shall not surely die: 5: For God doth know that in the day ye eat thereof, then your eyes shall be opened, and ye shall be as gods, knowing good and evil.

6: And when the woman saw that the tree was good for food, and that it was pleasant to the eyes, and a tree to be desired to make one wise, she took of the fruit thereof, and did eat, and gave also unto her husband with her; and he did eat. 7: And the eyes of them both were opened, and they knew that they were naked; and they sewed fig leaves together, and made themselves aprons. 8: And they heard the voice of the Lord God walking in the garden in the cool of the day: and Adam and his wife hid themselves from the presence of the Lord God amongst the trees of the garden. 9: And the Lord God called unto Adam, and said unto him, Where art thou? 10: And he said, I heard thy voice in the garden, and I was afraid, because I was naked; and I hid myself. 11: And he said, Who told thee that thou wast naked? Hast thou eaten of the tree, whereof I commanded thee that thou shouldest not eat? 12: And the man said, The woman whom thou gavest to be with me, she gave me of the tree, and I did eat. 13: And the Lord God said unto the woman, What is this that thou hast done? And the woman said, The serpent beguiled me, and I did eat. 14: And the Lord God said unto the serpent, Because thou hast done this, thou art cursed above all cattle, and above every beast of the field; upon thy belly shalt thou go, and dust shalt thou eat all the days of thy life ... 16: Unto the woman he said, I will greatly multiply thy sorrow and thy conception; in sorrow thou shalt bring forth children; and thy desire shall be to thy husband, and he shall rule over thee. 17: And unto Adam he said, Because thou hast hearkened unto the voice of thy wife, and hast eaten of the tree, of which I commanded thee, saying, Thou shalt not eat of it: cursed is the ground for thy sake; in sorrow shalt thou eat of it all the days of thy life; 18: Thorns also and thistles shall it bring forth to thee; and thou shalt eat the herb of the field; 19: In the sweat of thy face shalt thou eat bread, till thou return unto the ground; for out of it wast thou taken: for dust thou art, and unto dust shalt thou return ... 22: And the Lord God said, Behold, the man is become as one of us, to know good and evil: and now, lest he put forth his hand, and take also of the tree of life, and eat, and live for ever: 23: Therefore the Lord God sent him forth from the garden of Eden, to till the ground from whence he was taken. 24: So he drove out the man; and he placed at the east of the garden of Eden Cherubims, and a flaming sword which turned every way, to keep the way of the tree of life.

—Genesis 3:1–24

The first man, named Adam, was placed in a garden in Eden, with Eve, his wife: there they ate the fruit of the tree of the knowledge of good and evil, against the Lord's command; for which they were expelled from the garden, and became subject to diseases and death; but received promises of mercy through a Redeemer.

Left: *Adam and Eve are expelled from the Garden of Eden.*

Below: *Cherubim with flaming swords guard the Garden of Eden; Adam and Eve must make their own way in the rest of the world.*

Above: *Cain and Abel make their sacrifices to the Lord.*

Adam and Eve had two sons, Cain, a tiller of the land who grew crops, and Abel, a shepherd. Since, after being expelled from the Garden of Eden, Adam and Eve were unable to talk directly to God, they built an altar of stones and burned gifts to the Lord, praying for forgiveness of their sins. Cain offered the fruit of the ground; Abel the firstborn of his flock. But while God accepted Abel's sacrifice, he rejected Cain's.

Angry at this gross injustice, Cain killed his brother in a fit of fury, but this made things much worse for him. God cursed Cain henceforth to be a fugitive and a vagabond – and, in response to Cain's pleas that he would inevitably be killed, the Lord set a mark upon him and promised that whoever killed him would in turn suffer vengeance sevenfold. So Cain set out in despair to dwell in the land of Nod.

Adam and Eve had another child, Seth, among whose descendants was Enoch (the seventh generation from Adam and Eve), a good, pious man who spent his life in the fellowship of the Lord, "walking with God." Great-grandfather of Noah, he

4003 The birth of Cain, the first who was born of a woman; Abel is born soon after.
3875 Abel is murdered by Cain, because his sacrifice was more acceptable to God.
3874 Seth is born, whose offspring are called the children of God, by way of distinction from those of Cain, who are named the children of men.
3017 Enoch, who "walked with God," is translated to Heaven without tasting death.

Above: *His brother dead, Cain realizes that he must endure the wrath of the Lord.*

3: And in process of time it came to pass, that Cain brought of the fruit of the ground an offering unto the Lord 4: And Abel, he also brought of the firstlings of his flock and of the fat thereof. And the Lord had respect unto Abel and to his offering: 5: But unto Cain and to his offering he had not respect. And Cain was very wroth, and his countenance fell.
6: And the Lord said unto Cain, Why art thou wroth? and why is thy countenance fallen? 7: If thou
doest well, shalt thou not be accepted? and if thou doest not well, sin lieth at the door. And unto thee
shall be his desire, and thou shalt rule over him. 8: And Cain talked with Abel his brother: and it came
to pass, when they were in the field, that Cain rose up against Abel his brother, and slew him. 9: And
the Lord said unto Cain, Where is Abel thy brother? And he said, I know not: Am I my brother's keep-
er? 10: And he said, What hast thou done? the voice of thy brother's blood crieth unto me from the
ground. 11: And now art thou cursed from the earth, which hath opened her mouth to receive thy
brother's blood from thy hand; 12: When thou tillest the ground, it shall not henceforth yield unto
thee her strength; a fugitive and a vagabond shalt thou be in the earth. 13: And Cain said unto the
Lord, My punishment is greater than I can bear. 14: Behold, thou hast driven me out this day from
the face of the earth; and from thy face shall I be hid; and I shall be a fugitive and a vagabond in the
earth; and it shall come to pass, that every one that findeth me shall slay me. 15: And the Lord said
unto him, Therefore whosoever slayeth Cain, vengeance shall be taken on him sevenfold. And the
Lord set a mark upon Cain, lest any finding him should kill him. 16: And Cain went out from the presence of the Lord, and dwelt in the land of Nod, on the east of Eden.

— *Genesis 4:3–16*

prophesied that God would bring all sinners to judgment, and, like Elijah, he did not die but was taken up to Heaven by God.

Right: *Enoch is taken up to Heaven.*

THE EARLY PATRIARCHS

3874 BC Seth	*2348 BC The Flood*
3769 BC Enos	2346 BC Arphaxad
3679 BC Cainan	2311 BC Salah
3609 BC Mahalaleel	2281 BC Eber
3544 BC Jared	2247 BC Peleg
3382 BC Enoch	2217 BC Reu
3317 BC Methuselah	2185 BC Serug
3130 BC Lamech	2156 BC Nahor
2948 BC Noah	2126 BC Terah
2448 BC Japheth	1996 BC Abram
2445 BC Shem	

Above: *The construction of the Ark.*

When the generations of Man multiplied and began to fill the Earth, God saw such wickedness among humanity that he repented creating man and determined to destroy all living things. But Noah, a righteous man, found grace in the eyes of the Lord, and God instructed him to build an Ark, telling him that He was about to bring such a flood upon the Earth that all flesh would perish.

However, God made a covenant with Noah, telling him to bring into the Ark his family and a male and a female of every sort of living thing that is unclean; and sevenfold of clean creatures and fowl of the air. These were to survive the deluge and repopulate the Earth afresh, which would thus be cleansed of the wickedness that had arisen. Noah constructed the Ark according to God's directions and embarked his family and the animals God ordained to be saved.

SPECIFICATIONS OF THE ARK	
Fabrication	Gopher wood
Length	300 cubits
Breadth	50 cubits
Height	30 cubits
Decks	3 with compartments
Roof	Set in from the hull by 1 cubit
Apertures	Window and door

2464 God informs Noah of the future flood, and commissions him to preach repentance, 120 years before the deluge.

12: And God looked upon the earth, and, behold, it was corrupt; for all flesh had corrupted his way upon the earth. 13: And God said unto Noah, The end of all flesh is come before me; for the earth is filled with violence through them; and, behold, I will destroy them with the earth. 14: Make thee an ark of gopher wood; rooms shalt thou make in the ark, and shalt pitch it within and without with pitch. 17: And, behold, I, even I, do bring a flood of waters upon the earth, to destroy all flesh, wherein is the breath of life, from under heaven; and every thing that is in the earth shall die. 18: But with thee will I establish my covenant; and thou shalt come into the ark, thou, and thy sons, and thy wife, and thy sons' wives with thee. 19: And of every living thing of all flesh, two of every sort shalt thou bring into the ark, to keep them alive with thee; they shall be male and female. 20: Of fowls after their kind, and of cattle after their kind, of every creeping thing of the earth after his kind, two of every sort shall come unto thee, to keep them alive.

— *Genesis, 6:12–14, 17–20*

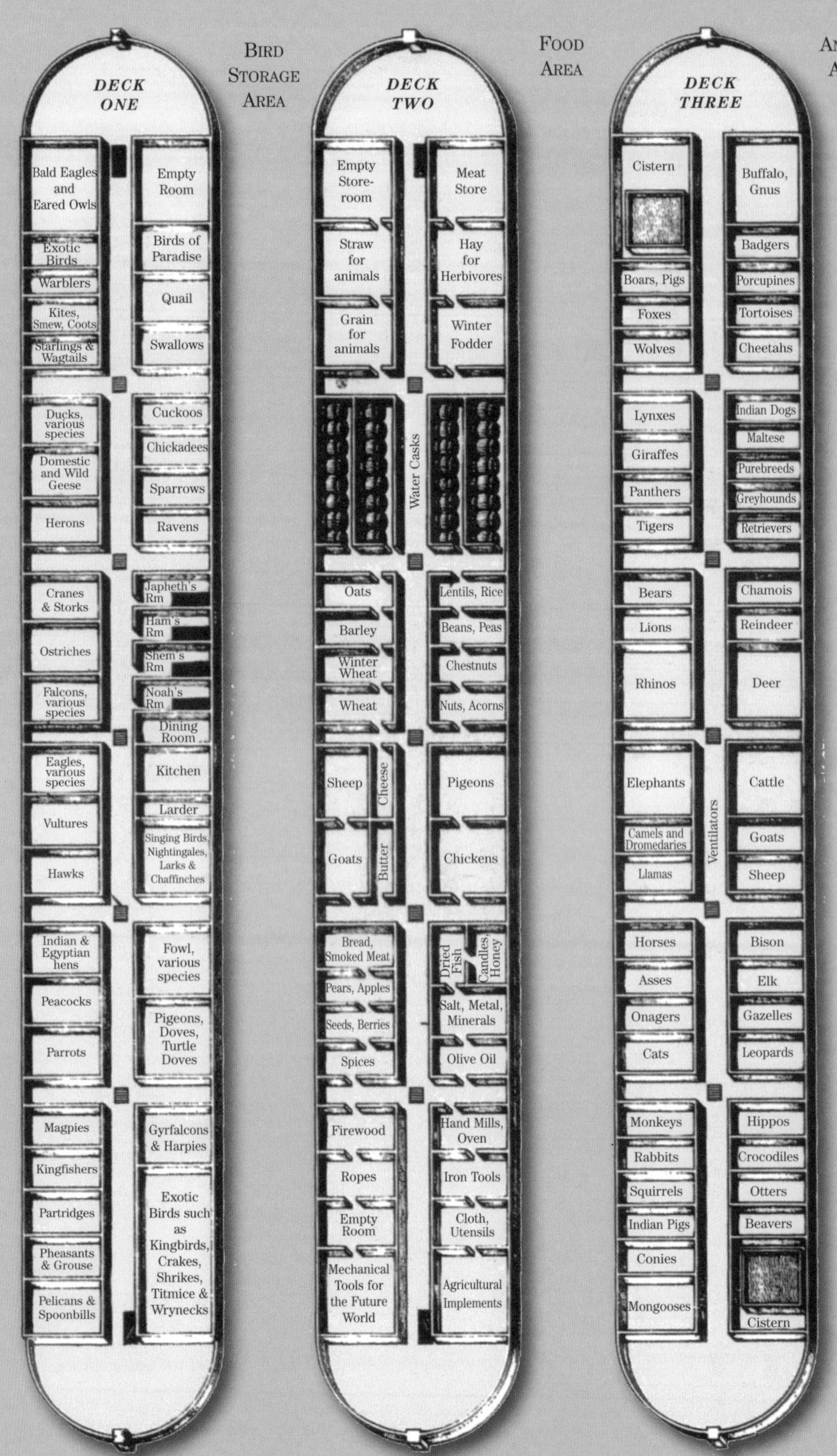

Bird Storage Area
Food Area
Anim
Are
DECK ONE
Bald Eagles and Eared Owls
Empty Room
Exotic Birds
Birds of Paradise
Warblers
Quail
Kites, Smew, Coots
Swallows
Starlings & Wagtails
Ducks, various species
Cuckoos
Chickadees
Domestic and Wild Geese
Sparrows
Herons
Ravens
Cranes & Storks
Japheth's Rm
Ham's Rm
Ostriches
Shem's Rm
Falcons, various species
Noah's Rm
Dining Room
Eagles, various species
Kitchen
Larder
Vultures
Singing Birds, Nightingales, Larks & Chaffinches
Hawks
Indian & Egyptian hens
Fowl, various species
Peacocks
Pigeons, Doves, Turtle Doves
Parrots
Magpies
Gyrfalcons & Harpies
Kingfishers
Exotic Birds such as Kingbirds, Crakes, Shrikes, Titmice & Wrynecks
Partridges
Pheasants & Grouse
Pelicans & Spoonbills
DECK TWO
Empty Store-room
Meat Store
Straw for animals
Hay for Herbivores
Grain for animals
Winter Fodder
Water Casks
Oats
Lentils, Rice
Barley
Beans, Peas
Winter Wheat
Chestnuts
Wheat
Nuts, Acorns
Sheep
Cheese
Pigeons
Goats
Butter
Chickens
Bread, Smoked Meat
Dried Fish
Candles, Honey
Pears, Apples
Salt, Metal, Minerals
Seeds, Berries
Spices
Olive Oil
Firewood
Hand Mills, Oven
Ropes
Iron Tools
Empty Room
Cloth, Utensils
Mechanical Tools for the Future World
Agricultural Implements
DECK THREE
Cistern
Buffalo, Gnus
Badgers
Boars, Pigs
Porcupines
Foxes
Tortoises
Wolves
Cheetahs
Lynxes
Indian Dogs
Maltese
Giraffes
Purebreeds
Panthers
Greyhounds
Tigers
Retrievers
Bears
Chamois
Lions
Reindeer
Rhinos
Deer
Elephants
Cattle
Ventilators
Camels and Dromedaries
Goats
Llamas
Sheep
Horses
Bison
Asses
Elk
Onagers
Gazelles
Cats
Leopards
Monkeys
Hippos
Rabbits
Crocodiles
Squirrels
Otters
Indian Pigs
Beavers
Conies
Mongooses
Cistern

Left: *An early reconstruction of the deck plan of the Ark based upon measurements in Genesis by the 17th-century scholar Kircher.*

Below: *The animals enter the Ark.*

2348 God commands Noah to prepare to enter the ark. Noah enters the Ark with his wife, his sons, and their wives.

1: And the Lord said unto Noah, Come thou and all thy house into the ark; for thee have I seen righteous before me in this generation. 2: Of every clean beast thou shalt take to thee by sevens, the male and his female: and of beasts that are not clean by two, the male and his female. 3: Of fowls also of the air by sevens, the male and the female; to keep seed alive upon the face of all the earth. 4: For yet seven days, and I will cause it to rain upon the earth forty days and forty nights; and every living substance that I have made will I destroy from off the face of the earth. 5: And Noah did according unto all that the Lord commanded him. 6: And Noah was six hundred years old when the flood of waters was upon the earth. 7: And Noah went in, and his sons, and his wife, and his sons' wives with him, into the ark, because of the waters of the flood. 8: Of clean beasts, and of beasts that are not clean, and of fowls, and of every thing that creepeth upon the earth, 9: There went in two and two unto Noah into the ark, the male and the female, as God had commanded Noah. 10: And it came to pass after seven days, that the waters of the flood were upon the earth. 11: In the six hundredth year of Noah's life, in the second month, the seventeenth day of the month, the same day were all the fountains of the great deep broken up, and the windows of heaven were opened. 12: And the rain was upon the earth forty days and forty nights. 13: In the selfsame day entered Noah, and Shem, and Ham, and Japheth, the sons of Noah, and Noah's wife, and the three wives of his sons with them, into the ark; 14: They, and every beast after his kind, and all the cattle after their kind, and every creeping thing that creepeth upon the earth after his kind, and every fowl after his kind, every bird of every sort. 15: And they went in unto Noah into the ark, two and two of all flesh, wherein is the breath of life. 16: And they that went in, went in male and female of all flesh, as God had commanded him: and the Lord shut him in. 17: And the flood was forty days upon the earth; and the waters increased, and bare up the ark, and it was lift up above the earth. —*Genesis 7:1–17*

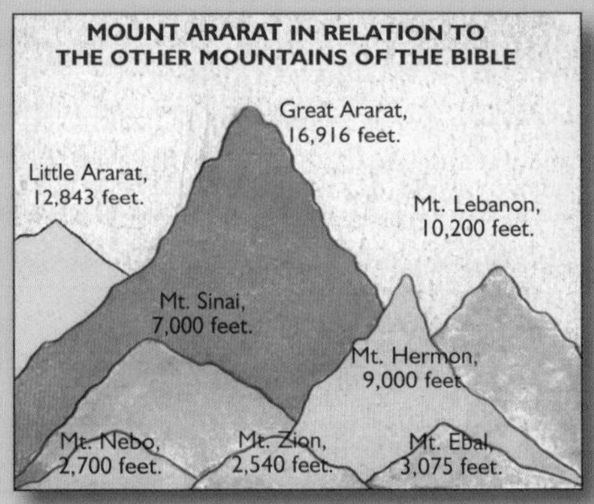
MOUNT ARARAT IN RELATION TO THE OTHER MOUNTAINS OF THE BIBLE
Great Ararat, 16,916 feet.
Little Ararat, 12,843 feet.
Mt. Lebanon, 10,200 feet.
Mt. Sinai, 7,000 feet.
Mt. Hermon, 9,000 feet.
Mt. Nebo, 2,700 feet.
Mt. Zion, 2,540 feet.
Mt. Ebal, 3,075 feet.

Then came the flood, rain that lasted 40 days and 40 nights, until the waters covered the entire Earth and even the mountains. For 150 days Noah and the Ark were afloat before God caused the waters to recede. Noah sent out a raven and then a dove, but neither could find land; after another seven days, when Noah sent forth the dove, it returned with an olive leaf, demonstrating the existence of dry land. The face of the Earth had become dry, and the Ark came to rest upon Mount Ararat.

Above left: *The dove's first flight proves fruitless.*

Below left: *Next time Noah sends out the dove it returns bearing an olive twig.*

Rain on the Earth for forty days.
The waters continue on the Earth 150 days.
The Ark rests on the mountain of Ararat.
Forty days afterwards, Noah sends forth the raven.
Seven days afterwards, Noah sends out the dove, and it returns.
Seven days afterwards he sends it out again; it returns in the evening, bringing an olive branch in its bill.
Seven days afterwards he sends it forth again; it returns no more.

17: And the flood was forty days upon the earth; and the waters increased, and bare up the ark, and it was lift up above the earth. 18: And the waters prevailed, and were increased greatly upon the earth; and the ark went upon the face of the waters. 19: And the waters prevailed exceedingly upon the earth; and all the high hills, that were under the whole heaven, were covered. 20: Fifteen cubits upward did the waters prevail; and the mountains were covered. 21: And all flesh died that moved upon the earth, both of fowl, and of cattle, and of beast, and of every creeping thing that creepeth upon the earth, and every man: 22: All in whose nostrils was the breath of life, of all that was in the dry land, died. 23: And every living substance was destroyed which was upon the face of the ground, both man, and cattle, and the creeping things, and the fowl of the heaven; and they were destroyed from the earth: and Noah only remained alive, and they that were with him in the ark. 24: And the waters prevailed upon the earth an hundred and fifty days. *—Genesis 7:17–24*

1: And God remembered Noah, and every living thing, and all the cattle that was with him in the ark: and God made a wind to pass over the earth, and the waters asswaged; 2: The fountains also of the deep and the windows of heaven were stopped, and the rain from heaven was restrained; 3: And the waters returned from off the earth continually: and after the end of the hundred and fifty days the waters were abated. 4: And the ark rested in the seventh month, on the seventeenth day of the month, upon the mountains of Ararat. 5: And the waters decreased continually until the tenth month: in the tenth month, on the first day of the month, were the tops of the mountains seen. 6: And it came to pass at the end of forty days, that Noah opened the window of the ark which he had made: 7: And he sent forth a raven, which went forth to and fro, until the waters were dried up from off the earth. 8: Also he sent forth a dove from him, to see if the waters were abated from off the face of the ground; 9: But the dove found no rest for the sole of her foot, and she returned unto him into the ark, for the waters were on the face of the whole earth: then he put forth his hand, and took her, and pulled her in unto him into the ark. 10: And he stayed yet other seven days; and again he sent forth the dove out of the ark; 11: And the dove came in to him in the evening; and, lo, in her mouth was an olive leaf pluckt off: so Noah knew that the waters were abated from off the earth. 12: And he stayed yet other seven days; and sent forth the dove; which returned not again unto him any more. 13: And it came to pass in the six hundredth and first year, in the first month, the first day of the month, the waters were dried up from off the earth: and Noah removed the covering of the ark, and looked, and, behold, the face of the ground was dry. 14: And in the second month, on the seven and twentieth day of the month, was the earth dried. *—Genesis 8:1–14*

Above: *The animals leave the Ark.*

2347 Noah being now 601 years old, takes off the roof of the Ark.
Noah quits the Ark.
He offers sacrifices of thanksgiving.
God permits man the use of flesh as food and sends a rainbow as a pledge that he will send no more universal deluge.

Left: *Noah offers burnt offerings to the Lord; the rainbow appears as a symbol of God's Covenant with the Earth and its inhabitants.*

15: And God spake unto Noah, saying, 16: Go forth of the ark, thou, and thy wife, and thy sons, and thy sons' wives with thee. 17: Bring forth with thee every living thing that is with thee, of all flesh, both of fowl, and of cattle, and of every creeping thing that creepeth upon the earth; that they may breed abundantly in the earth, and be fruitful, and multiply upon the earth. 18: And Noah went forth, and his sons, and his wife, and his sons' wives with him: 19: Every beast, every creeping thing, and every fowl, and whatsoever creepeth upon the earth, after their kinds, went forth out of the ark. 20: And Noah builded an altar unto the Lord; and took of every clean beast, and of every clean fowl, and offered burnt offerings on the altar. 21: And the Lord smelled a sweet savour; and the Lord said in his heart, I will not again curse the ground any more for man's sake; for the imagination of man's heart is evil from his youth; neither will I again smite any more every thing living, as I have done. 22: While the earth remaineth, seedtime and harvest, and cold and heat, and summer and winter, and day and night shall not cease. — *Genesis 8:15–22*

1: And God blessed Noah and his sons, and said unto them, Be fruitful, and multiply, and replenish the earth. 2: And the fear of you and the dread of you shall be upon every beast of the earth, and upon every fowl of the air, upon all that moveth upon the earth, and upon all the fishes of the sea; into your hand are they delivered. 3: Every moving thing that liveth shall be meat for you; even as the green herb have I given you all things. 8: And God spake unto Noah, and to his sons with him, saying, 9: And I, behold, I establish my covenant with you, and with your seed after you; 10: And with every living creature that is with you, of the fowl, of the cattle, and of every beast of the earth with you; from all that go out of the ark, to every beast of the earth. 11: And I will establish my covenant with you; neither shall all flesh be cut off any more by the waters of a flood; neither shall there any more be a flood to destroy the earth. 12: And God said, This is the token of the covenant which I make between me and you and every living creature that is with you, for perpetual generations: 13: I do set my bow in the cloud, and it shall be for a token of a covenant between me and the earth. 14: And it shall come to pass, when I bring a cloud over the earth, that the bow shall be seen in the cloud: 15: And I will remember my covenant, which is between me and you and every living creature of all flesh; and the waters shall no more become a flood to destroy all flesh. 16: And the bow shall be in the cloud; and I will look upon it, that I may remember the everlasting covenant between God and every living creature of all flesh that is upon the earth. 17: And God said unto Noah, This is the token of the covenant, which I have established between me and all flesh that is upon the earth.
— *Genesis 9:1–17*

THE DESCENDANTS OF NOAH AND THE REPOPULATING OF THE EARTH
AS DEDUCED FROM THE BOOK OF GENESIS

JAPHETH Asia Minor, Caucasus, Europe	**Gomer** Russians, Gauls, Germans, Britons	**Magog** Scythians
HAM Arabia, Egypt, North Africa	**Cush** Ethiopians	**Mizraim** Egyptians
SHEM Middle East	**Elam** Elamites (Persians)	**Asshur** Assyrians

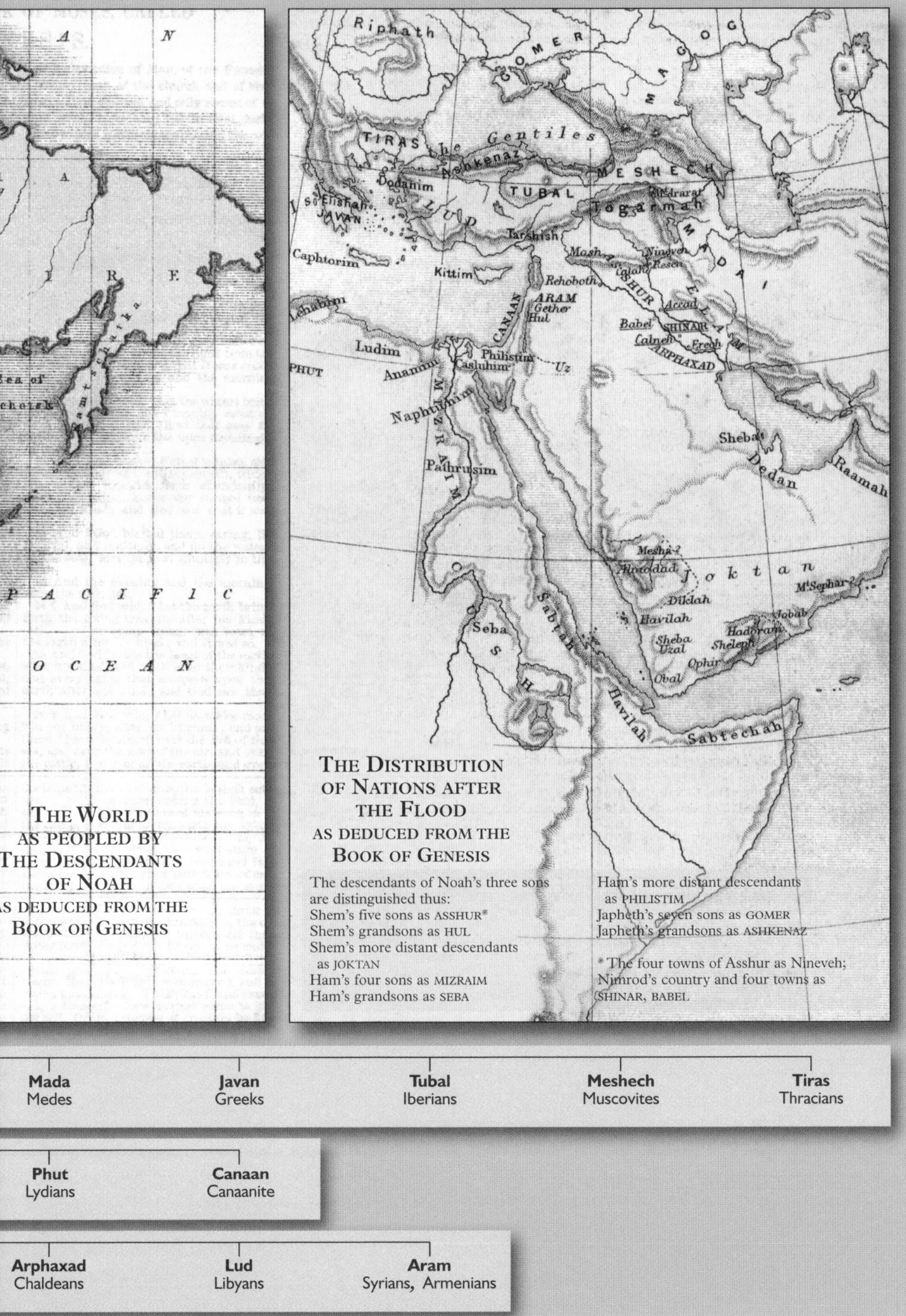
THE WORLD
AS PEOPLED BY
THE DESCENDANTS
OF NOAH
AS DEDUCED FROM THE
BOOK OF GENESIS
PACIFIC
OCEAN
THE DISTRIBUTION
OF NATIONS AFTER
THE FLOOD
AS DEDUCED FROM THE
BOOK OF GENESIS
The descendants of Noah's three sons are distinguished thus:
Shem's five sons as ASSHUR*
Shem's grandsons as HUL
Shem's more distant descendants as JOKTAN
Ham's four sons as MIZRAIM
Ham's grandsons as SEBA
Ham's more distant descendants as PHILISTIM
Japheth's seven sons as GOMER
Japheth's grandsons as ASHKENAZ
* The four towns of Asshur as Nineveh;
Nimrod's country and four towns as SHINAR, BABEL
Riphath
GOMER
MAGOG
TIRAS
the Gentiles
Ashkenaz
MESHECH
Dodanim
TUBAL
Elishah
JAVAN
LUD
Togarmah
Tarshish
Caphtorim
Kittim
Rehoboth
ARAM
Gether
Hul
CANAAN
Babel
SHINAR
Calneh
Erech
ARPHAXAD
Accad
Ludim
PHUT
Anamim
Philistim
Casluhim
Uz
Naphtuhim
MIZRAIM
Pathrusim
Sheba
Dedan
Raamah
Joktan
Hazarmaveth
Diklah
Havilah
Sheba
Uzal
Hadoram
Sheleph
Ophir
Obal
Jobab
Seba
Sabtah
CUSH
Havilah
Sabtechah
Mada
Medes
Javan
Greeks
Tubal
Iberians
Meshech
Muscovites
Tiras
Thracians
Phut
Lydians
Canaan
Canaanite
Arphaxad
Chaldeans
Lud
Libyans
Aram
Syrians, Armenians

From the location of the Ark, the descendants of Noah's sons moved and, as their numbers increased, began to spread out. Their migration took them toward the site of what would one day be Babylon, or Babel, and here they decided to build a great Tower, to establish their reputations before contact was lost between them, and to reach up to Heaven. Since they could find no suitable stone in the area, they made bricks, and instead of mortar used bitumen. The Tower grew but was never completed, for God saw what they were doing. This was a deviation from the way he had planned for man, so instead of simply throwing down their tower, he caused them to speak many different languages, so that they could not all understand one another. Work on the Tower was thrown into confusion and stopped. Meanwhile the different individuals who found that they spoke the same tongue formed groups and began to separate themselves from the rest. Thus mankind spread over the Earth.

2247 The Tower of Babel is built about this time in the valley of Shinar, but God miraculously confounds their language, and thus disperses them into different nations.

1: And the whole earth was of one language, and of one speech. 2: And it came to pass, as they journeyed from the east, that they found a plain in the land of Shinar; and they dwelt there. 3: And they said one to another, Go to, let us make brick, and burn them throughly. And they had brick for stone, and slime had they for morter. 4: And they said, Go to, let us build us a city and a tower, whose top may reach unto heaven; and let us make us a name, lest we be scattered abroad upon the face of the whole earth. 5: And the Lord came down to see the city and the tower, which the children of men builded. 6: And the Lord said, Behold, the people is one, and they have all one language; and this they begin to do: and now nothing will be restrained from them, which they have imagined to do. 7: Go to, let us go down, and there confound their language, that they may not understand one another's speech. 8: So the Lord scattered them abroad from thence upon the face of all the earth: and they left off to build the city. 9: Therefore is the name of it called Babel; because the Lord did there confound the language of all the earth: and from thence did the Lord scatter them abroad upon the face of all the earth.

— *Genesis 11:1–9*

Left: An impression of the Tower of Babel as it might have looked when completed.

Right: At work building the Tower.

In Ur of the Chaldees there dwelt a man called Abram, who was to become the first of the Patriarchs. God told him to move away from his kindred, promising that he would make a great nation from him. So Abram and his wife Sarai, with his nephew Lot and family, moved to Canaan. This land, God promised him, would belong to him and to his offspring. In a vision, God appeared to Abram and, indicating the stars above them, told him that his descendants were to number more than these. But, Abram asked God, how could this be so? He was childless, his wife barren. God reassured him that he would indeed have children and made a Covenant with him. He would have a son and a land in which to live; in return, Abram promised faithfully to serve the Lord. Henceforth, God told him, he would be named Abraham, "Father of Many Nations"; and his wife would be called Sarah; and all the males of God's chosen must be circumcised.

1996 Abram, the Patriarch, born at Ur, in Chaldaea.
1927 Sarah, wife to Abram, born.
1925 Chedorlaomer, king of Elam, subdues the five kings of Sodom, Gomorrah, Adama, Seboim, and Zoar.
1921 Abram called by God. He travels to Charre, or Haran, in Mesopotamia. His father Terah dies there, aged 205 years.
1921 Second calling of Abram from Haran. God makes a Covenant with him and he goes into Canaan with Sarah, his wife, and nephew Lot, and dwells at Sichem.

Left: *Abram sets out from Ur.*

Above: *The journey to Canaan.*

Right: *God likens the multitudes of Abram's descendants to the stars above him.*

1: Now the Lord had said unto Abram, Get thee out of thy country, and from thy kindred, and from thy father's house, unto a land that I will shew thee: 2: And I will make of thee a great nation, and I will bless thee, and make thy name great; and thou shalt be a blessing: 3: And I will bless them that bless thee, and curse him that curseth thee: and in thee shall all families of the earth be blessed. 4: So Abram departed, as the Lord had spoken unto him; and Lot went with him: and Abram was seventy and five years old when he departed out of Haran. 5: And Abram took Sarai his wife, and Lot his brother's son, and all their substance that they had gathered, and the souls that they had gotten in Haran; and they went forth to go into the land of Canaan; and into the land of Canaan they came. 6: And Abram passed through the land unto the place of Sichem, unto the plain of Moreh. And the Canaanite was then in the land. 7: And the Lord appeared unto Abram, and said, Unto thy seed will I give this land: and there builded he an altar unto the Lord, who appeared unto him. — *Genesis 12: 1–7*

Above: *Abraham and Lot separate, the former to Hebron, Lot to Sodom.*

When, forced by famine, Abraham took Sarah to Egypt, he was fearful that her beauty would cause jealousy and result in his death; so he persuaded her to make out that she was his sister. Her beauty brought the attention of the Pharaoh, and they were treated well until the Pharaoh's household became ill, and the newcomers were blamed and sent away.

When they returned, Abraham's fortunes improved, and he became so wealthy, with much livestock, that the time came for Lot to part company with his flocks, moving down to the plain of Jordan, while Abram stayed in Canaan.

Lot eventually settled not far from Sodom, a city fast gaining a reputation for vice and sin. On one occasion he became caught up in war between the coastal cities and was taken prisoner; but his uncle rescued him.

During a time of famine, Abraham and his family seek refuge in Egypt.
They return the next year and separate, Abraham going to Hebron, Lot to Sodom.
1912 Five kings rebelling against King Chedorlaomer of Elam are defeated by him. He plunders Sodom and carries off Lot captive. Abraham pursues and defeats Chedorlaomer, and rescues Lot. On his return, he receives the benediction of Melchizedek, king of Salem, the priest of the Most High God.

***Right:** The beauty of Sarah excites the admiration of the Egyptians.*

8: And there went out the king of Sodom, and the king of Gomorrah, and the king of Admah, and the king of Zeboiim, and the king of Bela (the same is Zoar;) and they joined battle with them in the vale of Siddim; 9: With Chedorlaomer the king of Elam, and with Tidal king of nations, and Amraphel king of Shinar, and Arioch king of Ellasar; four kings with five. 10: ... and the kings of Sodom and Gomorrah fled, and fell there; and they that remained fled to the mountain. 11: And they took all the goods of Sodom and Gomorrah, and all their victuals, and went their way. 12: And they took Lot, Abram's brother's son, who dwelt in Sodom, and his goods, and departed. 13: And there came one that had escaped, and told Abram the Hebrew; for he dwelt in the plain of Mamre the Amorite, brother of Eschol, and brother of Aner: and these were confederate with Abram. 14: And when Abram heard that his brother was taken captive, he armed his trained servants, born in his own house, three hundred and eighteen, and pursued them unto Dan. 15: And he divided himself against them, he and his servants, by night, and smote them, and pursued them unto Hobah, which is on the left hand of Damascus. 16: And he brought back all the goods, and also brought again his brother Lot, and his goods, and the women also, and the people. 17: And the king of Sodom went out to meet him after his return from the slaughter of Chedorlaomer, and of the kings that were with him, at the valley of Shaveh, which is the king's dale. 18: And Melchizedek king of Salem brought forth bread and wine: and he was the priest of the most high God. 19: And he blessed him, and said, Blessed be Abram of the most high God, possessor of heaven and earth: 20: And blessed be the most high God, which hath delivered thine enemies into thy hand. And he gave him tithes of all.

— Genesis 14: 8–20

Nearby were two cities, Sodom and Gomorrah, which were becoming dens of wickedness and vice. Seeing this, God determined to destroy them, but he set a test whereby they could be saved if only he could find fifty good men there. Abraham, realizing that his nephew Lot lived there and might be caught up in the destruction, appealed to God, who agreed to reduce his quota of virtuous men to ten. When God's angels entered Sodom Lot welcomed them, and, finding that he was the only good man there, they warned him that he must quickly leave the city, for it was about to be destroyed. But neither he nor his family must look back as they flee. So Lot, with his wife and daughters, departed in haste – but his wife did look back and was at once turned into a pillar of salt.

1: Now Sarai Abram's wife bare him no children: and she had an handmaid, an Egyptian, whose name was Hagar. 2: And Sarai said unto Abram, Behold now, the Lord hath restrained me from bearing: I pray thee, go in unto my maid; it may be that I may obtain children by her. And Abram hearkened to the voice of Sarai. 3: And Sarai Abram's wife took Hagar her maid the Egyptian, after Abram had dwelt ten years in the land of Canaan, and gave her to her husband Abram to be his wife. 4: And he went in unto Hagar, and she conceived: and when she saw that she had conceived ... 15: And Hagar bare Abram a son: and Abram called his son's name, which Hagar bare, Ishmael. 16: And Abram was fourscore and six years old, when Hagar bare Ishmael to Abram. — *Genesis 16: 1–4, 15–16*

1910 Ishmael is born to Abraham by Hagar.
1897 The Covenant is renewed by God with Abram, in memorial of which circumcision is instituted, and his name changed to Abraham.
The cities of Sodom and Gomorrah are destroyed for their wickedness by fire from Heaven. Lot, with his wife and two daughters, leave Sodom beforehand, being warned: but his wife, looking back, is turned into a pillar of salt.

Abraham and Sarah had a servant called Hagar, and since Sarah was barren, it was agreed that Abraham should father a child with Hagar; this child was named Ishmael. But God assured Abraham that Sarah would indeed bear him a child, and his name was Isaac.

***Left:** Following the agreement of God's Covenant, Abraham builds an altar.*

***Right:** The escape from Sodom and Gomorrah; but Lot's wife looks back and is turned into a pillar of salt.*

1: And when Abram was ninety years old and nine, the Lord appeared to Abram, and said unto him, I am the Almighty God; walk before me, and be thou perfect ... and thou shalt be a father of many nations. 5: Neither shall thy name any more be called Abram, but thy name shall be Abraham; for a father of many nations have I made thee. 6: And I will make thee exceeding fruitful, and I will make nations of thee, and kings shall come out of thee. 7: And I will establish my covenant between me and thee and thy seed after thee in their generations for an everlasting covenant, to be a God unto thee, and to thy seed after thee. 8: And I will give unto thee, and to thy seed after thee, the land wherein thou art a stranger, all the land of Canaan, for an everlasting possession; and I will be their God ... 19: And God said, Sarah thy wife shall bear thee a son indeed; and thou shalt call his name Isaac: and I will establish my covenant with him for an everlasting covenant, and with his seed after him. 20: And as for Ishmael, I have heard thee: Behold, I have blessed him, and will make him fruitful, and will multiply him exceedingly; twelve princes shall he beget, and I will make him a great nation. 21: But my covenant will I establish with Isaac, which Sarah shall bear unto thee at this set time in the next year. —*Genesis 17: 1–8, 19–21*

***Above:** Hagar and Ishmael in the wilderness.*

***Left:** Abraham prepares to sacrifice his son.*

1: And it came to pass after these things, that God did tempt Abraham, and said unto him ... Take now thy son, thine only son Isaac, whom thou lovest, and get thee into the land of Moriah; and offer him there for a burnt offering upon one of the mountains which I will tell thee of. 3: And Abraham rose up early in the morning, and saddled his ass, and took two of his young men with him, and Isaac his son, and clave the wood for the burnt offering, and rose up, and went unto the place of which God had told him ... 6: And Abraham took the wood of the burnt offering, and laid it upon Isaac his son; and he took the fire in his hand, and a knife; and they went both of them together ... 9: And they came to the place which God had told him of; and Abraham built an altar there, and laid the wood in order, and bound Isaac his son, and laid him on the altar upon the wood. 10: And Abraham stretched forth his hand, and took the knife to slay his son. 11: And the angel of the Lord called unto him out of heaven, and said, Abraham, Abraham ... Lay not thine hand upon the lad, neither do thou any thing unto him: for now I know that thou fearest God, seeing thou hast not withheld thy son, thine only son from me. 13: And Abraham lifted up his eyes, and looked, and behold behind him a ram caught in a thicket by his horns: and Abraham went and took the ram, and offered him up for a burnt offering in the stead of his son ... 15: And the angel of the Lord called unto Abraham out of heaven the second time, 16: And said, By myself have I sworn, saith the Lord, for because thou hast done this thing, and hast not withheld thy son, thine only son: 17: That in blessing I will bless thee, and in multiplying I will multiply thy seed as the stars of the heaven, and as the sand which is upon the sea shore; and thy seed shall possess the gate of his enemies; 18: And in thy seed shall all the nations of the earth be blessed; because thou hast obeyed my voice. *—Genesis 22:1–18*

One day God visited Abraham and Sarah, and promised that, despite her advancing years, Sarah would give birth to a son by Abraham, and some years later, Isaac was born. Meanwhile relations between Sarah and Hagar had deteriorated – at one point, Hagar, with child by Abraham, had fled into the desert, only to be met at a spring and told by God to go back. After the birth of Isaac, Sarah persuaded Abraham to send the servant and her son away. Not least was Sarah's concern that only Isaac should be Abraham's heir. Again Hagar struggled through the desert with her small child, and when her water ran out she despaired. But God appeared and reassured her that they were not outcasts in his eyes, and that her son had an important future, and they were saved. They settled in the area of Paran, and Ishmael grew up to be an archer and ancestor of twelve tribes, called Ishmaelites or Midianites.

Some time later God devised a terrible test of Abraham's faith. He told him to take his son, Isaac, to a nearby mountain and there offer him as a burnt sacrifice to the Lord. With Isaac bound on top of the pyre, Abraham took his knife to kill his son – but God stopped his hand, for Abraham had passed the test and God had thus demonstrated that he did not need human sacrifice.

Meanwhile Isaac had grown into a man, and it was important for the Covenant with God that he be found a wife. So Abraham sent out one of his servants to search for such a woman in his old homeland. One day, at a well, he encountered a young woman whom he asked for a drink, which was gladly given. The girl was Rebekah, the granddaughter of Abraham's brother Nahor, beautiful and unbetrothed. This was seen as a sign from God, and her family readily agreed to the match.

***Right:** Rebekah comes to marry Isaac.*

1896 Isaac born to Abraham by Sarah.
1891 Ishmael, sent away, with Hagar, by Abraham, takes up his abode in the wilderness of Paran. From him are descended some of the Arabian tribes.
1871 The faith of Abraham is proved in offering to sacrifice his son Isaac, then 25 years old.
1856 Isaac, being now 40 years old, marries Rebekah, the grand-daughter of Nahor, Abraham's brother.
1854 Abraham marries Keturah, by whom he has several children, and they became heads of different nations in the East.
1837 Rebekah continuing barren for nineteen years, Isaac intercedes for her, and God grants her conception.

For some years, Isaac and Rebekah failed to conceive, and it was only after Isaac prayed to the Lord for help that Rebekah at last gave birth to twin sons – Esau and Jacob. While Esau was beloved of Isaac, Jacob was Rebekah's favorite. When they grew into manhood, there took place an incident that would change their futures. When Esau, firstborn of the twins,

10: And Jacob went out from Beer-sheba ... and tarried there all night, because the sun was set ... 12: And he dreamed, and behold a ladder set up on the earth, and the top of it reached to heaven: and behold the angels of God ascending and descending on it. 13: And, behold, the Lord stood above it, and said, I am the Lord God of Abraham thy father, and the God of Isaac: the land whereon thou liest, to thee will I give it, and to thy seed; 14: And thy seed shall be as the dust of the earth, and thou shalt spread abroad to the west, and to the east, and to the north, and to the south: and in thee and in thy seed shall all the families of the earth be blessed. 15: And, behold, I am with thee, and will keep thee in all places whither thou goest, and will bring thee again into this land; for I will not leave thee, until I have done that which I have spoken to thee of. — *Genesis 28:10–15*

***Above:** Jacob's deceit – Isaac, believing him to be Esau, gives Jacob his blessing.*

returned from the fields tired and hungry, Jacob offered him bread and pottage of lentils but demanded that Esau give up his birthright in return. Esau carelessly agreed.

Rebekah, observing this, conspired with Jacob to go further. Isaac was now old, with not long to live, and both his eyesight and hearing were poor. While Esau was out in the fields, Jacob went to Isaac, offering him his favorite food and asking for his father's blessing, which was really due to Esau. The old man, reaching out and touching hairy flesh, was deceived into thinking that this was the elder of the two, so he gave his blessing, which amounted to making Jacob his heir. But the smooth-skinned Jacob had clad himself in goatskin and his brother's clothes, which convinced Isaac.

Esau's return revealed the deception, but it was too late. Jacob fled his brother's wrath, moving to the land of Laban, Rebekah's brother, in Haran. There he worked for his uncle and fell in love with his daughter, Rachel. When he asked for her hand in marriage, it was happily given, for Jacob was seen to be favored by

God. But now deception was practiced on Jacob, and by sleight of hand Laban married him to Leah, Rachel's elder sister. On realizing who was under the bridal veil, Jacob protested, but polygamy was customary at this time, and Laban promised that after a time he should marry Rachel too.

And so things turned out, and Leah bore Jacob children, six boys and a girl; only after some years did Rachel conceive and give birth to a son, Joseph, who was obviously very special to her and to Jacob.

As time passed, Jacob's relationship with Laban deteriorated, and he decided to move back to his homeland, leaving without telling Laban, who pursued him. When he caught up, there was an argument, but eventually they were reconciled and Jacob's party continued, only to encounter an angry Esau, with hundreds of followers. But again there was reconciliation.

Violence did break out later, after Leah's daughter, Dinah, was raped by a neighbor, Shechem. Following a feigned acceptance of this and agreement with Shechem and his family, the sons of Jacob fell on the Shechemites and slaughtered them.

God meanwhile appeared to Jacob and assured him that, as with Abraham and Isaac, his forebears, he would be father to a great nation; henceforth, he would be called Israel.

Rachel eventually gave birth to another son, whom Jacob called Benjamin; like his brother Joseph, he would play an important role in the story of Jacob's children. But Rachel died in childbirth.

1836 Esau and Jacob (twins) are born to Isaac by Rebekah, after more than nineteen years' barrenness.
1821 Abraham dies.
1773 Death of Ishmael.
1759 Isaac blesses Jacob instead of Esau. Jacob withdraws into Mesopotamia, to his uncle Laban. Here he marries Leah, and afterwards Rachel.
1747 Joseph born, son of Jacob and Rachel, Jacob being 90 years old.
1745 Rachel dies giving birth to Benjamin, Jacob's twelfth son.
1739 Jacob resolves to return to his parents in Canaan. Laban pursues him and overtakes him at Mount Gilead. Esau comes to meet him and receives him with much affection. Jacob arrives at Shechem.
1731 Dinah, Jacob's daughter, is ravished by Shechem. He and all his people are treacherously put to death on the third day after circumcision, by Simeon and Levi.

24: And Jacob was left alone; and there wrestled a man with him until the breaking of the day. 25: And when he saw that he prevailed not against him, he touched the hollow of his thigh; and the hollow of Jacob's thigh was out of joint, as he wrestled with him. 26: And he said, Let me go, for the day breaketh. And he said, I will not let thee go, except thou bless me. 27: And he said unto him, What is thy name? And he said, Jacob. 28: And he said, Thy name shall be called no more Jacob, but Israel: for as a prince hast thou power with God and with men, and hast prevailed. 29: And Jacob asked him, and said, Tell me, I pray thee, thy name. And he said, Wherefore is it that thou dost ask after my name? And he blessed him there. — *Genesis 32: 24–29*

Of Jacob's children, those borne by Rachel were especially dear to their father, Joseph receiving such attentions that this engendered the jealousy of his brothers, made worse when Jacob presented him with a coat of many colors. At an early age, too, Joseph showed a talent for interpreting dreams, beginning with his own, which seemed to glorify the dreamer, further irritating his brethren. Indeed, his brothers disliked him and determined to get rid of him. Their opportunity came one day when Joseph went to join them in the fields, whereupon they seized him and sold him into slavery to a passing band of Ishmaelites. Taking his ornamented robe, they bloodied it and presented it to their father as evidence that Joseph had been attacked and devoured by a wild beast.

***Top left:** Jacob gives his favorite son, Joseph, an ornamented robe, the coat of many colors; it will prove an object of jealousy for his brothers, and later will be used as false evidence of his death.*

***Left:** Joseph sold into slavery.*

***Below:** Joseph explains his fellow prisoners' dreams.*

The merchants took Joseph to Egypt, where he was sold as a slave to Potiphar, Pharaoh's chamberlain. Joseph grew to be tall and handsome, attracting the attention of the chamberlain's wife, who clandestinely propositioned him but was repeatedly rejected. In rage at being thus humiliated by a mere slave, she denounced the young man to his master as having attempted to lie with her, and he was cast into prison.

There he encountered two of Pharaoh's staff, his Chief Butler (a man of high rank) and his Chief Baker, who had engendered the wrath of their lord. Now Joseph's talent for explaining dreams came to the rescue of his fortunes: when they told him what they had dreamt, Joseph explained that they foretold the release of one of them, the Chief Butler, in three days' time, and the condemnation of the other. This proved true, and the Chief Butler was released.

Some time later the Pharaoh himself suffered a bout of disturbing dreams, which he could not understand. Remembering Joseph, still languishing in prison, the Chief Butler brought him before Pharaoh.

1728 Joseph, being seventeen years old, tells his father Jacob of his brothers' faults; they hate him, and sell him to passing Ishmaelites, who take him into Egypt. Joseph sold there as a slave to Potiphar.
1718 Joseph tempted by the wife of his master Potiphar, refuses her and is put in prison.
1716 Isaac dies, at the age of 180 years.

1: And it came to pass at the end of two full years, that Pharaoh dreamed: and, behold, he stood by the river. 2: And, behold, there came up out of the river seven well favoured kine and fatfleshed; and they fed in a meadow. 3: And, behold, seven other kine came up after them out of the river, ill favoured and leanfleshed; and stood by the other kine upon the brink of the river. 4: And the ill favoured and leanfleshed kine did eat up the seven well favoured and fat kine. So Pharaoh awoke. 5: And he slept and dreamed the second time: and, behold, seven ears of corn came up upon one stalk, rank and good. 6: And, behold, seven thin ears and blasted with the east wind sprung up after them. 7: And the seven thin ears devoured the seven rank and full ears. And Pharaoh awoke, and, behold, it was a dream. 8: And it came to pass in the morning that his spirit was troubled; and he sent and called for all the magicians of Egypt, and all the wise men thereof: and Pharaoh told them his dream; but there was none that could interpret them unto Pharaoh ... 14: Then Pharaoh sent and called Joseph, and they brought him hastily out of the dungeon: and he shaved himself, and changed his raiment, and came in unto Pharaoh. — *Genesis 41: 1–8, 14*

***Right:** Joseph finds himself brought before Pharaoh of Egypt.*

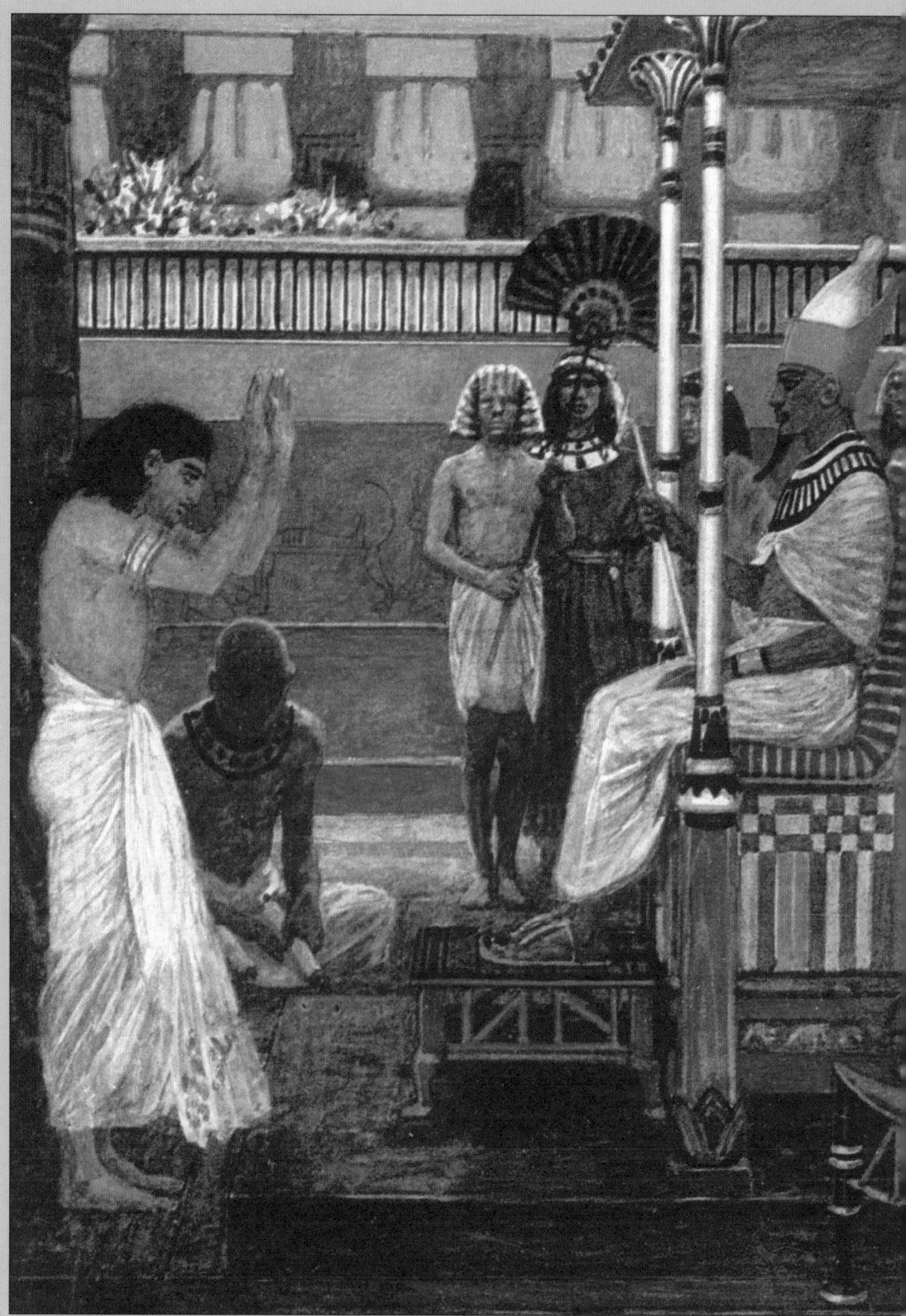

Joseph interpreted the dreams – there would be seven good years followed by seven years of famine. Pharaoh found this credible and saw it as a timely warning that the abundance of the good years should not be squandered but some stored for harder times. He appointed Joseph to take the necessary measures so that when famine came the land should not suffer.

1715 Joseph interprets Pharaoh's dreams, and is promoted. The seven years of plenty begin.
1715 The beginning of the seven years of plenty foretold by Joseph.
1708 The beginning of the seven years of scarcity, foretold by Joseph.

15: And Pharaoh said unto Joseph, I have dreamed a dream, and there is none that can interpret it: and I have heard say of thee, that thou canst understand a dream to interpret it. 16: And Joseph answered Pharaoh, saying, It is not in me: God shall give Pharaoh an answer of peace. 17: And Pharaoh said unto Joseph, In my dream, behold, I stood upon the bank of the river: 18: And, behold, there came up out of the river seven kine, fatfleshed and well favoured; and they fed in a meadow: 19: And, behold, seven other kine came up after them, poor and very ill favoured and leanfleshed, such as I never saw in all the land of Egypt for badness: 20: And the lean and the ill favoured kine did eat up the first seven fat kine: 21: And when they had eaten them up, it could not be known that they had eaten them; but they were still ill favoured, as at the beginning. So I awoke. 22: And I saw in my dream, and, behold, seven ears came up in one stalk, full and good: 23: And, behold, seven ears, withered, thin, and blasted with the east wind, sprung up after them: 24: And the thin ears devoured the seven good ears: and I told this unto the magicians; but there was none that could declare it to me. 25: And Joseph said unto Pharaoh, The dream of Pharaoh is one: God hath shewed Pharaoh what he is about to do. 26: The seven good kine are seven years; and the seven good ears are seven years: the dream is one. 27: And the seven thin and ill favoured kine that came up after them are seven years; and the seven empty ears blasted with the east wind shall be seven years of famine. 28: This is the thing which I have spoken unto Pharaoh: What God is about to do he sheweth unto Pharaoh. 29: Behold, there come seven years of great plenty throughout all the land of Egypt: 30: And there shall arise after them seven years of famine; and all the plenty shall be forgotten in the land of Egypt; and the famine shall consume the land; 31: And the plenty shall not be known in the land by reason of that famine following; for it shall be very grievous. 32: And for that the dream was doubled unto Pharaoh twice; it is because the thing is established by God, and God will shortly bring it to pass. 33: Now therefore let Pharaoh look out a man discreet and wise, and set him over the land of Egypt. 34: Let Pharaoh do this, and let him appoint officers over the land, and take up the fifth part of the land of Egypt in the seven plenteous years. 35: And let them gather all the food of those good years that come, and lay up corn under the hand of Pharaoh, and let them keep food in the cities. 36: And that food shall be for store to the land against the seven years of famine, which shall be in the land of Egypt; that the land perish not through the famine. 37: And the thing was good in the eyes of Pharaoh, and in the eyes of all his servants. 38: And Pharaoh said unto his servants, Can we find such a one as this is, a man in whom the Spirit of God is? 39: And Pharaoh said unto Joseph, Forasmuch as God hath shewed thee all this, there is none so discreet and wise as thou art: 40: Thou shalt be over my house, and according unto thy word shall all my people be ruled: only in the throne will I be greater than thou.

— Genesis 41: 15–39

***Left:** Joseph tells Pharaoh the meaning of his dreams. Egypt will be saved from the worst effects of the famine to come; and the fortunes of Joseph's family will be changed dramatically.*

Joseph proved himself an excellent servant to Pharaoh and rose in his lord's esteem so that he became rich and powerful in Egypt, second in all the land: "And Pharaoh called Joseph's name Zaphnath-paaneah; and he gave him to wife Asenath the daughter of Poti-pherah priest of On". *(Genesis 41:45)* His prudent actions in building up stores of grain in the granaries during the good years staved off the effects of the famine when it came; he also took all the land of Egypt into the royal ownership, then gave it back to the people on condition that they remit a fifth of their produce to Pharaoh.

41: And Pharaoh said unto Joseph, See, I have set thee over all the land of Egypt. 42: And Pharaoh took off his ring from his hand, and put it upon Joseph's hand, and arrayed him in vestures of fine linen, and put a gold chain about his neck; 43: And he made him to ride in the second chariot which he had; and they cried before him, Bow the knee: and he made him ruler over all the land of Egypt. 44: And Pharaoh said unto Joseph, I am Pharaoh, and without thee shall no man lift up his hand or foot in all the land of Egypt. 45: And Pharaoh called Joseph's name Zaphnath-paaneah; and he gave him to wife Asenath the daughter of Poti-pherah priest of On. And Joseph went out over all the land of Egypt. 46: And Joseph was thirty years old when he stood before Pharaoh king of Egypt. And Joseph went out from the presence of Pharaoh, and went throughout all the land of Egypt. 47: And in the seven plenteous years the earth brought forth by handfuls. 48: And he gathered up all the food of the seven years, which were in the land of Egypt, and laid up the food in the cities: the food of the field, which was round about every city, laid he up in the same. 49: And Joseph gathered corn as the sand of the sea, very much, until he left numbering; for it was without number. 50: And unto Joseph were born two sons before the years of famine came, which Asenath the daughter of Poti-pherah priest of On bare unto him. 51: And Joseph called the name of the firstborn Manasseh: For God, said he, hath made me forget all my toil, and all my father's house. 52: And the name of the second called he Ephraim: For God hath caused me to be fruitful in the land of my affliction. 53: And the seven years of plenteousness, that was in the land of Egypt, were ended. 54: And the seven years of dearth began to come, according as Joseph had said: and the dearth was in all lands; but in all the land of Egypt there was bread. 55: And when all the land of Egypt was famished, the people cried to Pharaoh for bread: and Pharaoh said unto all the Egyptians, Go unto Joseph; what he saith to you, do. 56: And the famine was over all the face of the earth: and Joseph opened all the storehouses, and sold unto the Egyptians; and the famine waxed sore in the land of Egypt. 57: And all countries came into Egypt to Joseph for to buy corn; because that the famine was so sore in all lands. — *Genesis 41: 41–57*

Left: *Joseph oversees the harvest during the good years, ensuring that plenty is put in store, ready for the hard times to come.*

Right: *Joseph rides high in Pharaoh's favor, becoming both rich and powerful.*

In Canaan, meanwhile, the famine hit hard, and just as Abraham had done many years before, the sons of Jacob set out for Egypt to find help. There they were sent before Pharaoh's great servant but failed to recognize him as the brother they had sold into slavery. Nor did he reveal his identity to them, but sent them back to Jacob with food, keeping one of the brothers, Simeon, as hostage, and directing them to bring before him the youngest of the family.

When they returned with Benjamin to Egypt, Joseph organized a feast for them, and still they did not realize the identity of their host. Now Joseph planned a trick: when they set off back to Canaan, he planted a silver cup in Benjamin's sack, then sent men to bring the brothers back, accusing them of theft.

***Left:** Joseph, mighty in the land of Egypt, gives audience to his brothers, who, not recognizing him, grovel and beg for food.*

***Right:** Reuben, the eldest of the brothers, pleads with Joseph – he sees that Joseph's demand that they bring him Benjamin will deeply upset their father.*

***Far right:** On Joseph's orders, a silver cup is hidden in Benjamin's sack before they set out for Canaan.*

1: Now when Jacob saw that there was corn in Egypt, Jacob said unto his sons, Why do ye look one upon another? 2: And he said, Behold, I have heard that there is corn in Egypt: get you down thither, and buy for us from thence; that we may live, and not die. 3: And Joseph's ten brethren went down to buy corn in Egypt. 4: But Benjamin, Joseph's brother, Jacob sent not with his brethren; for he said, Lest peradventure mischief befall him.
5: And the sons of Israel came to buy corn among those that came: for the famine was in the land of Canaan. 6: And Joseph was the governor over the land, and he it was that sold to all the people of the land: and Joseph's brethren came, and bowed down themselves before him with their faces to the earth. 7: And Joseph saw his brethren, and he knew them, but made himself strange unto them, and spake roughly unto them; and he said unto them, Whence come ye? And they said, From the land of Canaan to buy food. 8: And Joseph knew his brethren, but they knew not him. — *Genesis 42: 1–8*

1707 The famine prevailing, and reaching Canaan, Jacob sends all his sons, except Benjamin, into Egypt, to buy corn.

1: And he commanded the steward of his house, saying, Fill the men's sacks with food, as much as they can carry, and put every man's money in his sack's mouth.
2: And put my cup, the silver cup, in the sack's mouth of the youngest, and his corn money. And he did according to the word that Joseph had spoken. 3: As soon as the morning was light, the men were sent away, they and their asses. 4: And when they were gone out of the city, and not yet far off, Joseph said unto his steward, Up, follow after the men; and when thou dost overtake them, say unto them, Wherefore have ye rewarded evil for good? 5: Is not this it in which my lord drinketh, and whereby indeed he divineth? ye have done evil in so doing. 6: And he overtook them, and he spake unto them these same words ... 11: Then they speedily took down every man his sack to the ground, and opened every man his sack. 12: And he searched, and began at the eldest, and left at the youngest: and the cup was found in Benjamin's sack. 13: Then they rent their clothes, and laded every man his ass, and returned to the city.
— *Genesis 44: 1–5, 11–13*

Joseph Reveals he is their Brother and is Reunited with his Father

The silver cup was discovered, and Simeon offered himself in Benjamin's place for punishment. Joseph, in effect, had his moral revenge; he now revealed his identity to his astonished brothers and sent them off to Canaan, telling them to bring their father to Egypt.

Jacob was reunited with his favorite son, and Pharaoh's minister settled the family in Egypt, in a place called Goshen. There, under his protection, they flourished, and when Jacob died he left Joseph's second son, Ephraim, as his heir. Jacob was taken to be buried in Hebron with his forebears, Abraham, Sarah, Isaac, and Rebekah.

***Above left:** The brothers before Joseph, this time accused of theft.*

***Left:** Jacob is reunited with the son he has long thought dead.*

22: And Joseph dwelt in Egypt, he, and his father's house: and Joseph lived an hundred and ten years. 23: And Joseph saw Ephraim's children of the third generation: the children also of Machir the son Manasseh were brought up upon Joseph's knees. 24: And Joseph said unto his brethren, I die: and God will surely visit you, and bring you out of this land unto the land which he sware to Abraham, to Isaac, and to Jacob. 25: And Joseph took an oath of the children of Israel, saying, God will surely visit you, and ye shall carry up my bones from hence. 26: So Joseph died, being an hundred and ten years old: and they embalmed him, and he was put in a coffin in Egypt. — *Genesis 50: 22–26*

Right: Joseph at last reveals his identity to his brothers.

1: Then Joseph could not refrain himself before all them that stood by him; and he cried, Cause every man to go out from me. And there stood no man with him, while Joseph made himself known unto his brethren. 2: And he wept aloud: and the Egyptians and the house of Pharaoh heard. 3: And Joseph said unto his brethren, I am Joseph; doth my father yet live? And his brethren could not answer him; for they were troubled at his presence. 4: And Joseph said unto his brethren, Come near to me, I pray you. And they came near. And he said, I am Joseph your brother, whom ye sold into Egypt. 5: Now therefore be not grieved, nor angry with yourselves, that ye sold me hither: for God did send me before you to preserve life. 6: For these two years hath the famine been in the land: and yet there are five years, in the which there shall neither be earing nor harvest. 7: And God sent me before you to preserve you a posterity in the earth, and to save your lives by a great deliverance. 8: So now it was not you that sent me hither, but God: and he hath made me a father to Pharaoh, and lord of all his house, and a ruler throughout all the land of Egypt. 9: Haste ye, and go up to my father, and say unto him, Thus saith thy son Joseph, God hath made me lord of all Egypt: come down unto me, tarry not: 10: And thou shalt dwell in the land of Goshen, and thou shalt be near unto me, thou, and thy children, and thy children's children, and thy flocks, and thy herds, and all that thou hast: 11: And there will I nourish thee; for yet there are five years of famine; lest thou, and thy household, and all that thou hast, come to poverty. — *Genesis 45: 1–11*

1706 Joseph's brethren return into Egypt with their brother Benjamin. Joseph reveals himself, and persuades them to settle in Egypt with their father Jacob, then 130 years old.

1702 The property of all the lands in Egypt is sold to Joseph, who lets them out with a perpetual tax of the fifth part of their produce.

1701 The end of the seven years of scarcity. Joseph returns the Egyptians their cattle and their lands on condition that they pay the king the fifth part of the produce.

1689 Jacob on his deathbed adopts Manasseh and Ephraim, the two sons of Joseph; and collecting all his children, blesses them, and foretells many things, particularly the coming of the Messiah he dies aged 147, having resided seventeen years in Egypt.

1635 After Jacob's death, Joseph continues to rule over Egypt. Before his death, he calls for his brothers, and makes them promise not to bury him among the Egyptians, but to embalm his body, and carry it into Canaan, when they should return there.

1635 Joseph foretells the Exodus of the Israelites from Egypt and dies aged 110, having being prefect of Egypt for eighty years. His death concludes the book of Genesis, which contains a period of 2,369 years.

The Hebrews, now living in Egypt, multiplied, but their high standing with Pharaoh declined over the centuries; Jacob and Joseph became distant memories, and the people gradually became forced labor, working on the vast building projects for the government. But their numbers grew such that the Pharaoh became concerned abut the security of his kingdom with such an increasing "alien" population in the borderlands. So he sought a cruel solution: all male children of the Hebrews were to be put to death at birth, a measure the Hebrew midwives could frustrate only temporarily.

Among the victims of this drastic measure was a Levite couple, who, doubtless like many others, tried to hide their newborn son. When at last they saw they could no longer avoid the Egyptian murderers, they abandoned the baby in a floating basket in the rushes along the banks of the River Nile, hoping that the plight of the child would touch a sympathetic heart. And indeed it did, for the basket was discovered by Pharaoh's daughter, who, in defiance of her father's decree, adopted the baby, taking him back to the palace and naming him Moses.

The child thus grew up in a privileged world, educated and set apart from

Above: *The Hebrews at work making bricks.*
Below: *Pharaoh's daughter discovers the infant Moses.*

his fellow Hebrews. As he grew to manhood, his identity and loyalties must have troubled him, and this exploded in violence when he chanced upon the sight of a Hebrew being beaten by an Egyptian. In a fit of anger, Moses killed the Egyptian; then, realizing that he must in time be found out, despite his position, he fled into the Moabite desert, where he eluded the vengeance of Pharaoh. There he joined the family of Jethro, a priest, and married his daughter, Zipporah.

Time passed, and those who sought his death died. Then one day as he was near Mount Horeb, tending to his father-in-law's flock of sheep, he beheld a bush that seemed afire yet was not consumed by the flames. Fascinated, he drew near and heard the voice of God.

The Lord told him that he had seen and lamented the miserable situation of his chosen people; now, however, he would release them from bondage and lead them to "a land flowing with milk and honey." And Moses would be his instrument.

Three Miracles for Moses

❊ ***The serpent staff.*** God told Moses to cast his staff on the ground, whereupon it turned into a serpent. He told Moses to pick it up by the tail and it became a staff again.

❊ ***The leprous hand.*** God told Moses to put his hand into the folds of his garment; when he drew it out again, his hand was diseased and leprous. When he repeated this, the hand was healthy again.

❊ ***Water into blood.*** If those miracles were not enough, Moses was to draw water from the Nile and pour it onto the ground, where it would turn to blood.

In vain did Moses protest his inadequacy for such a huge task. He would not be believed by anybody: but God demonstrated three miracles that would persuade them. And, Moses objected, he was not eloquent; to which God, becoming impatient, replied that he should have the services of his elder brother, Aaron, as spokesman.

And so Moses returned to Egypt to begin God's work.

1574 Aaron born.
The year after, Pharaoh publishes an edict for drowning all male children of the Israelites.
1571 Moses born, and three months later is exposed among the bulrushes on the banks of the river, where he is found by Thermutis, Pharaoh's daughter, who adopts and educates him.
1531 Moses, being 40 years of age, visits the Israelites, his brethren, and observing their oppression, kills an Egyptian, whom he found beating a Hebrew.
He flees to Midian, where he lives for 40 years, and marries Zipporah, the daughter of Jethro.
1491 The Lord appears to Moses in a burning bush, while he is tending to his father-in-law's flock.
God sends Moses into Egypt to deliver Israel from bondage.

***Above:** God speaks to Moses from a burning bush.*

Having proved to the Hebrew elders, by means of the three miracles, that he was indeed the instrument of God, Moses went with Aaron to Pharaoh, and demanded that the Hebrews be free to leave Egypt. But Pharaoh was unyielding: why should he part with his work force? Instead he increased the burden upon the slaves by making them gather their own straw for their brick-making instead of providing it as before. Life became harder for the Hebrews, who did not hesitate to complain to Moses for what he had brought about.

But God commanded Moses and Aaron to go back to Pharaoh and this time demonstrate the miracle of

turning Aaron's staff into a serpent. This Pharaoh's magicians could also do: whereupon Aaron's staff ate all of theirs. And again, Pharaoh was intransigent. So God told Moses that he would bring down a series of plagues upon Egypt, which would eventually force the Egyptians to let the Hebrews leave. Confronting the king, Moses turned the river to blood, and then called up an infestation of frogs. Again the Egyptian magicians could match this.

1491 Moses and Aaron announce God's demands to Pharaoh, which he rejects.
Plagues afflict Egypt.
The Passover instituted as the Angel of Death slaughters the Egyptian firstborn.
The Hebrews depart from Egypt.

Left: *Moses and Aaron demand that Pharaoh let the Hebrews depart from Egypt.*

Below left: *Aaron's staff turned into a serpent eats those of the court magicians.*

Right: *The river turns to blood.*

THE PLAGUES OF EGYPT

- River of Blood
- Frogs
- Lice
- Flies
- Murrain of animals
- Boils (on animals and humans)
- Hail, rain, and storm
- Locusts
- Darkness for three days
- Death of firstborn

However, the Egyptian magicians could not imitate the plagues that followed, and for each plague Pharaoh seemed to give way but then hardened his heart once more. The disease to livestock did not

Above: The plague of flies.

Above: The plague of boils.

affect the Hebrews' herds and flocks; the boils did not affect them; and when hail, rain, and tempest thrashed down on Egypt, destroying crops and the harvest, no storm hit Goshen, where the Hebrews lived. The locusts destroyed what was left of the Egyptian harvest; and then God turned the

Above: The plague of locusts.

land dark for three days – except in Goshen.

It was now time for God's final punishment of the Egyptians, the death of the firstborn in every household. At midnight, the Angel of the Lord would strike; but God instructed Moses that all his people should roast and eat lamb that night, with unleavened bread; and they should paint their door frames with the lamb's blood, as a sign. This became the feast of the Passover, to be commemorated each year, as it is among Jews today.

This was the final straw for Pharaoh, whose own son was among the dead. He bid Moses take his people away. Laden with gold and jewels donated as an encouragement to leave by the ordinary Egyptians, who just wanted an end to the plagues, the Hebrews set out to the east, guided by a great pillar of cloud, into the desert.

Above: *The death of the firstborn – Pharaoh finds his son dead. But the Hebrews (inset) have painted their door frames with lamb's blood as a mark to the Angel of the Lord, and so are spared.*

Right: *At last, Pharaoh bids the Hebrews to be gone.*

God, knowing that a direct approach to the Promised Land would bring conflict with the Philistines, and that the Hebrews might falter, led them instead towards the Red Sea. Meanwhile Pharaoh was regretting his decision to allow the Hebrews to leave, despite the suffering that had been caused to Egypt. With infantry, cavalry, and chariots he set out in pursuit of the children of Israel.

Left: *The waters part to allow the Hebrews to cross.*

Below: *They reach the other side and the waters close behind them.*

At the shores of the sea, the Hebrews paused, only to look back and see the Egyptian army closing fast. They seemed to be trapped. But the pillar of cloud moved between them and their pursuers, turning night into day for the Hebrews. That night Moses obeyed God's instructions to stretch his hand over the sea: and the waters divided, the Hebrews passing across the dry seabed with a wall of water to each side. Once they were safely across, Moses stretched out again and the waters closed upon the pursuing Egyptians, engulfing them. After more than four centuries, the Hebrews were finally out of Egypt.

1491 Pharaoh pursues the Hebrews but is thwarted at the Red Sea.

23: And the Egyptians pursued, and went in after them to the midst of the sea, even all Pharaoh's horses, his chariots, and his horsemen. 24: And it came to pass, that in the morning watch the Lord looked unto the host of the Egyptians through the pillar of fire and of the cloud, and troubled the host of the Egyptians, 25: And took off their chariot wheels, that they drave them heavily ... 26: And the Lord said unto Moses, Stretch out thine hand over the sea, that the waters may come again upon the Egyptians, upon their chariots, and upon their horsemen. 27: And Moses stretched forth his hand over the sea, and the sea returned to his strength when the morning appeared; and the Egyptians fled against it; and the Lord overthrew the Egyptians in the midst of the sea. 28: And the waters returned, and covered the chariots, and the horsemen, and all the host of Pharaoh that came into the sea after them; there remained not so much as one of them. 29: But the children of Israel walked upon dry land in the midst of the sea; and the waters were a wall unto them on their right hand, and on their left. 30: Thus the Lord saved Israel that day out of the hand of the Egyptians; and Israel saw the Egyptians dead upon the sea shore. 31: And Israel saw that great work which the Lord did upon the Egyptians: and the people feared the Lord, and believed the Lord, and his servant Moses. —*Exodus 14:23–31*

The Red Sea behind them, the Israelites set out into the desert of Shur. Before long, however, grumbles reached Moses' ears about the lack of food and water. At Elim they found an oasis, but deeper into the desert of Sin the murmuring grew such that Moses appealed to God for help. God replied that he would provide: and that evening a great flock of quail settled about the camp. In the mornings, the dew dried to reveal a white flaky substance, which the Israelites could gather and make into bread. This they called manna: little did they realize that they would have to live on this for forty years.

At Rephidim they were attacked by the Amalekites and driven off with God's help. And at Rephidim too Moses received a visit from his father-in-law, Jethro, who brought Moses' wife and children. They feasted, and Jethro saw the strain put upon Moses by his great responsibilities, so he suggested he appoint officials, including judges, among the people to help him.

In the third month of their exodus, the Israelites came to the desert of Sinai and camped before Mount Sinai. Here, upon the mountain, God spoke to Moses, telling him that he would now give him the Laws of his Covenant.

God now confirmed the Covenant to Moses and set out the Laws, which Moses wrote into a book and read aloud to the assembled people. After building an altar and making sacrifices, Moses ascended the mountain with Aaron, his two sons and forty elders, where they met God and ate and drank with him to seal the Covenant. Then Moses went up alone again for forty days and nights and God put the Laws on tablets of stone.

Left: *Quail and manna are sent by God to feed the starving Israelites.*

Right: *At Rephidim water again becomes critical, but once more God provides. He tells Moses to go to the rock called Horeb and strike it, whereupon a spring gushes forth.*

Above: *On the appointed day, thunder and lightning crash above Mount Sinai, its top shrouded by a thick black cloud, and the ground trembles violently. Moses ascends into the darkness, while the fearful people, forbidden to approach farther than the foothills, watch and listen in awe.*

THE LAWS OF THE COVENANT

God's laws were specific and many, including:

- ✖ **Other gods** and idols were forbidden; this God stressed.
- ✖ **Altars** must be built to exact specifications.
- ✖ Conduct concerning Hebrew **servants**.
- ✖ **Injuries to the person:** including murder, manslaughter, kidnap, cursing, serious violence, beating and inflicting serious injury, with penalties:

  23: And if any mischief follow, then thou shalt give life for life, 24: Eye for eye, tooth for tooth, hand for hand, foot for foot, 25: Burning for burning, wound for wound, stripe for stripe. (Exodus 21:23–25)
- ✖ **Property**, theft and accident liabilities.
- ✖ **Social responsibilities** of many kinds.
- ✖ **Justice** for slander, bribery, etc.
- ✖ **The Sabbath**, the seventh day, to be a day of rest.
- ✖ **Land** to lie fallow each seventh year.

1491 Amalekites defeated at Rephidim.
1491 At Mount Sinai, God makes his Covenant with Israel and gives Moses the Ten Commandments and the Laws.

1: And God spake all these words, saying, 2: I am the Lord thy God, which have brought thee out of the land of Egypt, out of the house of bondage. 3: Thou shalt have no other gods before me. 4: Thou shalt not make unto thee any graven image, or any likeness of any thing that is in heaven above, or that is in the earth beneath, or that is in the water under the earth: 5: Thou shalt not bow down thyself to them, nor serve them: for I the Lord thy God am a jealous God, visiting the iniquity of the fathers upon the children unto the third and fourth generation of them that hate me; 6: And shewing mercy unto thousands of them that love me, and keep my commandments. 7: Thou shalt not take the name of the Lord thy God in vain; for the Lord will not hold him guiltless that taketh his name in vain. 8: Remember the sabbath day, to keep it holy. 9: Six days shalt thou labour, and do all thy work: 10: But the seventh day is the sabbath of the Lord thy God: in it thou shalt not do any work, thou, nor thy son, nor thy daughter, thy manservant, nor thy maidservant, nor thy cattle, nor thy stranger that is within thy gates: 11: For in six days the Lord made heaven and earth, the sea, and all that in them is, and rested the seventh day: wherefore the Lord blessed the sabbath day, and hallowed it. 12: Honour thy father and thy mother: that thy days may be long upon the land which the Lord thy God giveth thee. 13: Thou shalt not kill. 14: Thou shalt not commit adultery. 15: Thou shalt not steal. 16: Thou shalt not bear false witness against thy neighbour. 17: Thou shalt not covet thy neighbour's house, thou

shalt not covet thy neighbour's wife, nor his manservant, nor his maidservant, nor his ox, nor his ass, nor any thing that is thy neighbour's.

—*Exodus 20:1–17*

***Left:** Moses returns from Mount Sinai with the tablets of the Law.*

***Below:** The impatient Israelites construct and begin to worship a golden calf idol.*

***Right:** Moses smashes the tablets in frustration.*

***Below right:** Carrying the Ark of the Covenant.*

So long was Moses on Mount Sinai that the Israelites lost patience and faith. They prevailed upon Aaron to make a new god for them to worship, so he gathered jewelry from among them and made of it a golden calf. This the Israelites began worshipping.

So when he at last came down from the mountain, it was a blasphemous scene that met Moses' eyes. God had warned him that this was happening, but it did not prevent Moses becoming angry and smashing down the tablets from God. Only Moses' intercession stopped God destroying all his chosen people. Moses now issued an ultimatum – the people must be for God or against him. At once the Levites pledged their loyalty, and to them Moses allotted the task of slaying the blasphemous ringleaders and destroying the golden calf.

God also commanded Moses to construct a place where God could dwell and be with the Israelites on their journey, and issued very specific details of its construction and layout, together with rules for the priesthood and worship. The Levites were put in charge of this and of transporting it as the Israelites marched on toward the Promised Land.

1491 Moses comes down fro the mountain and, finding the people dancing about their golden calf, he throws the tablets of stone on the ground, and breaks them. Coming into the camp, he destroys the calf and slays, by the sword of the Levites, the Israelites who had worshipped this idol.
1491 The day following, Moses again goes up the mountain, and, by his prayers, obtains from God the pardon of his people. God orders him to prepare new tablets for the Law and promises not to forsake Israel.
1491 Moses comes down and prepares new tablets; he goes up again the day following; God shows him his glory. He continues again forty days and forty nights on the mountain, and God writes a second time his Law on the tablets of stone.
1491 After forty days, Moses comes down, not knowing that his face shines with glory. He puts a veil over his face, speaks to the people, and proposes to erect a Tabernacle to the Lord; to accomplish this he taxes each Israelite at half a shekel. This occasions a numbering of the people, who amount to 603,550 men. He appoints Bezaleel and Aholiab to oversee the work of the Tabernacle.
1490 Construction of the Tabernacle after the Exodus and the second numbering of the people. Consecration of the Tabernacle, the altars, and the priests.

Above: The Tabernacle in the wilderness, built according to God's instructions.

THE TABERNACLE

The Tabernacle is the meeting-point between God and his people: it symbolizes God's presence and is where he communicates to the Hebrews. This is a portable Holy Place for worshipping God while the Hebrews are on their journey to the Promised Land. It stands always at the center of the Hebrew encampment, with the tents of Moses and Aaron on the eastern side, and those of the other priestly families on the other three sides: Merari to the north, Gershon to the west, Kohath to the south. The entire edifice is transportable, the Levite tribe being responsible for its carriage. Responsibility for the construction is placed upon Bezaleel and Aholiab, and the Tabernacle is completed in the second year after leaving Egypt. God's presence is shown by a pillar of smoke and fire above the Most Holy Place.

THE OUTER COURTYARD

- Measures 100 cubits by 50, the perimeter curtained upon a framework of acacia pillars. This area is accessible to all.
- The Altar of Burnt Offering stands at the eastern end of the courtyard. It is a hollow box 5 cubits square and 3 cubits high, lined inside and out with bronze, but light enough to be portable.
- The Altar Fire is never allowed to go out.
- The Basin, set between the Altar and the Tabernacle itself, is where the priests ritually cleanse themselves before and after making sacrifices.

THE HOLY PLACE

- This is entered only by priests and contains three items of furniture:
- The Table of the Bread of the Presence (or Shewbread Table) measures 2 cubits by 1 and is a cubit and a half high. Each Sabbath, 12 prepared loaves are sprinkled with frankincense (symbolizing God's provision for the twelve tribes) and placed on the table. These are of unleavened wheat flour and are eaten by the priests in the sanctuary.
- The Lamp is a seven-branched lampstand (*menorah*), designed to take olive-oil burning lamps made in the shape of a blossoming almond-flower.
- The Altar of Incense, or Gold Altar, is a square box of acacia overlaid with gold, a cubit square and 2 cubits high. Incense is burned in the morning and in the evening, the fragrance rising as a sweet smoke symbolizing prayers to God.

THE MOST HOLY PLACE

- This is where God meets Man, and contains the Ark of the Covenant.
- It is entered only by the High Priest, once a year on the Day of Atonement, when he sprinkles blood on the cover of the Ark of the Covenant.
- It is entirely dark within.
- The Ark of the Covenant is the symbol of God's relationship with his people, the covenant, or agreement whereby he protects, guides and provides for his people in return for their faith in Him.
- The Ark is 2½ cubits by 1½ and 1½ cubits high. On the corners are gold rings to take the poles for carrying it on the shoulders of the Levites.
- The top of the Ark has a lid (sometimes called the "mercy seat", upon which are two large Cherubim facing one another. Between them is Shekinah, "God's Presence."
- The Ark contains the two tablets of stone on which the Ten Commandments are inscribed, plus a golden jar containing manna, miraculously preserved. In the Ark or nearby is a copy of the Law as taken down by Moses on Mount Sinai.

A priesthood was also instituted, with Aaron as High Priest, and his sons Nadab and Abihu also became priests. But they flouted God's very precise rules on worship, burning incense before the Lord when they should not; as a result, God made examples of them by burning them to death.

This was not the only family tragedy for Moses, for his sister Miriam had made uncomplimentary remarks about Moses and his Cushite wife, questioning Moses' position. In punishment, God brought leprosy upon her for seven days, during which she was banished from the camp.

The Israelites continued their trek, led by an angel and now taking with them the Tabernacle, including the Ark of the Covenant, which contained a new set of stone tablets bearing God's Laws. When they camped, Moses would have a special tent, the Tent of Meeting, set up just outside the camp; it was here that God would visit him.

1452 After wandering in the wilderness of Arabia-Petraea and Idumea for 37 years, they return to Mozeroth, near Kadesh-barnea; in the 39th year after the Exodus.
1452 Moses sends ambassadors to the king of Edom, asking passage through his territories; he refuses.
The Israelites complain for want of water, and Moses brings it forth from a rock; but because he, as well as Aaron, have shown some distrust, God tells them they shall not enter the Promised Land.

Below: *The twelve tribes in their allotted encampments around the Tabernacle.*

***Left:** The spies return from the Promised Land laden with its fruit but fearing its inhabitants.*

Nearing Canaan, twelve men were sent on an intelligence-gathering expedition, one man for each of the tribes. Returning, they revealed that the land was indeed fertile and rich – they brought back fruit to demonstrate this – but they also reported that the inhabitants were many, living in large fortified cities. The story got worse in the telling, and soon the camp was alive with rumors of giants there. Panic set in among the people, who saw only disaster before them; some even wanted to return to Egypt. Moses was reviled and almost stoned to death.

This lack of faith yet again sealed the Israelites' fate, for God now decreed that they should be condemned to forty years more of wandering in the wilderness. Of those who had left Egypt, only their children and grandchildren would enter the Promised Land; save just two men, Caleb and Joshua (Moses' assistant), who had reported positively about the prospects of invading Canaan. In vain the people changed their mind; but when they went forward it was without God's blessing, and they were severely repulsed by Amalekites and Canaanites. Dismayed, the Israelites trudged back into the desert, and disaffection grew. Three Levites, Korah, Dathan and Abiram, eventually set themselves at the head of 250 respected community leaders and came to Moses and Aaron, demanding they step down. God alone would judge, replied Moses, which he duly did. The people were warned to keep away from the offenders: then the earth opened up and swallowed them, including their households. The 250 were burned to death; and a plague finished off those rebels who remained.

To emphasize God's leadership, Aaron was now confirmed as High Priest, by miraculous means. A staff from each of the twelve tribes was planted in the ground before the Tabernacle; next day, the staff that bore the name of Aaron had sprouted and bore almonds. In time the Israelites found themselves once more in the desert of Sin, and it was here, on Mount Hor, that Aaron died, to be succeeded by his son, Eleazar.

1451 Og, King of Bashan, attacks Israel, but is defeated.
War against the Midianites.
Moses renews the Covenant of Israel with the Lord.

Right: *Aaron's staff sprouts and produces almonds overnight, a demonstration to the people that God is with him and with Moses.*

The resentment of the Israelites at their plight was not stilled, however. When their complaints became loud, God reacted by sending venomous snakes among them. Only when Moses interceded did he relent. Moses was to make an effigy of a serpent in bronze and place it on a pole; any who had been bitten could look upon this and be healed.

Increasingly the Israelites were finding their route blocked by established communities: Edom refused them passage, but when opposed by Amorites and Bashan, they fought and won, defeating King Og at Edrei.

One of the kingdoms that began to feel threatened by the proximity of the migrating Israelites was Moab, whose king, Balak, decided to attempt a pre-emptive measure against possible invasion. He sent his messengers to a prophet called Balaam, asking him to pronounce a curse upon the Israelites. He had to send several envoys for this because in a dream Balaam received instructions from God not to do this. Eventually he was persuaded, and set out with the king's men for a high place, from where the curse could be made most effectively. On the way, however, the donkey he was riding began to behave erratically, and when he beat it the animal miraculously spoke to him, complaining. Suddenly Balaam could see what the donkey had already seen – an armed angel barring the way, who told him that the donkey was the only reason he would not kill Balaam. He could proceed, Balaam was told, but now Balaam was repenting his decision to make the curse. Instead, he blessed the Israelites; when the king tried to get him to make the curse twice more, again Balaam blessed the Israelites, the spirit of God having come upon him.

Moab meanwhile attempted a more subtle strategy, as Moabite women sought to subvert the Israelites; and indeed many fell under their spell, even taking to the worship of Baal. God sent a plague in punishment, and after a second census of the tribes, Moses attacked Moab, destroying them; in the process Balaam himself fell.

Now the Israelites were ready to move into Canaan. But Moses, as God had foretold, was not permitted to enter the Promised Land; he was allowed to gaze over the fertile land from afar; and then he died, Joshua becoming the leader of the Israelites for the conquest of Canaan.

1451 Moses, at the age of 120, dies on Mount Nebo, in the land of Moab, having first taken a view of the Promised Land. Balaam commissioned by the king of Moab to curse Israel.

Above: *Moses looks out over the Promised Land. Like all but two of his companions who had left Egypt all those years ago, he was to die without entering it.*

Left: *Moses and the brazen serpent.*

Right: *Balaam blesses the Israelites against the wishes of King Balak of Moab.*

Moses' successor as leader of the Israelites was Joshua, long his closest companion and one of the two spies sent into Canaan who reported positively. It was now Joshua's task to lead his people in the conquest of the Promised Land.

The first step was the crossing of the River Jordan, then in flood. Miraculously, however, as soon as the priests leading the crossing stepped into the water, the waters subsided, and the Israelites crossed safely. To commemorate this, Joshua decreed that a memorial be built in the middle of the river.

Those of military age who entered Canaan were uncircumcised, for the generations that had made the Exodus from Egypt were now dead. So at Gilgal the whole nation was circumcised, signalling a new beginning. The manna that had fed them for so long ceased, and the day after the celebration of the Passover they ate for the first time the produce of the land of milk and honey.

Jericho was the first city to fall, and as with all the conquest, God's hand was visible in the outcome: he instructed Joshua to march his troops around the impregnable-looking walls of the city for six days; on the seventh they were to do

13: And it came to pass, when Joshua was by Jericho, that he lifted up his eyes and looked, and, behold, there stood a man over against him with his sword drawn in his hand: and Joshua went unto him, and said unto him, Art thou for us, or for our adversaries? 14: And he said, Nay; but as captain of the host of the LORD am I now come. And Joshua fell on his face to the earth, and did worship, and said unto him, What saith my lord unto his servant? 15: And the captain of the LORD's host said unto Joshua, Loose thy shoe from off thy foot; for the place whereon thou standest is holy. And Joshua did so. — *Joshua 5:13–15*

Above left: *Crossing the Jordan.*

Above: *Trumpets around the walls of Jericho.*

the same but the priests should blow their trumpets, and the walls would collapse. And so it happened, and Jericho fell to the Israelites.

The city of Ai followed, totally destroyed and all its people killed, according to God's instruction for total annihilation. Joshua then turned south, conquering the cities there, before advancing north as far as Sidon. Then Joshua set about allocating the newly conquered land to the twelve tribes.

By the time of his death, all Canaan had been taken. At Shechem, the Covenant was renewed, and Joshua was buried. And at Shechem they buried the bones of Joseph, which they had brought out of Egypt, at the plot of land Jacob had bought.

1451 The Israelites under Joshua pass the River Jordan and enter Canaan. Jericho is taken by Joshua, and after that the city of Ai. He makes a treaty with Gibeon and defeats the five kings of the Amorites, while the sun and moon stand still. The Israelites begin to till the lands they have conquered.
1445 Joshua makes a division of the land of Canaan among the tribes of Israel and rests from his conquests.
1426 Joshua dies in retirement at Timnath-serah, aged 110.

Right: *"Then spake Joshua to the Lord in the day when the Lord delivered up the Amorites before the children of Israel, and he said in the sight of Israel, Sun, stand thou still upon Gibeon; and thou, Moon, in the valley of Ajalon. And the sun stood still, and the moon stayed, until the people had avenged themselves upon their enemies. Is not this written in the book of Jasher? So the sun stood still in the midst of heaven, and hasted not to go down about a whole day. And there was no day like that before it or after it, that the Lord hearkened unto the voice of a man: for the Lord fought for Israel." (Joshua 10:12–14)*

Right: *Taking the city of Ai.*

Conquest does not necessarily bring peace. During the period following the death of Joshua, the Israelites lapsed into idolatry and gradually forgot their Covenant with God. The twelve tribes were also increasingly divided among themselves. As a result, they found themselves beset by enemies and often defeated, becoming subjects of other kings and states. This became a cycle, interrupted by God's appointment of a series of Judges, each of whom brought the people back to God and successfully defeated Israel's enemies.

Of those Judges, one was a woman named Deborah, whose practice it was to sit beneath a palm tree and there dispense advice to the people. She also had prophetic powers. When the depredations

THE SIX SERVITUDES OF ISRAEL

	Date	Oppressor king/state	Years
1	1413	Chusan of Mesopotamia	8
2	1343	Eglin of Moab	18
3	1305	Jabin of Canaan	20
4	1252	Midianites	7
5	1206	Philistines and Amorites	18
6	1156	Philistines	40

***Above left:** Deborah under the palm tree.*

***Above:** Gideon's noisy attack panics the Midianites.*

> 10: And ... there arose another generation after them, which knew not the Lord, nor yet the works which he had done for Israel. 11: And the children of Israel did evil in the sight of the Lord, and served Baalim: 12: And they forsook the Lord God of their fathers, which brought them out of the land of Egypt, and followed other gods, of the gods of the people that were round about them, and bowed themselves unto them, and provoked the Lord to anger ... 14: And the anger of the Lord was hot against Israel, and he delivered them into ... the hands of their enemies round about, so that they could not any longer stand before their enemies. 15: Whithersoever they went out, the hand of the Lord was against them for evil, as the Lord had said, and as the Lord had sworn unto them: and they were greatly distressed. 16: Nevertheless the Lord raised up judges, which delivered them out of the hand of those that spoiled them ... 18: And when the Lord raised them up judges, then the Lord was with the judge, and delivered them out of the hand of their enemies all the days of the judge ... 19: And it came to pass, when the judge was dead, that they returned, and corrupted themselves more than their fathers, in following other gods to serve them, and to bow down unto them; they ceased not from their own doings, nor from their stubborn way. — *Judges 2:10–19*

of the Canaanites became insupportable, she recruited a general, Barak. He was cautious, but Deborah directed him and told him that because of his vacillation the glory of the victory would not be wholly his; the enemy general would die by the hand of a woman. The battle duly won, the fleeing enemy general, Sisera, took refuge in the tent of Jael, wife of Heber, who offered him protection. When the exhausted Sisera lay down to sleep, Jael drove a tent peg through his temple.

THE FOURTEEN JUDGES OF ISRAEL

1 Othniel	7 Jair	13 Eli
2 Ehud	8 Jephthah	14 Samuel
3 Shamgar	9 Ibzan	
4 Deborah	10 Elon	* *Interrupted*
5 Gideon*	11 Abdon	*by Abimelech as*
6 Tola	12 Samson	*king, 3 years*

This victory led to the destruction of the Canaanite king and peace for forty years; but then the Israelites turned their faces from the Lord again. And again God raised up a Judge, this time a man called Gideon, who, armed with faith, won a great victory over the Midianites against great odds. As a demonstration to the people that the victory was due to God rather than to numbers, God told Gideon to attack the Midianites with just 300 men. Dividing his force into three, he equipped them with trumpets and jars with torches inside. Approaching the enemy camp they set up such a noise that the Midianites fled.

Forty years of peace ensued before the death of Gideon, after which one of his sons, Abimelech, bribed and killed his way to power and made himself king for three years, before perishing during a siege when a woman threw down a millstone upon his head.

And Israel meanwhile relapsed, losing the favor of the Lord and leading to subjection and humiliation, only to be rescued each time by a Judge raised up by God.

1413 The Israelites, having sunk into idolatry after the death of Joshua, are now in servitude under Chushan, king of Mesopotamia.
1405 Othniel, the first of the Judges, defeats Chushan, and frees Israel.
1390 The tribe of Benjamin is almost totally destroyed by the other eleven tribes, for their cruel usage of the wife of a Levite.
1325 Ehud the Benjamite kills Eglon, and so relieves them from their second bondage.
1285 Deborah the prophetess, and third Judge of Israel, with Barak, general of the Israelites, defeats the Canaanites under Sisera, at the Battle of Megiddo. Sisera is killed by Jael, the wife of Heber. Upon the battle is composed the beautiful "Song of Victory", in Judges, chapter 5.
1245 Gideon routs the Midianites with only 300 men and slays their two kings, Zebah and Zalmunna. He is offered the kingdom of Israel, which he refuses.
1236 Upon Gideon's death, Abimelech, his natural son, murders his seventy brothers and makes himself king of Israel for three years.
1206 The Israelites, being given to idolatry again, are delivered by God into the hands of the Philistines and Ammonites.
1188 Jephtha defeats the Ammonites and rashly makes a vow that deprives him of his daughter. He chastises the insolence of the Ephraimites, having killed 42,000 of them in a battle.

Top left: *Samson wrestles a lion to death.*

Above: *Captured by the Philistines, he is humiliated at a mill grinding corn.*

Left: *He pushes down the pillars of the Philistines' temple.*

28: And Samson called unto the Lord, and said, O Lord God, remember me, I pray thee, and strengthen me, I pray thee, only this once, O God, that I may be at once avenged of the Philistines for my two eyes. 29: And Samson took hold of the two middle pillars upon which the house stood, and on which it was borne up, of the one with his right hand, and of the other with his left. 30: And Samson said, Let me die with the Philistines. And he bowed himself with all his might; and the house fell upon the lords, and upon all the people that were therein. So the dead which he slew at his death were more than they which he slew in his life.

—*Judges 16: 28–30*

One of the Judges of Israel was Samson, in whom the spirit of the Lord had manifested itself as great strength combined with great virtue, for he was dedicated to God at his birth, never to imbibe wine, touch anything dead or cut his hair. His wonderful feats of strength included wrestling with a lion, carrying off the gates of the Philistine city of Gaza and, armed with nothing more than the jawbone of an ass, killing a host of Philistines. Unwisely, he married a Philistine, named Delilah, whom her countrymen paid to discover the secret of his might. And eventually she found out that if his hair were cut this would constitute breaking his Covenant vow; so this she did while her husband slept.

Shorn of his hair and now deprived of his great strength, Samson was captured by the enemy, blinded and set to work at a grinding mill. But as his hair grew back, so returned his power. Then, one day the Philistines decided to show him off in their Temple of Dagon. Chained there, he prayed to God, who gave him back his mighty strength to push down the massive pillars of the temple, killing all 3,000 Philistines within.

Right: *Delilah cuts Samson's hair.*

Ruth was a Moabite woman who became part of an illustrious lineage. She lived in Moab with her mother-in-law, Naomi, and sister-in-law, Orpah, both also widows. During a time of famine, Naomi returned to her native Bethlehem, accompanied by Ruth, and at harvest-time, Ruth gleaned leftover grain in the fields of Boaz, a local rich farmer. Seeing her in the fields, he fell in love with her and took her to wife. Their son, Obed, was the father of Jesse, the father of King David.

Right: *Ruth in the fields near Bethlehem.*

1136 Samson slays 1,000 Philistines with the jawbone of an ass.
1117 Samson is betrayed by Delilah and deprived of his strength; upon its return, he pulls down the Temple of Dagon on the heads of his enemies, the Philistines.
The Israelites take up arms but lose 4,000 men in one battle, and the Philistines capture the Ark of the Covenant. Among the dead are Hophni and Phinehas, sons of Eli, Judge of Israel and High Priest; this has been prophesied because of their corruption. The news of their death and the capture of the Ark kills Eli.
1117 To the time of Eli is referred the history of Ruth, great-grandmother of King David.

The last of the Judges was the greatest, for Samuel would be prophet and priest as well as Judge. His mother, Hannah, despaired of having a child until God interceded, and in thanks she dedicated the boy to God, his name meaning "Heard by God."

Meanwhile the Judge and High Priest, Eli, had two sons, who also became priests but whose abhorrent behavior aroused the wrath of God, especially when Eli failed to restrain them. One night, God spoke to the young Samuel, telling him that he would punish these two worthless men.

This punishment was meted out when the Philistines captured the Ark of the Covenant, a dreadful disaster for the Israelites. During the battle, Eli's sons were killed, and on hearing the shocking news, the old man fell off his chair, breaking his neck, and died.

The Philistines took the Ark back to Ashdod, and set it in the Temple of their great god, Dagon, as a trophy. But within two days the statue of the god had disintegrated, and the Philistines began to suffer from the plague. In vain they moved the Ark to Gath, only to have the plague break out there. So they returned the Ark to the Israelites, who repented their foolishness and idolatry, putting away the idols of Baal and Ashtaroth they had been worshipping, and listening instead to their new Judge, Samuel. And when the Philistines attacked the assembled Israelites at Mizpeh, God inflicted a great defeat upon them, and the

26: And Samuel said unto Saul, I will not return with thee: for thou hast rejected the word of the Lord, and the Lord hath rejected thee from being king over Israel. 27: And as Samuel turned about to go away, he laid hold upon the skirt of his mantle, and it rent. 28: And Samuel said unto him, The Lord hath rent the kingdom of Israel from thee this day, and hath given it to a neighbour of thine, that is better than thou. —*I Samuel 15:26–28*

> 13: So the Philistines were subdued, and they came no more into the coast of Israel: and the hand of the Lord was against the Philistines all the days of Samuel. 14: And the cities which the Philistines had taken from Israel were restored to Israel, from Ekron even unto Gath; and the coasts thereof did Israel deliver out of the hands of the Philistines. And there was peace between Israel and the Amorites. 15: And Samuel judged Israel all the days of his life. —*I Samuel 7:13–15*

***Far left:** Hannah presents her son Samuel to Eli, dedicating his life to God.*

***Near left:** When God first speaks to Samuel, he thinks it is Eli calling and awakens the old priest.*

Israelites recovered the lands they had previously lost to their enemy.

When he became old, Samuel appointed his sons as Judges, making the same mistake as Eli, for both were unworthy. The elders came to tell him so and demanded that the nation be ruled by a king. Samuel consulted God, who told him to listen to the people, and so set out to find a suitable candidate for the throne. God directed him to Saul, a tall, 30-year old Benjamite, who was acclaimed king.

Saul began his reign well, relieving the Ammonite siege of Jabesh, but in the next encounter with the Philistines his generalship, although successful in the end, was poor, and Samuel rebuked him. Saul continued campaigning on all sides, but there came a battle with the Amalekites at which he captured the enemy king, Agag. The Amalekite host had been destroyed, but Saul spared their ruler, and his men took the livestock of their foes as plunder. This was contrary to the instructions of God, however, who had specified total destruction. Samuel again remonstrated and had Agag put to death. And now God rejected Saul.

1116 Samuel, the twelfth and last Judge of Israel, for 21 years.
The Philistines, having placed the Ark of the Covenant in the Temple of Dagon, are smitten with emerods, and send it back after seven months' possession.
1096 The Philistines are defeated by Samuel.
1095 The Israelites ask for a king, which is granted them, though with God's displeasure; and Saul is anointed by Samuel to be their king.
1093 Saul defeats the Philistines. But Saul is rejected by God for disobedience with regard to Amalekites.

***Above:** Samuel slays King Agag.*

Left: David plays the harp for the despairing and now God-forsaken Saul. Twice, in outbursts of violent rage, he hurled a javelin at David, but missed.

God now led Samuel to David, youngest son of Jesse, whom he had chosen to be king in Saul's place – but not yet. In the meantime, with God's favor withdrawn from Saul, an evil spirit tormented him. When David entered the royal court, the melancholy king found that the young man's harp-playing soothed him.

During another campaign against the Philistines, David visited the camp bringing provisions and heard the Philistine champion Goliath challenge the Israelites to single combat; hearing the challenge, he volunteered and faced the giant armour-

41: And the Philistine came on and drew near unto David; and the man that bare the shield went before him. 42: And when the Philistine looked about, and saw David, he disdained him: for he was but a youth, and ruddy, and of a fair countenance. 43: And the Philistine said unto David, Am I a dog, that thou comest to me with staves? And the Philistine cursed David by his gods. 44: And the Philistine said to David, Come to me, and I will give thy flesh unto the fowls of the air, and to the beasts of the field. 45: Then said David to the Philistine, Thou comest to me with a sword, and with a spear, and with a shield: but I come to thee in the name of the Lord of hosts, the God of the armies of Israel, whom thou hast defied. 46: This day will the Lord deliver thee into mine hand; and I will smite thee, and take thine head from thee ... 49: And David put his hand in his bag, and took thence a stone, and slang it, and smote the Philistine in his forehead, that the stone sunk into his forehead; and he fell upon his face to the earth ... And when the Philistines saw their champion was dead, they fled. *— I Samuel 17: 41–46, 49–51*

clad champion with no more than a sling. With one stone he killed Goliath. David now attained high rank at court and led armies in the field against the Philistines with great success, but Saul increasingly saw the hand of the Lord – while he himself had been deserted, God's favor was all too clearly to be seen with David. In fits of depression, he twice nearly killed David, who fled, pursued into the hills by Saul with troops. Several attempts were made on David's life, but he managed to escape, helped by his intimate friendship with Saul's son Jonathan.

On two occasions, David managed to infiltrate Saul's camp and took evidence that he had been in Saul's tent and could have killed the king but did not. Each

time Saul repented outwardly, but he was increasingly alone. Samuel, who had turned away from him, had now died, but Saul consulted a witch at Endor, who raised Samuel's spirit, and Saul asked him for help. But Samuel had no words of comfort and predicted that his end was near.

These words came true very shortly afterwards: at the battle near Mount Gilboa, the Philistines were successful, Jonathan and Saul's other sons perishing in the battle. Saul, in despair at the defeat and his loss, fell upon his sword.

1085 Birth of David, son of Jesse.
David, when 22 years old, is anointed by Samuel to be king after Saul.
1074 War of Saul against the Amalekites.
1062 David, finding that Saul seeks to take his life, retires into the deserts of Judah.
1056 David retires among the Philistines, who give him Ziklag, where he lives for one year and four months.
1055 Saul consults the Witch of Endor, and is totally defeated by the Philistines next day at Mount Gilboa; three of his sons are slain, upon which he kills himself.

Left: David, penetrating Saul's camp, has power of life or death over the sleeping king.

Below: Saul at the battle of Mount Gilboa: defeated, forsaken by God, his sons killed, he takes his own life.

Upon the death of Saul, the king's fourth son, Ish-bosheth (Esh-baal), was proclaimed king by the general of the army, Abner. David meanwhile moved from Ziklag to Hebron, where the elders of Judah anointed him king. The Israelites were thus split, and civil war became inevitable. After seven years of fighting, Abner (the power behind the throne of the feeble Ish-bosheth) quarreled with his king over a former concubine of Saul, and Abner transferred his allegiance to David.

They came to an agreement, part of which was that David's wife Michal (daughter of Saul) be restored to him. Abner did not long outlive the meeting at Hebron, however, slain by Joab, one of David's nephews, in pursuance of a long-standing feud. David was careful to distance himself from the act, did not punish the assassin, but instead laid a curse upon Joab's family.

Not long after this, Ish-bosheth was himself assassinated, and the elders of the northern tribes came to Hebron to anoint David king at last of all the Jews.

The Philistines, realizing that a united kingdom would be more difficult to keep in check, attacked twice but were soundly defeated and repulsed. David could now set about consolidating his kingdom.

His first move was to attack and capture Jerusalem, the city of the Jebusites, which stood at the border between the previously warring kingdoms. A strong site, Jerusalem would become the city of David, both religious

Left: *David's troops storm Jerusalem.*

Right: *David anointed king at Hebron. He had been anointed three times: first, by Samuel; then by the tribe of Judah; and finally by the elders of all the tribes.*

1053 Ish-bosheth proclaimed king of Israel.
1048 Ish-bosheth assassinated. David acknowledged king over all Israel. He is consecrated a third time at Hebron.
1047 Jerusalem taken from the Jebusites by David, who makes it the capital of the united kingdom.

1: Then came all the tribes of Israel to David unto Hebron, and spake, saying, Behold, we are thy bone and thy flesh. 2: Also in time past, when Saul was king over us, thou wast he that leddest out and broughtest in Israel: and the Lord said to thee, Thou shalt feed my people Israel, and thou shalt be a captain over Israel. 3: So all the elders of Israel came to the king to Hebron; and king David made a league w ith them in Hebron before the Lord: and they anointed David king over Israel. 4: David was thirty years old when he began to reign, and he reigned forty years. 5: In Hebron he reigned over Judah seven years and six months: and in Jerusalem he reigned thirty and three years over all Israel and Judah. 6: And the king and his men went to Jerusalem unto the Jebusites, the inhabitants of the land: which spake unto David, saying, Except thou take away the blind and the lame, thou shalt not come in hither: thinking, David cannot come in hither. 7: Nevertheless David took the strong hold of Zion: the same is the city of David. 8: And David said on that day, Whosoever getteth up to the gutter, and smiteth the Jebusites, and the lame and the blind, that are hated of David's soul, he shall be chief and captain. Wherefore they said, The blind and the lame shall not come into the house. 9: So David dwelt in the fort, and called it the city of David. And David built round about from Millo and inward. 10: And David went on, and grew great, and the Lord God of hosts was with him. —*2 Samuel 5: 1–10.*

and administrative capital of his kingdom. The Ark of the Covenant, captured by the Philistines many years earlier, then restored to the Israelites, had lain neglected at Kiriath-jearim for some half a century. Now, as part of David's plan to make Jerusalem the religious heart of his kingdom, it was brought to the city and installed in a new Tabernacle. Its arrival was a scene of much rejoicing, as David

Left: *King David dances as the Ark of the Covenant is brought to Jerusalem.*

1: And David consulted with the captains of thousands and hundreds, and with every leader. 2: And David said unto all the congregation of Israel, If it seem good unto you, and that it be of the Lord our God, let us send abroad unto our brethren every where, that are left in all the land of Israel, and with them also to the priests and Levites which are in their cities and suburbs, that they may gather themselves unto us: 3: And let us bring again the ark of our God to us: for we inquired not at it in the days of Saul. 4: And all the congregation said that they would do so: for the thing was right in the eyes of all the people. 5: So David gathered all Israel together ... to bring up thence the ark of God the LORD, that dwelleth between the cherubims, whose name is called on it. 7: And they carried the ark of God in a new cart out of the house of Abinadab: and Uzza and Ahio drave the cart. 8: And David and all Israel played before God with all their might, and with singing, and with harps, and with psalteries, and with timbrels, and with cymbals, and with trumpets. — *1 Chronicles 13:1–8*

danced before the Ark. But Michal condemned the king for unseemly behavior, only to be told that what she saw as vulgar was appropriate in the eyes of the Lord. And God responded by making the queen barren.

Military conquest beyond the borders of the kingdom now became David's primary concern. First he defeated the Philistines decisively, so that they were no longer a major power in the region (although he would later have to fight a campaign to prevent their resurgence). He attacked Moab, Syria, Edom, and the Ammonites, expanding his realm and creating a substantial empire which commanded trade routes north via Damascus and south via the Red Sea port of Ezion-Geber. Now equipped with a strong force of chariots, the kingdom of Israel had become the dominant power in the region.

The glory of David's reign was now to be tarnished by a grievous sin, however. While his main army was fighting the Ammonites, David happened to see a beautiful woman bathing, called her to his presence, and they lay together. This was Bathsheba, wife of Uriah, a Hittite in David's royal guard then active at the siege of Rabbah. The king then sent a message to Joab, in command of the siege, to place Uriah in the forefront of the fighting, but then to ensure he became isolated from his comrades and was killed. This Joab did. Uriah died; Bathsheba mourned; and after a time became wife to David and bearing him a son.

But God was displeased at this ruthless act and sent Nathan to the king. Nathan told David a parable analogous to the king's own wicked behavior, the listener unwittingly declaring that the perpetrator should die. Then Nathan revealed the message of the story and judgment – that David had himself sinned and would be punished by the Lord.

1046 David eliminates the Philistines as a military rival and makes further conquests.
1045 David brings the Ark from Kirjath-jearim to Jerusalem and commits it to Abinadab. After three months, David brings it to his own palace.
1035 David commits adultery with Bathsheba and engineers the death of Uriah, her husband. For this sin he is reproved by Nathan.

1: And the Lord sent Nathan unto David. And he came unto him, and said unto him, There were two men in one city; the one rich, and the other poor. 2: The rich man had exceeding many flocks and herds: 3: But the poor man had nothing, save one little ewe lamb, which he had bought and nourished up: and it grew up together with him, and with his children; it did eat of his own meat, and drank of his own cup, and lay in his bosom, and was unto him as a daughter. 4: And there came a traveller unto the rich man, and he spared to take of his own flock and of his own herd, to dress for the wayfaring man that was come unto him; but took the poor man's lamb, and dressed it for the man that was come to him. 5: And David's anger was greatly kindled against the man; and he said to Nathan, As the Lord liveth, the man that hath done this thing shall surely die: 6: And he shall restore the lamb fourfold, because he did this thing, and because he had no pity. 7: And Nathan said to David, Thou art the man. —*2 Samuel 12: 1–7*

Above: *King David repents his adultery with Bathsheba and mourns the death of their son.*

David repented, but God caused his son by Bathsheba to die.
More tragedies were to follow, for a callous rape then set in motion a sequence of grave family troubles for the House of David. Amnon, his eldest son by Ahinoam, raped his half-sister, Tamar, who fled to her brother Absalom. David's anger at this was, fatally, not followed by action, allowing Absalom's resentment to fester until, two years later, his men murdered Amnon. Absalom fled the king's wrath to Geshur, where he remained in exile for three years. Meanwhile David grieved at this family tragedy and the loss of his beloved son – until persuaded to allow his return. Even then, it was another two years before father and son would meet face to face.

In time, Absalom became accepted again in Jerusalem and began to assume the position of heir-apparent, openly soliciting the goodwill of the people. Meanwhile he quietly built up his own personal following and set in plan a well-concealed conspiracy.

When the time seemed ripe, Absalom struck, staging a coup that took David completely by surprise. David fled with

1034 Solomon born.
1023 Absalom rebels against David and takes Jerusalem but is defeated and killed by Joab.

Above: *Absalom seeks popularity in Jerusalem.*

Below: *David escapes from Jerusalem as Absalom takes control of the city.*

8: For the battle was there scattered over the face of all the country: and the wood devoured more people that day than the sword devoured. 9: And Absalom met the servants of David. And Absalom rode upon a mule, and the mule went under the thick boughs of a great oak, and his head caught hold of the oak, and he was taken up between the heaven and the earth; and the mule that was under him went away. 10: And a certain man saw it, and told Joab, and said, Behold, I saw Absalom hanged in an oak. 11: And Joab said unto the man that told him, And, behold, thou sawest him, and why didst thou not smite him there to the ground? and I would have given thee ten shekels of silver, and a girdle. 12: And the man said unto Joab, Though I should receive a thousand shekels of silver in mine hand, yet would I not put forth mine hand against the king's son: for in our hearing the king charged thee and Abishai and Ittai, saying, Beware that none touch the young man Absalom. 13: Otherwise I should have wrought falsehood against mine own life: for there is no matter hid from the king, and thou thyself wouldest have set thyself against me. 14: Then said Joab, I may not tarry thus with thee. And he took three darts in his hand, and thrust them through the heart of Absalom, while he was yet alive in the midst of the oak. 15: And ten young men that bare Joab's armour compassed about and smote Absalom, and slew him. *—2 Samuel 18:8–15*

his household, and Absalom took control of Jerusalem.

Ahithophel, Bathsheba's grandfather, had been one of David's wisest advisors, but had disapproved of the king's treatment of his daughter. Now he stayed in Jerusalem to counsel Absalom and advised Absalom to sleep with those of David's concubines that had remained in the city, which he did, committing a deep public insult to his father that ensured there could be no reconciliation between them.

Left: *Absalom's death.*

Above: *David grieves for his son.*

But David sent back spies, the leader of whom, Hushai, soon won the trust of the usurper king. His military advice prevailed: that Absalom should gather his strength before attacking David rather than follow Ahithophel's advice and send a flying column to capture him and thereby risk ambush and the bad impression that losses would cause. This gave David time to rally his forces so that when Absalom's army met his, in a great battle in the forest of Ephraim, the usurper's forces were defeated. Absalom's short-lived reign ended in an accident – riding through the forest, he was caught by a branch, where David's men found the dangling king and dispatched him.

David returned to his capital, but another ill effect of his son's rebellion was soon to show itself – a break between Judah and the northern tribes. David's main supporters in putting down the revolt were from Judah, and when he returned to Jerusalem these troops accompanied him, arousing jealousy among the northerners. One of them, a Benjamite named Sheba, incited a further mutiny but won scant support. Cornered in Abel Beth Maacah, he was beheaded by the unsympathetic inhabitants and his head thrown over the

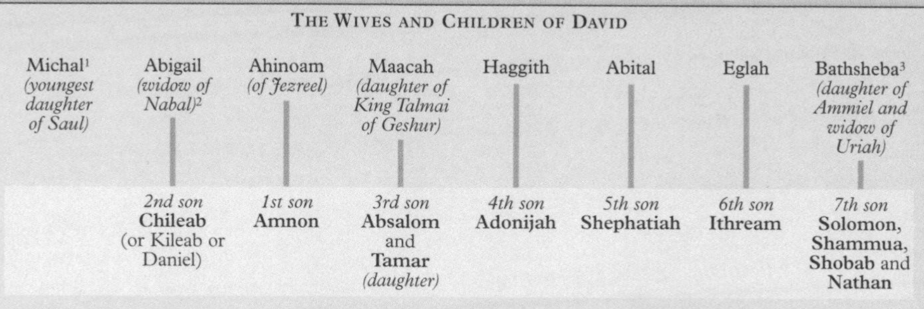

THE WIVES AND CHILDREN OF DAVID

Michal[1] *(youngest daughter of Saul)*	Abigail *(widow of Nabal)*[2]	Ahinoam *(of Jezreel)*	Maacah *(daughter of King Talmai of Geshur)*	Haggith	Abital	Eglah	Bathsheba[3] *(daughter of Ammiel and widow of Uriah)*
	2nd son **Chileab** (or Kileab or Daniel)	*1st son* **Amnon**	*3rd son* **Absalom** and **Tamar** *(daughter)*	*4th son* **Adonijah**	*5th son* **Shephatiah**	*6th son* **Ithream**	*7th son* **Solomon, Shammua, Shobab** and **Nathan**

David's first five sons were born at Hebron, when it was his capital for seven and a half years. He had other sons by concubines incuding: Ibhar, Elishua, Nogah, Nepheg, Japhia, Elishama, Eliada and Eliphelet.

1 – Michal aided David's escape from a trap set by Saul; she was later given to Paltiel by Saul but returned to David by Abner. She was estranged after criticizing David during the return of the Ark of the Covenant to Jerusalem.

2 – Nabal was a farmer who refused David's troops supplies while he was in conflict with Saul, despite David's troops protecting his flocks; Abigail took food to the troops and apologized to David. Nabal died soon after and David took her to wife.

3 – Bathsheba was also granddaughter of Ahithophel.

The Gibeonites – Last Years of David

1: Then there was a famine in the days of David three years, year after year; and David inquired of the Lord. And the Lord answered, It is for Saul, and for his bloody house, because he slew the Gibeonites. 2: And the king called the Gibeonites, and said unto them; (now the Gibeonites were not of the children of Israel, but of the remnant of the Amorites; and the children of Israel had sworn unto them: and Saul sought to slay them in his zeal to the children of Israel and Judah.) 3: Wherefore David said unto the Gibeonites, What shall I do for you? and wherewith shall I make the atonement, that ye may bless the inheritance of the Lord? 4: And the Gibeonites said unto him, We will have no silver nor gold of Saul, nor of his house; neither for us shalt thou kill any man in Israel. And he said, What ye shall say, that will I do for you. 5: And they answered the king, The man that consumed us, and that devised against us that we should be destroyed from remaining in any of the coasts of Israel, 6: Let seven men of his sons be delivered unto us, and we will hang them up unto the Lord in Gibeah of Saul, whom the Lord did choose. And the king said, I will give them. 7: But the king spared Mephibosheth, the son of Jonathan the son of Saul, because of the Lord's oath that was between them, between David and Jonathan the son of Saul. 8: But the king took the two sons of Rizpah the daughter of Aiah, whom she bare unto Saul, Armoni and Mephibosheth; and the five sons of Michal the daughter of Saul, whom she brought up for Adriel the son of Barzillai the Meholathite: 9: And he delivered them into the hands of the Gibeonites, and they hanged them in the hill before the Lord: and they fell all seven together, and were put to death in the days of harvest, in the first days, in the beginning of barley harvest. 10: And Rizpah the daughter of Aiah took sackcloth, and spread it for her upon the rock, from the beginning of harvest until water dropped upon them out of heaven, and suffered neither the birds of the air to rest on them by day, nor the beasts of the field by night. 11: And it was told David what Rizpah the daughter of Aiah, the concubine of Saul, had done. 12: And David went and took the bones of Saul and the bones of Jonathan his son from the men of Jabesh-gilead, which had stolen them from the street of Beth-shan, where the Philistines had hanged them, when the Philistines had slain Saul in Gilboa: 13: And he brought up from thence the bones of Saul and the bones of Jonathan his son; and they gathered the bones of them that were hanged. 14: And the bones of Saul and Jonathan his son buried they in the country of Benjamin in Zelah, in the sepulchre of Kish his father: and they performed all that the king commanded. And after that God was intreated for the land.

—*2 Samuel 21:1–14.*

walls to the royal troops preparing to besiege the place.

A famine struck the kingdom and lasted three years before David appealed to God, to be told that this was punishment upon the people for Saul's sin, committed many years earlier, against the Gibeonites, a number of whom Saul had treacherously slain. The sin must be expiated, so David had the representatives of the Gibeonites brought to his court in order to offer amends. They specified that seven male descendants of Saul be given up for execution and then their bodies exposed at Gibeon.

When David took a census of the fighting men in his realm, God was displeased and gave him a choice of three punishments: three years of famine; three months of fleeing his enemies; or three days of plague. The latter ensued until God directed David to the threshing-floor of Araunah, which he purchased and there built an altar for burnt sacrifice. The plague stopped. But David now decided that here he would build a proper, stone temple to house the Ark of the Covenant. It was not to be in his lifetime, however, but he set out detailed instructions for Solomon, his chosen successor, to follow.

1021 Famine strikes Israel; David appeases God's wrath by compensating for the sin committed on the Gibeonites.
1017 David takes a census: there are 800,000 fighting men in Israel; 500,000 in Judah.
1017 David purchases the site for the Temple.
1015 David dies.

***Left:** David purchases Araunah's threshing floor, watched by an angel in the sky with unsheathed sword.*

***Above:** David in extreme old age, comforted by his last concubine, Abishag.*

Influenced by Bathsheba, David chose as his successor Solomon, her eldest surviving son. He inherited a realm that was strong, prosperous, and at peace. Solomon's reign was a golden age of Israel, fed by bountiful trade, and famous for its dazzling wealth.

Solomon's first actions were to secure his throne, which included the execution of his half-brother Adonijah, the rightful heir to the throne in terms of simple primogeniture, who had insolently asked for the hand of the old king's concubine, Abishag. Solomon doubtless saw him as a threat to his throne.

At Gibeon, God appeared to Solomon, and the new king asked for guidance and a discerning heart to govern God's people and to distinguish between right and wrong, which pleased the Lord. And indeed, wisdom, quite apart from wealth, was the quality that impressed visitors – not only sound judgment in all things, but a knowledge and erudition on all manner of subjects.

***Left:** The judgment of Solomon – ordering that the child be cut in two reveals the true, caring mother.*

1016 Rehoboam born, son of Solomon.
1013 Solomon marries a daughter of the king of Egypt. Solomon gives a remarkable sentence in a case between two women.

5: In Gibeon the Lord appeared to Solomon in a dream by night ... 6: And Solomon said ... O LORD my God, thou hast made thy servant king instead of David my father: and I am but a little child: I know not how to go out or come in ... 9: Give therefore thy servant an understanding heart to judge thy people, that I may discern between good and bad: for who is able to judge this thy so great a people? 10: And the speech pleased the Lord ... 11: And God said unto him, Because thou hast asked this thing, and hast not asked for thyself long life; neither hast asked riches for thyself, nor hast asked the life of thine enemies ...12: Behold, I have done according to thy words: lo, I have given thee a wise and an understanding heart ... 14: And if thou wilt walk in my ways, to keep my statutes and my commandments ... then I will lengthen thy days. 15: And Solomon awoke ... And he came to Jerusalem, and stood before the ark of the covenant of the LORD, and offered up burnt offerings, and offered peace offerings, and made a feast to all his servants. *—I Kings 3:5–15*

16: Then came there two women, that were harlots, unto the king, and stood before him. 17: And the one woman said, O my lord, I and this woman dwell in one house; and I was delivered of a child with her in the house. 18: And it came to pass the third day after that I was delivered, that this woman was delivered also: and we were together; there was no stranger with us in the house, save we two in the house. 19: And this woman's child died in the night; because she overlaid it. 20: And she arose at midnight, and took my son from beside me, while thine handmaid slept, and laid it in her bosom, and laid her dead child in my bosom. 21: And when I rose in the morning to give my child suck, behold, it was dead: but when I had considered it in the morning, behold, it was not my son, which I did bear. 22: And the other woman said, Nay; but the living is my son, and the dead is thy son. And this said, No; but the dead is thy son, and the living is my son. Thus they spake before the king. 23: Then said the king, The one saith, This is my son that liveth, and thy son is the dead: and the other saith, Nay; but thy son is the dead, and my son is the living. 24: And the king said, Bring me a sword. And they brought a sword before the king. 25: And the king said, Divide the living child in two, and give half to the one, and half to the other. 26: Then spake the woman whose the living child was unto the king, for her bowels yearned upon her son, and she said, O my lord, give her the living child, and in no wise slay it. But the other said, Let it be neither mine nor thine, but divide it. 27: Then the king answered and said, Give her the living child, and in no wise slay it: she is the mother thereof. 28: And all Israel heard of the judgment which the king had judged; and they feared the king: for they saw that the wisdom of God was in him, to do judgment. *—I Kings 3:16–28*

The crowning centerpiece of Solomon's reign was the construction of the great Temple. Building began in the fourth year of his reign and took seven years. The Bible provides a very detailed description of its dimensions, decoration, and furnishings. Built of both stone and wood, it featured prominently the famed cedars of Lebanon, provided by Solomon's friend and ally, Hiram of Tyre. The general plan followed that of the Tabernacle, which had traveled through the Wilderness with Moses from Egypt to the Promised Land. In the inner sanctum was installed the Ark of the Covenant, which David had brought up to Zion. Solomon dedicated the Temple in a fourteen-day festival, during which he is recorded as having sacrificed 22,000 cattle and 120,000 sheep and goats.

The Temple

- The Temple was in three parts: the portico, main sanctuary and inner sanctuary, the latter containing the Ark of the Covenant. Around these rooms were smaller chambers for the priests.
- It took 7 years to build on Mount Moriah and measured 60 cubits long by 20 wide and 30 high.
- At the entrance were two great pillars, called Jachin and Boaz.
- The inner walls were lined with cedar wood, with rich carvings and much gold embellishment.
- Across the entrance to the inner sanctuary, the oracle, were gold chains, and there were two cherubim with outstretched wings, 10 cubits high and overlaid with gold.

For the second time, God appeared to Solomon, accepting his Temple, but issuing a stern warning against non-observance of his commands and decrees.

Left and right: *The dedication of the Temple. It would last more than 400 years until its destruction by Nebuchadnezzar. By that time, however, it was greatly decayed, much of the decoration having been used to pay off foreign conquerors.*

1012 Solomon lays the foundation of the Temple, 480 years after the Exodus from Egypt. Hiram, king of Tyre, supplies cedar wood and workmen to assist in building it.
1004 Temple of Solomon finished.
1004 The Temple is solemnly dedicated, 1,000 years before Christ and 3,000 years after Creation.
Zadok is rewarded for his loyalty to both David and Solomon by being appointed High Priest, a role that becomes hereditary in his family.

Solomon also built a great royal palace, similarly ornamented and fitted out in sumptuous style, and he made use of the expertise of Hiram's people to build a fleet of trading ships on the Red Sea coast. These vessels plied their trade in three-yearly voyages, returning with gold, silver, ivory, and even apes and baboons.

The brilliance of the realm and its ruler attracted the attention of surrounding nations, and Solomon's distinguished guests included the daughter of Pharaoh of Egypt, and the Queen of Sheba, who came from her country far to the south. She arrived with a huge caravan laden with spices, gold, and precious stones, and was afforded a spectacular welcome.

But in the end, for all his wisdom and wealth, Solomon did not live up to God's expectations of him. Significantly he failed to observe God's commandments forbidding intermarriage with foreigners, and the Bible tells us that he proceeded to take 700 wives of royal birth and 300 concubines. Worse, these women brought their own religions, which Solomon accommodated, so that he gradually ceased to be fully devoted to God. This angered God: Solomon and the Israelites had been warned repeatedly; God promised that upon Solomon's death he would tear the kingdom in two.

992 Solomon finishes the building of his palace, and that of his queen, the daughter of Pharaoh.
Visit of Queen of Sheba.

Left: *The reception of the Queen of Sheba.*

Above: *She questions Solomon on all manner of subjects.*

Below: *Solomon's trading fleet brings back the riches of the east.*

Upon the death of Solomon, Rehoboam became king, but, as God had told Solomon, there was to be punishment for Solomon's breaking of the Covenant and God's commands. Internal strife in the kingdom, provoked by the king's heavy handed imposition of taxes and promises of a stern rule, led to a rebellion of the ten northern tribes, who broke away, Jeroboam setting himself up as king of Israel, with his capital city at Samaria. This was to become a permanent division, despite efforts by several kings to reunite the Jews.

Jeroboam was fearful of the effect of the pilgrimages his subjects would make to Jerusalem and to the Temple there, so he took measures to create a new priesthood and bullcalf idols, which he set up at Bethel and Dan, thus subverting the people from their religion. He proceeded with this heedless of the warnings given him by the blind prophet Ahijah of Shiloh: his actions condemned him in the eyes of God, and his dynasty was doomed.

975 Solomon dies and the kingdom splits into Israel (north, the land of ten tribes) and Judah, with its capital at Jerusalem.
975(–958) Jeroboam king of Israel.
975(–958) Rehoboam king of Judah.
974 Jeroboam reproved by the prophet Shemaiah for establishing worship of golden calves in the kingdom of Israel at Bethel and Dan – "He made Israel to sin." The prophet also foretells of Josiah (639–610).
c.973 Priests and Levites leave the kingdom of Israel for that of Judah following Jeroboam's measures to stop religious ties with Jerusalem.

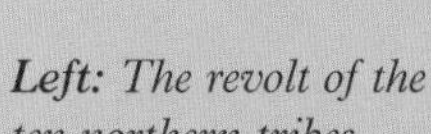

***Left:** The revolt of the ten northern tribes.*

***Right:** Shemaiah was another prophet who condemned Jeroboam for setting up idols in Israel.*

Elijah was one of the most forceful prophets, strong in his determination to champion the Hebrew God (his name literally meant "Yahweh is my God") and to turn the Israelites back from the worship of idols – for Ahab, king of Israel, listened to the entreaties of his Tyrian wife, Jezebel, and introduced the worship of Melkart, the Phoenician version of Baal. Elijah warned him that God's punishment would be a drought. When this came about, Elijah went into in the wilderness, reassured by God that he would find water from a stream and would be fed by bread and flesh brought him by ravens. Many in Israel perished, but at Zarephath Elijah came upon a widow and her child who were on the verge of starving to death; miraculously, her flour, oil, and water did not run out, and Elijah saved the life of the child.

Right: *Elijah confronts King Ahab and tells him that turning away from God in favor of Baal will surely bring down divine judgment upon his head. He predicts that Israel will suffer a terrible drought and famine.*

Left: *In the wilderness, as the famine strikes Israel, Elijah is fed by ravens.*

Right: *Elijah saves the life of the widow's child in Zarephath.*

971 Pharaoh Shishak of Egypt plunders Jerusalem.
958(–955) Abijam king of Judah.
957 Abijam defeats Jeroboam in battle.
955(–914) Asa king of Judah.
954(–953) Nadab king of Israel.
953(–930) Baasha usurps the throne of Israel.
945 Inspired by the prophet Azariah, King Asa eliminates idolatry in Judah and fortifies Judah. He repulses an attack by King Zerrah of Ethiopia (probably modern Sudan).
930(–929) Elah king of Israel.
929 Zimri usurps the throne of Israel, assassinating Elah, but is himself dethroned and killed by Omri (929–917). He builds a new capital city for the northern kingdom, called Samaria.*
917(–897) Ahab king of Israel. His wife, Jezebel, persuades him to impose the worship of her own Phoenician god Melkart (Baal).
914(–889) Jehosophat king of Judah; he builds strong defenses for the state, increases the army and ensures that the people are taught the law and stop worshipping foreign gods.
910 Elijah predicts famine in Israel, which comes to pass.

* All that remains today is a mound at Sebaste, near Nablus.

On returning to the king, Elijah challenged him to a contest of faith: two sacrificial altars were to be built, one to Baal, the other to the Hebrew God. This took place on Mount Carmel. The priests of Baal (the Bible accounts them as 450 prophets of Baal) set a bullock upon their altar, but despite a day of entreaties to their god could not provide divine fire to kindle the wood. Elijah's demonstration was made

Elijah mocks the priests of Baal: 26: And they took the bullock which was given them, and they dressed it, and called on the name of Baal from morning even until noon, saying, O Baal, hear us. But there was no voice, nor any that answered. And they leaped upon the altar which was made. 27: And it came to pass at noon, that Elijah mocked them, and said, Cry aloud: for he is a god; either he is talking, or he is pursuing, or he is in a journey, or peradventure he sleepeth, and must be awaked — *1 Kings 18: 26–27*

more demanding by thoroughly wetting the sacrifice, the wood and stones, and even by filling a trench around the altar with water. But when Elijah prayed, fire fell upon victim, wood, stone and even consumed the water. The people loudly acclaimed the victory of the Hebrew God; the priests of Baal were taken away and slaughtered.

Now came an end to the drought; heavy rain was about to fall, and Elijah warned the king. But he would not heed, and went off to eat and drink. When the rain fell, very heavily, the power of the Lord came upon Elijah and he ran faster than the king's chariot.

Left: *Divine fire descends upon Elijah's sacrifice on Mount Carmel.*

Above: *Elijah's servant sees a cloud like a man's hand out at sea, as the storm approaches.*

907 Elijah defeats the prophets of Baal in a sacrificial contest.

36: And it came to pass at the time of the offering of the evening sacrifice, that Elijah the prophet came near, and said, Lord God of Abraham, Isaac, and of Israel, let it be known this day that thou art God in Israel, and that I am thy servant, and that I have done all these things at thy word. 37: Hear me, O Lord, hear me, that this people may know that thou art the Lord God, and that thou hast turned their heart back again. 38: Then the fire of the Lord fell, and consumed the burnt sacrifice, and the wood, and the stones, and the dust and licked up the water that was in the trench. 39: And when all the people saw it, they fell on their faces: and they said, The Lord, he is the God; the Lord, he is the God. 40: And Elijah said unto them, Take the prophets of Baal; let not one of them escape. And they took them: and Elijah brought them down to the brook Kishon, and slew them there. 41: And Elijah said unto Ahab, Get thee up, eat and drink; for there is a sound of abundance of rain. 42: So Ahab went up to eat and to drink. And Elijah went up to the top of Carmel; and he cast himself down upon the earth, and put his face between his knees, 43: And said to his servant, Go up now, look toward the sea. And he went up, and looked, and said, There is nothing. And he said, Go again seven times. 44: And it came to pass at the seventh time, that he said, Behold, there ariseth a little cloud out of the sea, like a man's hand. And he said, Go up, say unto Ahab, Prepare thy chariot, and get thee down, that the rain stop thee not. 45: And it came to pass in the mean while, that the heaven was black with clouds and wind, and there was a great rain. And Ahab rode, and went to Jezreel. 46: And the hand of the Lord was on Elijah; and he girded up his loins, and ran before Ahab to the entrance of Jezreel.
— *1 Kings 18: 36–46*

Above: *Elijah, desolate in the wilderness mountains of Horeb.*

Seething with rage, meanwhile, Jezebel planned her revenge upon the prophet. But before her soldiers could seize him, Elijah fled into the southern wilderness of Judah. Despite the triumph of the two altars, Elijah felt desolate and hopeless and even asked God for death. But God sent an angel to minister to him, and eventually Elijah found refuge in a cave on Mount Horeb. Here a great wind, earthquake, and fire erupted all around before God revealed himself to the prophet in a "still small voice," reassuring him and revealing that Hazael would become king of Syria, Jehu king of Israel, and that Elisha would be Elijah's successor.

1: And Ahab told Jezebel all that Elijah had done, and withal how he had slain all the prophets with the sword. 2: Then Jezebel sent a messenger unto Elijah, saying, So let the gods do to me, and more also, if I make not thy life as the life of one of them by to morrow about this time. 3: And when he saw that, he arose, and went for his life, and came to Beer-sheba, which belongeth to Judah, and left his servant there. 4: But he himself went a day's journey into the wilderness, and came and sat down under a juniper tree: and he requested for himself that he might die; and said, It is enough; now, O Lord, take away my life; for I am not better than my fathers. 5: And as he lay and slept under a juniper tree, behold, then an angel touched him, and said unto him, Arise and eat. 6: And he looked, and, behold, there was a cake baken on the coals, and a cruse of water at his head. And he did eat and drink, and laid him down again. 7: And the angel of the Lord came again the second time, and touched him, and said, Arise and eat; because the journey is too great for thee. 8: And he arose, and did eat and drink, and went in the strength of that meat forty days and forty nights unto Horeb the mount of God. 9: And he came thither unto a cave, and lodged there; and, behold, the word of the LORD came to him, and he said unto him, What doest thou here, Elijah? 10: And he said, I have been very jealous for the Lord God of hosts: for the children of Israel have forsaken thy covenant, thrown down thine altars, and slain thy prophets with the sword; and I, even I only, am left; and they seek my life, to take it away. 11: And he said, Go forth, and stand upon the mount before the Lord. And, behold, the Lord passed by, and a great and strong wind rent the mountains, and brake in pieces the rocks before the Lord; but the Lord was not in the wind: and after the wind an earthquake; but the Lord was not in the earthquake: 12: And after the earthquake a fire; but the Lord was not in the fire: and after the fire a still small voice. 13: And it was so, when Elijah heard it, that he wrapped his face in his mantle, and went out, and stood in the entering in of the cave. And, behold, there came a voice unto him, and said, What doest thou here, Elijah? 14: And he said, I have been very jealous for the Lord God of hosts: because the children of Israel have forsaken thy covenant, thrown down thine altars, and slain thy prophets with the sword; and I, even I only, am left; and they seek my life, to take it away. 15: And the Lord said unto him, Go, return on thy way to the wilderness of Damascus: and when thou comest, anoint Hazael to be king over Syria: 16: And Jehu the son of Nimshi shalt thou anoint to be king over Israel: and Elisha the son of Shaphat of Abel-meholah shalt thou anoint to be prophet in thy room. 17: And it shall come to pass, that him that escapeth the sword of Hazael shall Jehu slay: and him that escapeth from the sword of Jehu shall Elisha slay. 18: Yet I have left me seven thousand in Israel, all the knees which have not bowed unto Baal, and every mouth which hath not kissed him. —*1 Kings 19: 1–18*

Despite the lesson of the two altars, King Ahab continued his wicked ways. A man called Naboth owned a particularly good vineyard in the region of Jezreel, and Ahab attempted to force him into selling it to the king. He refused, so Jezebel brought trumped-up charges against the poor man, accusing him of cursing the king and God. False witnesses acquired his committal and he was duly stoned to death. When Elijah heard about this, he confronted Ahab and his wife and assured them that they would pay for their sins; which, in time, they did. Upon Ahab's demise, Ahaziah proved as unworthy a successor as could be expected from this dynasty. One day a

Above left: *King Ahab attempts to force the purchase of Naboth's vineyard.*

Left: *God sends down fire to protect Elijah from the troops sent by Ahaziah.*

> 19: So he departed thence, and found Elisha the son of Shaphat, who was plowing with twelve yoke of oxen before him, and he with the twelfth: and Elijah passed by him, and cast his mantle upon him. 20: And he left the oxen, and ran after Elijah, and said, Let me, I pray thee, kiss my father and my mother, and then I will follow thee. And he said unto him, Go back again: for what have I done to thee? 21: And he returned back from him, and took a yoke of oxen, and slew them, and boiled their flesh with the instruments of the oxen, and gave unto the people, and they did eat. Then he arose, and went after Elijah, and ministered unto him. — *1 Kings 19: 19–21*

serious accident befell him and he sent to the priests for assurance of his recovery – not to the priests of God, but to those of Baal-zebub, the fly god. Elijah intercepted the messengers and sent back to Ahaziah the unwelcome message from God that he would assuredly die, so the king sent soldiers to seize him. Elijah called down fire upon two detachments of these troops; the third approached the prophet meekly, and he accompanied them back to court, where he stood, unafraid, and repeated the message of doom.

901 Samaria attacked by King Banhadad of Syria but repulsed.
899 The seizure of Naboth's vineyard; Elijah predicts divine justice for King Ahab of Israel and his wife Jezebel.
898 Ahab makes son Ahaziah co-ruler of Israel; Jehosophat of Judah similarly co-opts his son, Jehoram and sets about reforming Judah.
Ahab allies with Jehosophat, and his son Joram marries Athaliah, daughter of Ahab; this attempt to reunite the two kingdoms is, however, doomed.
897 Prophet Micaiah warns Ahab about false prophets, and the king is slain at Ramoth-Gilead as prophesied; Ahaziah becomes sole ruler of Israel (–985). The Moabites (who have been tributaries since the conquests of David) revolt.
895 Elijah reproves Ahaziah and predicts his sickness and death; troops sent to apprehend the prophet are slain by heavenly fire. Ahaziah dies as predicted and is succeeded as king of Israel by Jehoram (–884).

Right: *King Ahaziah of Israel meets his death in battle, as Elijah had prophesied.*

***Above:** A fiery chariot descends and in a whirlwind bears Elijah to Heaven, leaving Elisha to wear his mantle.*

The end of Elijah's prophetic ministry was as dramatic as the rest of his life. In company with Elisha, whom he knew to be his successor, he traveled from Bethel to Jericho and on across the Jordan, parting the waters in style by striking them with his cloak. Then a chariot of fire, pulled by fiery horses, descended and Elijah was taken up to Heaven in a whirlwind, leaving Elisha to take on the burden of his work.

895 Elijah taken alive into Heaven.
895 Jehosophat and Jehoram ally to suppress a revolt by the Moabites; they survive an extreme lack of water by following Elijah's advice.
889 Joram sole ruler of Judah (–885) upon the death of Jehosophat.

1: And it came to pass, when the Lord would take up Elijah into heaven by a whirlwind, that Elijah went with Elisha from Gilgal ... 7: And fifty men of the sons of the prophets went, and stood to view afar off: and they two stood by Jordan. 8: And Elijah took his mantle, and wrapped it together, and smote the waters, and they were divided hither and thither, so that they two went over on dry ground. 9: And it came to pass, when they were gone over, that Elijah said unto Elisha, Ask what I shall do for thee, before I be taken away from thee. And Elisha said, I pray thee, let a double portion of thy spirit be upon me. 10: And he said, Thou hast asked a hard thing: nevertheless, if thou see me when I am taken from thee, it shall be so unto thee; but if not, it shall not be so. 11: And it came to pass, as they still went on, and talked, that, behold, there appeared a chariot of fire, and horses of fire, and parted them both asunder; and Elijah went up by a whirlwind into heaven. 12: And Elisha saw it, and he cried, My father, my father, the chariot of Israel, and the horsemen thereof. And he saw him no more ... 13: He took up also the mantle of Elijah that fell from him, and went back, and stood by the bank of Jordan; 14: And he took the mantle of Elijah that fell from him, and smote the waters, and said, Where is the LORD God of Elijah? and when he also had smitten the waters, they parted hither and thither: and Elisha went over. 15: And when the sons of the prophets which were to view at Jericho saw him, they said, The spirit of Elijah doth rest on Elisha. And they came to meet him, and bowed themselves to the ground before him.

— *2 Kings 2:1–15*

***Left:** The fate of Jezebel. After killing her son, Joram, Jehu went to Jezreel. From a high window, Jezebel called him a murderer, and Jehu ordered her to be thrown out. Her body was devoured by dogs, as prophesied: "In the portion of Jezreel shall dogs eat the flesh of Jezebel: And the carcase of Jezebel shall be as dung upon the face of the field in the portion of Jezreel; so that they shall not say, This is Jezebel." (2 Kings 9: 36–37)*

Elisha's ministry as a prophet was characterized by gentle acts of mercy. People and kings came to him for help and intercession with God, and, after praying to God each time, he was able to perform miracles. For example, when a delegation asked him to cure the unhealthy water of their town, not far from Jericho, he asked for a bowl of salt and threw this into the spring in question, and the water immediately became wholesome.

885 Joram dies after a wicked reign (encouraged by his wife Athaliah, daughter of Ahab and Jezebel), his doom foretold in a letter from Elijah; Ahaziah succeeds him (–884) as king of Judah.
884 Elijah's predictions about Israel's royal family are fulfilled as Jehu conspires against Joram and kills him as well as Azahiah, ruling to 856.
884 Queen Mother Athaliah usurps the kingdom of Judah (–878) and murders all the

24: And it came to pass after this, that Ben-hadad king of Syria gathered all his host, and went up, and besieged Samaria. 25: And there was a great famine in Samaria: and, behold, they besieged it, until an ass's head was sold for fourscore pieces of silver, and the fourth part of a cab of dove's dung for five pieces of silver.

— 2 Kings 6:24–25

1: Then Elisha said, Hear ye the word of the Lord; Thus saith the Lord, To morrow about this time shall a measure of fine flour be sold for a shekel, and two measures of barley for a shekel, in the gate of Samaria ... 3: And there were four leprous men at the entering in of the gate: and they said one to another, Why sit we here until we die? 4: If we say, We will enter into the city, then the famine is in the city, and we shall die there: and if we sit still here, we die also. Now therefore come, and let us fall unto the host of the Syrians: if they save us alive, we shall live; and if they kill us, we shall but die. 5: And they rose up in the twilight, to go unto the camp of the Syrians: and when they were come to the uttermost part of the camp of Syria, behold, there was no man there. 6: For the Lord had made the host of the Syrians to hear a noise of chariots, and a noise of horses, even the noise of a great host: and they said one to another, Lo, the king of Israel hath hired against us the kings of the Hittites, and the kings of the Egyptians, to come upon us. 7: Wherefore they arose and fled in the twilight, and left their tents, and their horses, and their asses, even the camp as it was, and fled for their life. 8: And when these lepers came to the uttermost part of the camp, they went into one tent, and did eat and drink, and carried thence silver, and gold, and raiment, and went and hid it; and came again, and entered into another tent, and carried thence also, and went and hid it ... 10: So they came and called unto the porter of the city: and they told them, saying, We came to the camp of the Syrians, and, behold, there was no man there, neither voice of man, but horses tied, and asses tied, and the tents as they were ... 16: And the people went out, and spoiled the tents of the Syrians. So a measure of fine flour was sold for a shekel, and two measures of barley for a shekel, according to the word of the Lord. 17: And the king appointed the lord on whose hand he leaned to have the charge of the gate: and the people trode upon him in the gate, and he died, as the man of God had said, who spake when the king came down to him. 18: And it came to pass as the man of God had spoken to the king, saying, Two measures of barley for a shekel, and a measure of fine flour for a shekel, shall be to morrow about this time in the gate of Samaria

— 2 Kings 7:1–18

The Shunammite woman takes Elisha in: 8: And it fell on a day, that Elisha passed to Shunem, where was a great woman; and she constrained him to eat bread. And so it was, that as oft as he passed by, he turned in thither to eat bread. 9: And she said unto her husband, Behold now, I perceive that this is an holy man of God, which passeth by us continually. 10: Let us make a little chamber, I pray thee, on the wall; and let us set for him there a bed, and a table, and a stool, and a candlestick: and it shall be, when he cometh to us, that he shall turn in thither. 11: And it fell on a day, that he came thither, and he turned into the chamber, and lay there. 12: And he said to Gehazi his servant, Call this Shunammite. And when he had called her, she stood before him. *—2 Kings 4:8–12*

Elisha restores life to the woman's child: 18: And when the child was grown, it fell on a day, that he went out to his father to the reapers. 19: And he said unto his father, My head, my head. And he said to a lad, Carry him to his mother. 20: And when he had taken him, and brought him to his mother, he sat on her knees till noon, and then died. 21: And she went up, and laid him on the bed of the man of God, and shut the door upon him, and went out. 22: And she called unto her husband, and said, Send me, I pray thee, one of the young men, and one of the asses, that I may run to the man of God, and come again ... 27: And when she came to the man of God to the hill, she caught him by the feet ... And he arose, and followed her ... 32: And when Elisha was come into the house, behold, the child was dead, and laid upon his bed. 33: He went in therefore, and shut the door upon them twain, and prayed unto the Lord. 34: And he went up, and lay upon the child, and put his mouth upon his mouth, and his eyes upon his eyes, and his hands upon his hands: and he stretched himself upon the child; and the flesh of the child waxed warm. 35: Then he returned, and walked in the house to and fro; and went up, and stretched himself upon him: and the child sneezed seven times, and the child opened his eyes. 36: And he called Gehazi, and said, Call this Shunammite. So he called her. And when she was come in unto him, he said, Take up thy son. 37: Then she went in, and fell at his feet, and bowed herself to the ground, and took up her son ...
—2 Kings 4: 8–12, 18–37

Another miracle concerning water took place when the kings of Judah, Israel, and Edom took the field with armies to crush a revolt of the Moabites and found themselves in a critical situation with water running out. Elisha was called for, and he instructed the kings to dig trenches; next morning, these were filled with water.

The River Jordan too was the location of one of his miracles, when his companions persuaded him that they should build new dwellings by the river. As construction proceeded, one of them dropped an ax – which they had borrowed – into the river. Elisha threw his stick into the water, whereupon the ax-head surfaced and they hooked it out.

A Shunammite woman longing for a child asked Elisha to intercede with God, and she bore a son, who grew but then died. Elisha made haste to the woman's house, lay spreadeagled upon the body, and the child was miraculously brought back to life.

royal family save the child Joash, son of Ahaziah, who is protected in the temple by Jehoshabeath, daughter of Jehoram and wife of the High Priest, Jehoiada.

878 Jehoiada anoints Joash king of Judah (–839) and puts Athaliah and other idolatrous priests to death. Priests and Levites play a crucial role in this restoration of the rightful monarch. The people are recalled to God's Covenant.

856 Jehoiada, commanded by Joash, repairs the temple.

856(–839) Jehoahaz king of Israel.

845 Death and royal burial of Judah's High Priest, Jehoiada; Joash and Judah revert to idolatry.

840 Prophet Zechariah stoned.

839 Jehoahaz, king of Israel, afflicted by calamities (including widespread destruction wrought by King Hazael of Syria) and disease, is murdered by his servants; Joash, son of Jehoahaz, becomes king of Israel (–825).

17: Now after the death of Jehoiada came the princes of Judah, and made obeisance to the king. Then the king hearkened unto them. 18: And they left the house of the Lord God of their fathers, and served groves and idols: and wrath came upon Judah and Jerusalem for this their trespass. 19: Yet he sent prophets to them, to bring them again unto the Lord; and they testified against them: but they would not give ear. 20: And the Spirit of God came upon Zechariah the son of Jehoiada the priest, which stood above the people, and said unto them, Thus saith God, Why transgress ye the commandments of the Lord, that ye cannot prosper? because ye have forsaken the Lord, he hath also forsaken you. 21: And they conspired against him, and stoned him with stones at the commandment of the king in the court of the house of the Lord. 22: Thus Joash the king remembered not the kindness which Jehoiada his father had done to him, but slew his son. And when he died, he said, The Lord look upon it, and require it. — *2 Chronicles 24:17–22*

One day a widow appealed to Elisha to help with her late husband's debts. He told her to ask her neighbors if she could borrow empty jars and instructed her to pour oil into them. Miraculously, she kept pouring but the oil did not run out, so she was able to sell many jars of oil to pay off the debts. In a similar miracle, Elisha once fed a hundred people with but twenty loaves of bread.

Naaman, an officer in the army of the king of Aram, suffered from a bad skin disease, and his girl servant, who was a captive Israelite, suggested consulting the prophet. Elisha told the man to bathe seven times in the Jordan, which the officer did, with disappointing results, for he had expected instant relief. His servants rebuked him for his attitude and he went again to the Jordan and was cured. This story ends with the deceitful action of Elisha's sevant, Gehazi. When the officer

offered Elisha a reward for his cure, the prophet would have none of it. But later the servant returned to the officer, said Elisha had changed his mind, and received money. However, Gehazi could not hide his sin from Elisha: in punishment, his hand became leprous.

During a period of conflict between the Aramaeans and the kingdom of Israel, the Aramaeans became frustrated when they discovered that Elisha was able to warn the Jews of their enemy's deployments. So the king of Aram sent troops to seize the prophet, surrounding him at Doham. Elisha prayed to God, and the enemy were made blind, and he led them captive to the king of Israel, whose instinct was, of course, to kill them all. But Elisha stopped him, counseling him to feast and entertain them, which he reluctantly did. Then the Aramaeans were sent on their way and promised to stop their raids.

Left: *"And the Syrians had gone out by companies, and had brought away captive out of the land of Israel a little maid; and she waited on Naaman's wife. And she said unto her mistress, Would God my lord were with the prophet that is in Samaria! for he would recover him of his leprosy." (2 Kings 5:2–3)*

Right: *Elisha refuses the offer of payment for healing Naaman.*

839(–810) Amaziah king of Judah.
839 Amaziah defeats the Edomites and challenges Joash of Israel but is defeated and imprisoned; Joash plunders Jerusalem and the Temple and pulls down the city walls.

Even a prophet can run out of patience, however. On day Elisha was out walking when a gang of youths jeered at him; by now he had lost his hair, and they called him "thou bald head." Perhaps in slight over-reaction, Elisha called forth two bears, which proceeded to chase and maul the insulting youths.

When Elisha was on his death-bed, he received a visit from King Joash, who lamented the passing of the prophet (which was rich indeed, considering the nature of this king's reign). The old prophet told him to shoot an arrow through the east window (in the direction of Damascus), and told him that this was the arrow of victory he would win over Aram at Aphek. Then he told the king to strike the ground with his arrows, which he did, three times. Elisha told him those three blows symbolized three victories; but that he should have struck five times, and would then have won a complete victory.

839 King Joash of Israel visits the prophet Elisha, who is near to death, and is assured by him of victory over the Syrians.
825(–784) Jeroboam II king of Israel.
810(–758) Uzziah rules Judah upon assassination of Amaziah. During his reign a great earthquake shakes the region.

***Left:** King Joash at the deathbed of Elisha, as the old prophet makes his last prophecy.*

***Right:** King Uzziah strengthens the defenses of Jerusalem with engines of war.*

Jonah was a prophet who came probably from the area of Galilee. He was commanded by God to go to Nineveh, capital of the mighty Assyrian Empire, and announce God's impending judgment upon their wickedness.

But Jonah did not go. Not only did he believe that God would bring salvation only for the Jews; he feared that if the Assyrians did indeed repent, God would spare them. Jonah preferred that they should all meet the doom he believed they so richly deserved.

So instead of heading for Nineveh, he boarded a Phoenician ship bound for the other end of the Mediterranean, Tarshish (or Tartessus, modern Cadiz). En route, God called up a great storm, and, despite the best efforts of the mariners, the vessel could make no progress toward the safety of land. Then the crew began to realize that one of the people on board must have offended a god, and eventually Jonah admitted that he must be the guilty one. Reluctantly, and after further efforts to make landfall, the sailors followed Jonah's selfless advice to cast him overboard. At once the storm abated, and the ship made a safe course, the ship's crew acknowledging the power of the Hebrew God.

But this was not the end of Jonah, for he was swallowed by a great fish, and languished, contrite, in its belly for three days and nights, praying to God for forgiveness. At the end of that time, the fish vomited him onto the shore, and he received God's command again: to go to

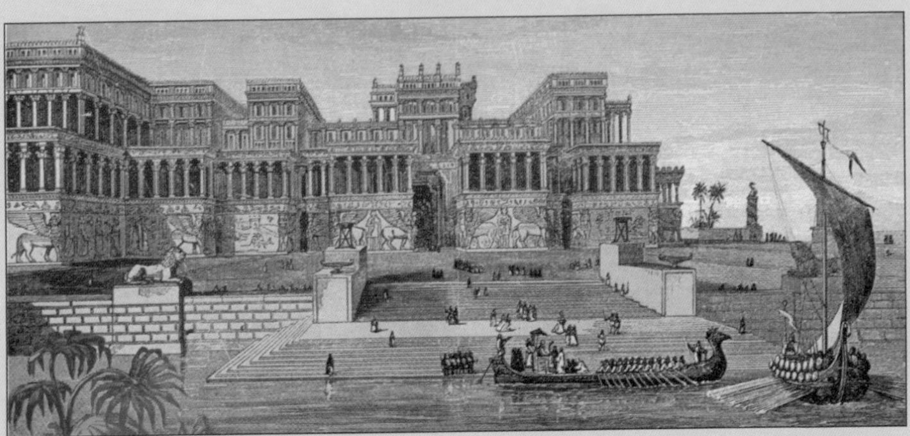

***Above:** Nineveh. **Top:** Jonah volunteers to be thrown overboard.*

Nineveh and warn them.

At Nineveh, Jonah found a receptive audience and the signs of repentance. But this did not please the prophet, and he sat gloomily outside the city walls. There God taught him another lesson. To shade him from the intense heat, a castor-oil plant miraculously shot up; but then it was devoured by a worm, and Jonah despaired, wilting in the dry torment of the sun. Then God told him his lesson: if Jonah could care for the wellbeing of a plant, which he had not planted or nourished himself, how much more must God care for the great city, with its people, children, and animals? God had love for all: Gentiles would repent if they were taught; and salvation was not only for the Jews.

***Right:** Jonah preaches in Nineveh.*

1: But it displeased Jonah exceedingly, and he was very angry. 2: And he prayed unto the Lord, and said, I pray thee, O Lord, was not this my saying, when I was yet in my country? Therefore I fled before unto Tarshish: for I knew that thou art a gracious God, and merciful, slow to anger, and of great kindness, and repentest thee of the evil. 3: Therefore now, O Lord, take, I beseech thee, my life from me; for it is better for me to die than to live. 4: Then said the Lord, Doest thou well to be angry? 5: So Jonah went out of the city, and sat on the east side of the city, and there made him a booth, and sat under it in the shadow, till he might see what would become of the city. 6: And the Lord God prepared a gourd, and made it to come up over Jonah, that it might be a shadow over his head, to deliver him from his grief. So Jonah was exceeding glad of the gourd. 7: But God prepared a worm when the morning rose the next day, and it smote the gourd that it withered. 8: And it came to pass, when the sun did arise, that God prepared a vehement east wind; and the sun beat upon the head of Jonah, that he fainted, and wished in himself to die, and said, It is better for me to die than to live. 9: And God said to Jonah, Doest thou well to be angry for the gourd? And he said, I do well to be angry, even unto death. 10: Then said the Lord, Thou hast had pity on the gourd, for the which thou hast not laboured, neither madest it grow; which came up in a night, and perished in a night: 11: And should not I spare Nineveh, that great city, wherein are more than sixscore thousand persons that cannot discern between their right hand and their left hand; and also much cattle? *—Jonah 4:1–11*

The prophet Amos, who was active during the reigns of Kings Uzziah and Jeroboam II, was a herdsman and tree-grower (a "pincher of sycamores") living a few miles south of Bethlehem when he was called by God to bear witness. Although a native of Judah, his main work was in the northern kingdom, beginning at Bethel, where he went for business and attended a religious feast.

He spoke out at a time of prosperity and relative peace against the way in which material concerns had blurred morality. Religious practices were still carried on, but the outward observance masked a divorce from morality. Bribery and corruption was widespread; the rich got richer, the poor poorer; justice was debased, and immorality was open and shameless. The people had forgotten God: but God, he said, sees all, even the greed, venality, and sharp practice, which would all be punished.

At Bethel, the High Priest, Amaziah, rudely told him to go back to Judah; Amos's response was that he was a simple man called by God. He wanted nothing from the "hireling prophets," whose words were dictated by political interest.

He experienced five visions that embodied the message:

- Devouring locusts sent by God; but upon Amos's pleading, God relented.
- Judgement by fire: again he interceded and God relented.
- God stands with a plumb-line to judge

> 21: I hate, I despise your feast days, and I will not smell in your solemn assemblies. 22: Though ye offer me burnt offerings and your meat offerings, I will not accept them: neither will I regard the peace offerings of your fat beasts. 23: Take thou away from me the noise of thy songs; for I will not hear the melody of thy viols. —*Amos 5:21–23*

how Israel had diverged from the upright path.

- A basket of ripe fruit: God told him that as the fruit was ripe, so was Israel for judgment.
- Finally, he saw God standing by the altar, and the Lord spoke to him about the coming total destruction he would bring.

For Amos, the sin lay less in the idolatry than the moral and social decline in the absence of righteousness. The greatest perils to nations came not by poverty but by prosperity. And God was not just the God of the Hebrews but God of the whole earth. Jews who thought that the day of judgment would bring justice in their favor and would strike other nations were misleading themselves: God would mete out justice upon them.

787 Amos prophesies against Jeroboam II.
784 Interregnum of 11–12 years upon death of Jeroboam II.
773(–772) Zechariah king of Israel.
772 Shallum usurps the throne of Israel but is himself deposed by Menahem, who imposes a cruel rule (–761).
771 Israel invaded by King Pul of Assyria and made tributary to the Assyrian Empire.

8: Behold, the eyes of the Lord God are upon the sinful kingdom, and I will destroy it from off the face of the earth; saving that I will not utterly destroy the house of Jacob, saith the Lord. 9: For, lo, I will command, and I will sift the house of Israel among all nations, like as corn is sifted in a sieve, yet shall not the least grain fall upon the earth. 10: All the sinners of my people shall die by the sword, which say, The evil shall not overtake nor prevent us. 11: In that day will I raise up the tabernacle of David that is fallen, and close up the breaches thereof; and I will raise up his ruins, and I will build it as in the days of old: 12: That they may possess the remnant of Edom, and of all the heathen, which are called by my name, saith the Lord that doeth this. 13: Behold, the days come, saith the Lord, that the plowman shall overtake the reaper, and the treader of grapes him that soweth seed; and the mountains shall drop sweet wine, and all the hills shall melt. 14: And I will bring again the captivity of my people of Israel, and they shall build the waste cities, and inhabit them; and they shall plant vineyards, and drink the wine thereof; they shall also make gardens, and eat the fruit of them. 15: And I will plant them upon their land, and they shall no more be pulled up out of their land which I have given them, saith the Lord thy God. — *Amos 9:8–15*

While Amos was born in Judah, Hosea (or Hoshea) was a native of the northern kingdom, who began prophesying a little after Amos began his ministry. His message was similar – that the people had forsaken their God and that retribution would surely come. But Hosea's message was colored by his own personal experience, so that his life was in a sense a metaphor for Israel.

God had directed him to marry a woman called Gomer, and she proved unfaithful to him. God, it seems, knew that this would be so, and her cheating led Hosea to the gradual realization that the children of their marriage were not in fact his children. Here the Book of Hosea uses

1: In the year that king Uzziah died I saw also the Lord sitting upon a throne, high and lifted up, and his train filled the temple. 2: Above it stood the seraphims: each one had six wings; with twain he covered his face, and with twain he covered his feet, and with twain he did fly. 3: And one cried unto another, and said, Holy, holy, holy, is the Lord of hosts: the whole earth is full of his glory. 4: And the posts of the door moved at the voice of him that cried, and the house was filled with smoke. 5: Then said I, Woe is me! for I am undone; because I am a man of unclean lips, and I dwell in the midst of a people of unclean lips: for mine eyes have seen the King, the Lord of hosts. 6: Then flew one of the seraphims unto me, having a live coal in his hand, which he had taken with the tongs from off the altar: 7: And he laid it upon my mouth, and said, Lo, this hath touched thy lips; and thine iniquity is taken away, and thy sin purged. 8: Also I heard the voice of the Lord, saying, Whom shall I send, and who will go for us? Then said I, Here am I; send me. 9: And he said, Go, and tell this people, Hear ye indeed, but understand not; and see ye indeed, but perceive not. 10: Make the heart of this people fat, and make their ears heavy, and shut their eyes; lest they see with their eyes, and hear with their ears, and understand with their heart, and convert, and be healed. 11: Then said I, Lord, how long? And he answered, Until the cities be wasted without inhabitant, and the houses without man, and the land be utterly desolate, 12: And the Lord have removed men far away, and there be a great forsaking in the midst of the land. 13: But yet in it shall be a tenth, and it shall return, and shall be eaten: as a teil tree, and as an oak, whose substance is in them, when they cast their leaves: so the holy seed shall be the substance thereof.

—Isaiah 6:1–13

metaphors: the children were named Jezreel (standing for bloodshed, this area having been fought over many times); Lo-ruhamah ("unloved"); and Lo-ammi ("not my people" or "not my kin"). Although Hosea realized her unfaithfulness, and at some stage she left and ended as a slave to another man, Hosea rescued her and brought her back "on probation." God had told him to keep loving her, just as he still loved his people. The people needed bringing back to loyalty to their God.

So Hosea's marriage was like the relationship between God and his people – Hosea pleaded with his unfaithful wife just as God addressed his faithless people. While the priests had failed to make God's Laws known and had enriched themselves at the public expense, a generation had grown to adulthood without knowing their true God. Israel, prophesied Hosea, would become a slave-nation to Assyria. The people would be sent dispossessed, wandering among the nations – a prediction that came to be the dominating aspect of Jewish history. But Hosea's contemporaries took no notice of him.

It was during the year that Uzziah, leper king of Judah, died that the prophet Isaiah received his calling from God. One of the greatest of the prophets, Isaiah was active for more than forty years, during the turbulent reigns of Uzziah, Jotham, Ahaz, Hezekiah, and Manasseh in Judah.

The most political of the prophets, he was probably of high birth and thus with access to the court, so that King Hezekiah in particular relied on his counsel. In addition to being a prophet, Isaiah was a statesman, reformer, teacher of kings, and a theologian. The theme of his ministry was set by God at the moment of his calling: that retribution was to come for the impieties and sins of the Jews – but that after suffering a new beginning would come.

761(–759) Pekahiah king of Israel
759 Pekahiah deposed and assassinated by one of his captains, Pekah (–739).
758 Uzziah, king of Judah, having burned incense in the temple and been punished with leprosy, dies; his son Jotham succeeds him (–742).
That same year Isaiah called by God.
742(–726) Ahaz king of Judah.

Above: *Hosea preaching. "O Israel, return unto the Lord thy God; for thou hast fallen by thine iniquity ... I will be as the dew unto Israel: he shall grow as the lily, and cast forth his roots ... His branches shall spread, and his beauty shall be as the olive tree ... They that dwell under his shadow shall return; they shall revive as the corn, and grow as the vine ..." (Hosea 14:1–7)*

Much of Isaiah's message had been foreshadowed by Amos – the social injustice of the times and the complacent, mechanical worship in the Temple, which had become the center of a fetishistic cult and a meaningless end in itself, adulterated by the importation of foreign practices and gods – and the sheer ingratitude of the people to God. But Isaiah had a more direct influence than Amos or Micah (his contemporary), largely because of his connections in high places, and he also gathered a group of disciples to perpetuate his teaching.

***Left:** Isaiah contemplates the vice and folly of Jerusalem.*

741 Pekah, king of Israel, allies with King Rezin of Syria to overthrow the monarchy in Judah; but the prophet Isaiah reassures King Ahaz that his line will succeed, since he prophesies that Immanuel, son of a virgin, shall yet spring from the stock of David.
740 Pekah, king of Israel, wins a great victory over Judah, as punishment for Ahaz and his kingdom's wickedness
Toward the close of Pekah's reign, inhabitants of the western and northern regions of Israel are carried off captive by the Assyrian king, Tiglath-pileser.
739 Pekah deposed and murdered by Hoshea, who rules Israel to 725.
736 Beside acting increasingly impiously, Ahaz allies with Assyria.

1: And there shall come forth a rod out of the stem of Jesse, and a Branch shall grow out of his roots:
2: And the spirit of the Lord shall rest upon him, the spirit of wisdom and understanding, the spirit
of counsel and might, the spirit of knowledge and of the fear of the Lord; 3: And shall make him of
quick understanding in the fear of the Lord: and he shall not judge after the sight of his eyes, neither
reprove after the hearing of his ears: 4: But with righteousness shall he judge the poor, and reprove
with equity for the meek of the earth: and he shall smite the earth with the rod of his mouth, and
with the breath of his lips shall he slay the wicked. 5: And righteousness shall be the girdle of his
loins, and faithfulness the girdle of his reins. 6: The wolf also shall dwell with the lamb, and the
leopard shall lie down with the kid; and the calf
and the young lion and the fatling together; and a
little child shall lead them. 7: And the cow and the
bear shall feed; their young ones shall lie down
together: and the lion shall eat straw like the ox.
8: And the sucking child shall play on the hole of
the asp, and the weaned child shall put his hand on
the cockatrice' den. 9: They shall not hurt nor
destroy in all my holy mountain: for the earth shall
be full of the knowledge of the Lord, as the waters
cover the sea. 10: And in that day there shall be a
root of Jesse, which shall stand for an ensign of
the people; to it shall the Gentiles seek: and his
rest shall be glorious. 11: And it shall come to pass
in that day, that the Lord shall set his hand again
the second time to recover the remnant of his
people, which shall be left ... 12: And he shall set
up an ensign for the nations, and shall assemble
the outcasts of Israel, and gather together the
dispersed of Judah from the four corners of the
earth ... 16: And there shall be an highway for the
remnant of his people, which shall be left, from
Assyria; like as it was to Israel in the day that he
came up out of the land of Egypt. — *Isaiah 11: 1–16*

Micah, who came from Moresheth in Judah, made his prophecies a little later than Amos and Hosea but was a contemporary of Isaiah. From small landowning stock, he addressed the lower orders of society, upbraiding the ruling classes and leaders, including wealthy landowners, always squeezing out smaller farmers, and judges and officials. The priests, he claimed, had misunderstood God: while practicing injustice, they yet relied on God or their own safety. In particular, he singled out the two capital cities of Jerusalem and Samaria for damnation.

His message was in the form of judgment, but then comfort and salvation. Man's moral sins offended God, and judgment would come. All was darkness, but yet there would be light with God. He prophesied that Jerusalem would one day become the religious center of the world; and he also made a prophecy that would resonate in the New Testament. From Bethlehem, he predicted, would come a Messiah, the ultimate deliverer, one greater even than David, who would rule over all God's people. This was the prophecy that would lead three wise men of the east to seek out the newborn Jesus seven centuries later.

But again, he was barely listened to by those in power and was stoned to death.

***Above:** Micah at work. His constituency was the smaller landowners and working classes.*

Micah and the Messiah 2: But thou, Bethlehem Ephratah, though thou be little among the thousands of Judah, yet out of thee shall he come forth unto me that is to be ruler in Israel; whose goings forth have been from of old, from everlasting. — *Micah 5:2*

Isaiah and the Messiah 10: Moreover the Lord spake again unto Ahaz, saying, 11: Ask thee a sign of the Lord thy God; ask it either in the depth, or in the height above. 12: But Ahaz said, I will not ask, neither will I tempt the Lord. 13: And he said, Hear ye now, O house of David; Is it a small thing for you to weary men, but will ye weary my God also? 14: Therefore the Lord himself shall give you a sign; Behold, a virgin shall conceive, and bear a son, and shall call his name Immanuel. 15: Butter and honey shall he eat, that he may know to refuse the evil, and choose the good. 16: For before the child shall know to refuse the evil, and choose the good, the land that thou abhorrest shall be forsaken of both her kings. — *Isaiah 7:10–16*

The New Testament reference 1: In those days came John the Baptist, preaching in the wilderness of Judaea, 2: And saying, Repent ye: for the kingdom of heaven is at hand. 3: For this is he that was spoken of by the prophet Esaias [Isaiah], saying, The voice of one crying in the wilderness, Prepare ye the way of the Lord, make his paths straight. — *Matthew 3:1–3*

During Isaiah's time, the kingdom of Israel was defeated, reduced, and eventually destroyed by the Assyrians. In addition to paying tribute to Assyria – which meant repeated raids on the Temple treasury – King Ahaz of Judah attempted to appease the Assyrians by allowing the introduction of other religions, including those concerned with the sun, moon, and stars, while an Assyrian-style altar replaced the original in the Temple courtyard. In vain did Isaiah tell Ahaz that he was in error. Alliances and political maneuvers would not work: the Jews must place their trust in the hands of God alone.

As the situation of Israel went from bad to worse, Judah watched fearfully under the direction of a new king. Hezekiah enjoyed a good relationship with Isaiah, and for more than a dozen years followed his wise counsel. He instituted a religious reformation of the kingdom, a root and branch destruction of the alien cults that had so corrupted Judah. Idols of alien gods were destroyed, altars pulled down, and even the brazen serpent melted down. This, dating from the time of Moses, had become, perversely, a religious symbol in its own right – the priests burned incense to it. For Hezekiah and Isaiah it was idolatry, a mere piece of bronze.

Hezekiah also celebrated the Passover, which seems again to have been neglected for a long time, and he encouraged the inhabitants of what remained of the northern kingdom to participate in the feast at Jerusalem.

Top right: *The worship of idols and graven images had again become widespread by the time of Ahaz.*

Right: *Hezekiah carried out a wholesale religious reformation and celebrated the Passover.*

728 Israel defeated and made tributary to Assyria by King Shalmaneser.
726(–698) Hezekiah king of Judah; he destroys idols, works to restore the faith of Judah and celebrates a remarkable Passover, inviting the people of Israel to join in it.
725 Hoshea, king of Israel, now allied to Egypt, defies Assyria; Shalmaneser defeats him, takes him captive and attacks Samaria.

Hezekiah also took measures to improve the defenses of Jerusalem, which had been badly damaged by an incursion by King Pekah of Israel some years before. And construction work was also undertaken to improve and secure the supply of water to the city, vital if it were to survive a long siege.

It was during the reign of Hezekiah that Judah witnessed the end of their fellow kingdom. Already reduced to little more than the city state of Samaria, the Israelites revolted against Assyria, bringing down the full weight of the mighty empire and their own destruction. The Assyrian king, Shalmaneser V, razed the city and deported the people, never to be heard of again. In their place the land was colonized from the east. These newcomers brought their own gods and cults, but they also intermarried with some of those Jews who remained, and a hybrid form of worship that included the Hebrew god evolved. These people became known as the Samaritans – but the lack of purity in their religion made them anathema to the Jews of Judah (which

Left: *The end of Samaria and the kingdom of Israel. The ten tribes are deported, but some come as refugees to Judah.*

explains the force of Christ's parable some seven centuries later). Meanwhile a precious few of the northern Jews came as refugees to Judah, increasing its population and strengthening it.

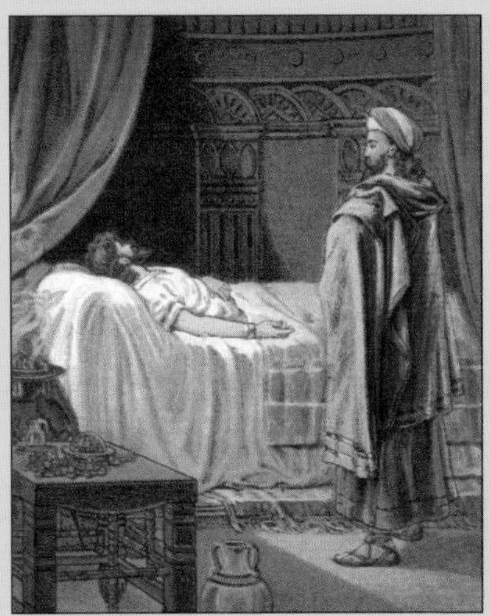

1: In those days was Hezekiah sick unto death. And Isaiah the prophet the son of Amoz came unto him, and said unto him, Thus saith the Lord, Set thine house in order: for thou shalt die, and not live. 2: Then Hezekiah turned his face toward the wall, and prayed unto the Lord, 3: And said, Remember now, O Lord, I beseech thee, how I have walked before thee in truth and with a perfect heart, and have done that which is good in thy sight. And Hezekiah wept sore. 4: Then came the word of the Lord to Isaiah, saying, 5: Go, and say to Hezekiah, Thus saith the Lord, the God of David thy father, I have heard thy prayer, I have seen thy tears: behold, I will add unto thy days fifteen years.
6: And I will deliver thee and this city out of the hand of the king of Assyria: and I will defend this city. 7: And this shall be a sign unto thee from the Lord, that the Lord will do this thing that he hath spoken; 8: Behold, I will bring again the shadow of the degrees, which is gone down in the sun dial of Ahaz, ten degrees backward. So the sun returned ten degrees, by which degrees it was gone down. — *Isaiah 38: 1–8*

721 Assyrians capture Samaria, ending the kingdom of Israel. The ten tribes are deported to distant parts while their own lands are colonized from without (giving rise to the Samaritans).
Hezekiah, king of Judah, celebrates a remarkable Passover, inviting the people remaining in the northern kingdom to participate.
Hezekiah is miraculously healed from a near-mortal illness
714 Hezekiah allies Judah with Egypt and Cush.
713 Judah forestalls invasion by King Sennacherib of Assyria by paying tribute.

Above: *The Assyrians appear before the walls of Jerusalem.*

Judah was now a very small, isolated country between the mighty, ambitious and menacing powers of Assyria and Egypt (the power of Babylon being yet to make itself felt). There was always an Egyptian presence in the court of Jerusalem, and eventually it succeeded in seducing Hezekiah into alliance – contrary to the vociferous advice of Isaiah. The result was an expedition by the Assyrian King Sennacherib, which deprived Judah of many of its cities and towns, including Lachish. Hezekiah paid out a substantial tribute to induce the Assyrians to retire; but it was not long before they were back, demanding the unconditional surrender of Jerusalem. Isaiah reassured Hezekiah, for God would come to their aid. The Assyrians departed to campaign elsewhere but were soon back in strength, encamped about the city, which was now under siege. As Isaiah had warned, the promises of help from Egypt did not prove forthcoming.

In this crisis, Hezekiah and Isaiah prayed for help. And God responded, sending an angel of death into the enemy camp. Miraculously rescued, Jerusalem watched the ruins of the Assyrian army depart. For a while, the city was saved; in Nineveh, a palace coup ended the reign of Sennacherib, and the threat from Assyria abated. But Isaiah's message, unheard in the celebration of the miracle, remained the same. Destruction and suffering were inescapable in the longer term. Babylon was no answer, for in time it would prove an even sterner tyrant than Assyria – princes of the throne of David, Isaiah predicted, would one day be mere palace slaves in Babylon.

But yet there was hope. After all the destruction and suffering, a remnant would rebuild God's city – a new Jerusalem would arise, righteous and faithful to the true God.

712 Hezekiah injudiciously offends Babylonian ambassadors; the captivity in Babylon is predicted.
710 The Assyrian king Sennacherib invades Judah but fails to take Jerusalem. Hezekiah and Isaiah pray to God for deliverance, whereupon an angel cuts off the invading army. Soon after, Sennacherib perishes by the hands of his sons in a palace coup. About this time the prophet Nahum predicts the fall of Nineveh.

Left: *The Assyrian envoy contemptuously demands the surrender of Jerusalem.*

Above: *Isaiah reassures the people: God will save them.*

Hezekiah's son Manasseh was, according to the ancient writers, the worst king Jerusalem ever had. Reversing his father's religious policies and attempting to appease Assyria, he allowed back the altars to Baal and much else, even including human sacrifice. Although he is said to have repented toward the end of his reign, the situation did not improve, for his successor, Amon, followed the same policies until, after only a short time, he was assassinated in his own palace.

Josiah came to the throne at the young age of eight. Having witnessed violence and civil war during his childhood years, by the time he was sixteen he was seeking God and became a passionate, perhaps fanatical, reformer. At the age of twenty he set out to purge Judah and Jerusalem, and six years later rebuilt the Temple. During the work on the Temple, the priest Hilkiah discovered an ancient scroll, which was found to be the document of the Covenant. Reading this was itself revealing: the people saw that

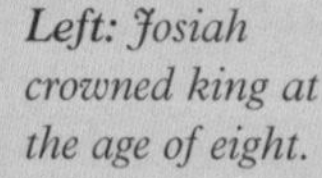

Left: *Josiah crowned king at the age of eight.*

Above right: *The rediscovered Book of the Law presented to King Josiah.*

God's support for his people was not unconditional but depended upon their observation of the Mosaic Law. This inspired Josiah to attempt a national revival, with the Temple at its center. The violence of the religious repression was most clearly seen at Bethel, where the priests were killed. He attempted to renew the Covenant; but despite all his efforts, it would not be enough to assuage God's anger with the Jews.

During Josiah's reign began the prophecies of Jeremiah, a humble, modest man who was forced to live a solitary life for much of the time, for God did not allow him to marry. His task was to be both a melancholy and a frustrating one, for God's mission to him was to carry a message to the people which they did not want to hear. It was an almost insupportable burden.

698 Manasseh king of Judah at age twelve, but his reign is a wicked one – he is one of Judah's least God-fearing kings, and is even said to have practiced human sacrifice. About 676 or 660 he is taken captive to Babylon. But he later repents, is restored to his kingdom and returns to the faith of God.
641 Amos king of Judah; his wickedness brings about his assassination after two years by his servants; his son, Josiah, succeeds at the age of eight, ruling to 610.
630 Josiah begins reform of Judah, even extending his reclaim to the north, the attentions of the Assyrians focused elsewhere at this time.
629 The prophet Jeremiah begins his work.
623 Josiah repairs the Temple; Hilkiah, the High Priest, discovers the book of the Law. Josiah is alarmed and consults the prophetess Huldah, who predicts the desolations of Judah and Jerusalem.

***Right:** Josiah's destruction of the idols.*

1: The word which came to Jeremiah from the Lord, saying, 2: Arise, and go down to the potter's house, and there I will cause thee to hear my words. 3: Then I went down to the potter's house, and, behold, he wrought a work on the wheels. 4: And the vessel that he made of clay was marred in the hand of the potter: so he made it again another vessel, as seemed good to the potter to make it. 5: Then the word of the Lord came to me, saying, 6: O house of Israel, cannot I do with you as this potter? saith the Lord. Behold, as the clay is in the potter's hand, so are ye in mine hand, O house of Israel. 7: At what instant I shall speak concerning a nation, and concerning a kingdom, to pluck up, and to pull down, and to destroy it; 8: If that nation, against whom I have pronounced, turn from their evil, I will repent of the evil that I thought to do unto them. 9: And at what instant I shall speak concerning a nation, and concerning a kingdom, to build and to plant it; 10: If it do evil in my sight, that it obey not my voice, then I will repent of the good, wherewith I said I would benefit them. 11: Now therefore go to, speak to the men of Judah, and to the inhabitants of Jerusalem, saying, Thus saith the Lord; Behold, I frame evil against you, and devise a device against you: return ye now every one from his evil way, and make your ways and your doings good.

—Jeremiah 18:1–11

1: Thus saith the Lord, Go and get a potter's earthen bottle, and take of the ancients of the people, and of the ancients of the priests; 2: And go forth ... and proclaim there the words that I shall tell thee, 3: And say, Hear ye the word of the Lord, O kings of Judah, and inhabitants of Jerusalem; Thus saith the Lord of hosts, the God of Israel; Behold, I will bring evil upon this place, the which whosoever heareth, his ears shall tingle. 4: Because they have forsaken me, and have estranged this place, and have burned incense in it unto other gods, whom neither they nor their fathers have known, nor the kings of Judah, and have filled this place with the blood of innocents; 5: They have built also the high places of Baal, to burn their sons with fire for burnt offerings unto Baal, which I commanded not ... 7: And I will make void the counsel of Judah and Jerusalem in this place; and I will cause them to fall by the sword before their enemies ... 8: And I will make this city desolate, and an hissing; every one that passeth thereby shall be astonished and hiss because of all the plagues thereof ... 10: Then shalt thou break the bottle in the sight of the men that go with thee, 11: And shalt say unto them, Thus saith the Lord of hosts; Even so will I break this people and this city, as one breaketh a potter's vessel, that cannot be made whole again: and they shall bury them in Tophet, till there be no place to bury.

— Jeremiah 19:1–11

His attitude toward Josiah's reforms seems to have been that the reforms would fail – they came from the will of the king rather than the conscience of the people. There was no inward turning toward God.

For most of Josiah's reign, Judah experienced some respite from the wars that surrounded and often engulfed it, including the great incursion of Scythian horseman who ravaged the Middle East as far as Egypt. With the destruction of the Assyrian power by the rising Babylonian Empire, Josiah harbored ambitions to reunite Judah with Israel, which had been conquered during the previous century by the Assyrians. He perished in battle at Megiddo against the Egyptian Pharaoh Necho, who was also taking advantage of the temporary power vacuum to try to extend Egypt's influence north.

Josiah's son, Jehoahaz, was soon

622 Josiah celebrates the Passover, much neglected in the past, with zeal; it is the climax of his reforms.
612 Assyrian Empire overcome: destruction of Nineveh by the Babylonians.
610 In battle with Pharaoh Necho of Egypt at Megiddo, Josiah dies, to the lamentations of his people. Jehoahaz, his second son, succeeds him, but within three months is captured and taken captive to Egypt by Necho; Jehoahaz's elder brother Jehoiakim is set on the throne of Judah (– 600) as a puppet ruler.

Below: *The death of Josiah at Megiddo.*

deposed in favor of his brother, Jehoiakim, who realigned the state with Egypt, provoking Nebuchadnezzar to turn his attention to Jerusalem. The priests and prophets of Judah persisted in assertions that God would protect them from this new threat, just as he had before. But Jeremiah warned that this was not so – Jerusalem would be destroyed – and he was branded a defeatist and a traitor. He condemned the false reliance on the Temple, thereby making enemies of the priests. Pashur, the Temple overseer, at one point had Jeremiah scourged and put in the stocks. Later, during the siege of Jerusalem, he was thrown into a cistern so that nobody had to listen to his depressing prophecies; but on the orders of King Zedekiah he was rescued.

Like Jeremiah, Zephaniah spoke out against the idolatry, violence, fraud, and generally wanton behavior into which the

6: And Jeremiah said, The word of the Lord came unto me, saying, 7: Behold, Hanameel the son of Shallum thine uncle shall come unto thee, saying, Buy thee my field that is in Anathoth: for the right of redemption is thine to buy it. 8: So Hanameel mine uncle's son came to me in the court of the prison according to the word of the Lord, and said unto me, Buy my field, I pray thee, that is in Anathoth, which is in the country of Benjamin: for the right of inheritance is thine, and the redemption is thine; buy it for thyself. Then I knew that this was the word of the Lord. 9: And I bought the field of Hanameel my uncle's son, that was in Anathoth, and weighed him the money, even seventeen shekels of silver. 10: And I subscribed the evidence, and sealed it, and took witnesses, and weighed him the money in the balances. 11: So I took the evidence of the purchase, both that which was sealed according to the law and custom, and that which was open: 12: And I gave the evidence of the purchase unto Baruch the son of Neriah, the son of Maaseiah, in the sight of Hanameel mine uncle's son, and in the presence of the witnesses that subscribed the book of the purchase, before all the Jews that sat in the court of the prison. 13: And I charged Baruch before them, saying, 14: Thus saith the Lord of hosts, the God of Israel; Take these evidences, this evidence of the purchase, both which is sealed, and this evidence which is open; and put them in an earthen vessel, that they may continue many days. 15: For thus saith the Lord of hosts, the God of Israel; Houses and fields and vineyards shall be possessed again in this land.

— Jeremiah 32: 6–15

Jews had sunk. Jerusalem, he said, had become such a place of abominable corruption that there was no other way but for God to destroy it. But the humble, faithful people, of which there were still some, would in time enjoy the Lord's blessings again.

When Nebuchadnezzar captured Jerusalem, the city was plundered but, since it had surrendered, not destroyed. The upper elements of society were

606 Nebuchadnezzar (joint king of Babylon with his father, Nabopolassar until the latter's death the following year) makes Judah tributary; the "70-Years" captivity of the Jews begins, the prophet Daniel being among those taken; many of the sacred vessels of the Temple are looted by the Babylonians.
603 Jehoiakim revolts against the Babylonians, and Obadiah prophesies against the Edomites about this time.
600(–598) Jehoiachin (Jeconiah, Jeconias, or Coniah) succeeds his father Jehoiakim, who is slain.
598–7 Nebuchadnezzar besieges Jerusalem; Jehoiachin and many other Jews are taken captive to Babylon; his uncle, Zedekiah, made king (–588). Ezekiel is among those deported to Babylon, as is Mordecai.

Far left: *Jeremiah rescued from the cistern.*

Center left: *Jeremiah's unwanted prophecies are burned by the king.*

Left: *The first capture of Jerusalem by the Babylonians. Judah is forced to accept the Babylonian yoke.*

deported to Babylon and Zedekiah, another of Josiah's sons, was placed on the throne. But when he rebelled against Babylon, Nebuchadnezzar showed no mercy. After a long siege, the city fell and was systematically destroyed; there were also more deportations.

Jeremiah was made captive but later set free and was not included in those sent to Babylon. During the siege of Jerusalem he had bought a plot of land at Anathoth as a token of his confidence that there would be a future for Jerusalem. He attempted to comfort his brethren in exile – it was possible to serve God in a foreign land; and one day the they would return to make a new beginning. In the end, after their trials and suffering, God would restore the

Jews to his favor, and the land would bloom once again. Then there was an attempted coup against Gedaliah, the local Governor appointed by Babylon, failed, and many remnants of Judah fled to Egypt; Jeremiah was one of them.

595 Ezekiel begins prophesying in Chaldaea.
593 Zedekiah allies with Egypt's Pharaoh, Hophra.
590 Nebuchadnezzar lays siege to Jerusalem upon Zedekiah's revolt; meanwhile Jeremiah continues to prophesy but the king fails to act upon his words.
589 The Babylonians repulse an Egyptian relief expedition.
587 Nebuchadnezzar takes Jerusalem and destroys it, including the Temple. This is seen as God's punishment of his chosen people, who have turned away from him too many times. Zedekiah's sons are killed before their father's eyes; he himself is then blinded and carried captive to Babylon.
584 The scattered remnant of the Jews carried off.

Left: *The destruction of Jerusalem.*

Above: *The cruel fate of King Zedekiah.*

Ezekiel was a younger contemporary of Jeremiah and was in training for the priesthood before he was carried off among the first group of deportees from Jerusalem to Babylon. He was to become God's messenger to the exiles, forecasting the destruction of Jerusalem (which was yet to come at that time), and later a hope of a new beginning.

His calling to be a prophet was dramatic indeed, the first of a series of visions or revelations. He saw what appeared to be a a great storm coming up from the north, a huge cloud lit suddenly by flashes of lightning, brilliant light and deafening noise. In the midst of this was a vast four-wheeled chariot, drawn by four cherubim and moving in all directions. Above there appeared a gigantic figure in the shape of a man, which he described as the glory of God – he was glimpsing the Almighty. God spoke. Addressing Ezekiel as the "Son of Man," he told him that he was to be God's messenger to the exiles.

The early visions were of God's judgment on his people, which Ezekiel had to relay to his fellow exiles partly by a sort of play-acting, symbolizing the end of Jerusalem, its siege and fall. He was also given a vision of the Temple, transported there to see how it was being violated by the worship of idols and alien gods. Horrified by the abominations he witnessed, Ezekiel then saw a great chariot-throne ascend and head eastward above the Mount of Olives. God's departure from the Temple and from Jerusalem was thus symbolized, a message to the exiles that he had come with them.

God also sent messages in the form of parables. One such told of a great forest fire to the south, indicating the destruction of the southern kingdom of Judah, just as the northern kingdom had perished before. Another concerned two adulterous sisters. Oholah, symbolizing Samaria, prostituted herself to Egyptians and Assyrians, but God handed her to the Assyrians for punishment. Her sister, Ohalibah, standing for Jerusalem, was no better and imitated her sister, but God meted out her punishment too.

After the fall of Jerusalem, and the further mass deportations, Ezekiel's visions took on a different tone, looking to a better future, which was in tune with the longings of the exiles. He saw a valley of dry bones into which God breathed life; and later a great vision of a city on a hill, centered upon a new Temple, which was described in considerable detail, particular attention being given to the priesthood. Only the descendants of Zadok, the High Priest of Solomon, would be allowed to enter the inner sanctum and perform the liturgy. The Levites, heretofore the keepers of the Temple (as they had been of the Tabernacle in Moses' time) were effectively demoted on account of their sin in tolerating and condoning idolatry in the Temple for so long; henceforth their role would be restricted to the more menial tasks. From the Temple flowed a life-giving river, its banks lined with fruit-bearing trees that never lost their leaves. The vision depicted God's return to a new Temple, to dwell among his people again in an earthly paradise.

1: The hand of the Lord was upon me, and carried me out in the spirit of the Lord, and set me down in the midst of the valley which was full of bones, 2: And caused me to pass by them round about: and, behold, there were very many in the open valley; and, lo, they were very dry. 3: And he said unto me, Son of man, can these bones live? And I answered, O Lord God, thou knowest. 4: Again he said unto me, Prophesy upon these bones, and say unto them, O ye dry bones, hear the word of the Lord. 5: Thus saith the Lord God unto these bones; Behold, I will cause breath to enter into you, and ye shall live: 6: And I will lay sinews upon you, and will bring up flesh upon you, and cover you with skin, and put breath in you, and ye shall live; and ye shall know that I am the Lord. 7: So I prophesied as I was commanded: and as I prophesied, there was a noise, and behold a shaking, and the bones came together, bone to his bone. 8: And when I beheld, lo, the sinews and the flesh came up upon them, and the skin covered them above: but there was no breath in them. 9: Then said he unto me, Prophesy unto the wind, prophesy, son of man, and say to the wind, Thus saith the Lord GOD; Come from the four winds, O breath, and breathe upon these slain, that they may live. 10: So I prophesied as he commanded me, and the breath came into them, and they lived, and stood up upon their feet, an exceeding great army. 11: Then he said unto me, Son of man, these bones are the whole house of Israel: behold, they say, Our bones are dried, and our hope is lost: we are cut off for our parts. 12: Therefore prophesy and say unto them, Thus saith the Lord God; Behold, O my people, I will open your graves, and cause you to come up out of your graves, and bring you into the land of Israel ... 14: And shall put my spirit in you, and ye shall live, and I shall place you in your own land: then shall ye know that I the Lord have spoken it, and performed it, saith the Lord ... Behold, I will take the children of Israel from among the heathen, whither they be gone, and will gather them on every side, and bring them into their own land: 22: And I will make them one nation in the land upon the mountains of Israel; and one king shall be king to them all: and they shall be no more two nations, neither shall they be divided into two kingdoms any more at all: 23: Neither shall they defile themselves any more with their idols, nor with their detestable things, nor with any of their transgressions: but I will save them out of all their dwellingplaces, wherein they have sinned, and will cleanse them: so shall they be my people, and I will be their God. 24: And David my servant shall be king over them; and they all shall have one shepherd: they shall also walk in my judgments, and observe my statutes, and do them. 25: And they shall dwell in the land that I have given unto Jacob my servant, wherein your fathers have dwelt; and they shall dwell therein, even they, and their children, and their children's children for ever: and my servant David shall be their prince for ever. 26: Moreover I will make a covenant of peace with them; it shall be an everlasting covenant with them: and I will place them, and multiply them, and will set my sanctuary in the midst of them for evermore. 27: My tabernacle also shall be with them: yea, I will be their God, and they shall be my people. — *Ezekiel 37: 1–27*

Not all the Jews taken to Babylon were miserably treated. Some, such as Daniel, and his three companions, Shadrach, Meshach and Abed-nego, rose to positions of prominence and wealth in the royal administration. They were among the early deportees, taken as children, educated and trained for official positions within the imperial administration. Daniel may even have been of royal blood. He grew to be a handsome young man, well proportioned and an asset to the kings he served – Nebuchadnezzar, Cyrus, and Darius.

Like Joseph, he was an interpreter of dreams, turning to God for help. One night the mighty king, Nebuchadnezzar, experienced a dream that puzzled and disturbed him, but none of his court magicians, astrologers, or other such luminaries could shed light on the king's

dream. The angry monarch ordered them all to be slaughtered, but fortunately someone mentioned this to Daniel, who interceded with the king. If he could interpret the dream, would the king rescind his command? That night Daniel consulted his three friends and prayed to God for help. By morning he had his answer, which he set before the king.

The dream had been of a vast statue, with a head of gold, chest and arms of silver, belly and thighs of bronze, legs of iron, and feet a mixture of iron and clay. Nebuchadnezzar had seen a rock, hewn not by human hands, smash the feet of the statue, whereupon the whole collapsed into tiny fragments and was blown away on the wind, while the rock grew to fill the world.

Daniel explained that, while no man could interpret this dream, God could. It was a vision of the future. The head was Nebuchadnezzar's own glorious empire, for he was the King of Kings; each of the other elements represented successor empires which would rise and fall, the last, that or iron and clay, being divided, with the strength of iron but the weakness of clay. The rock represented God's eternal kingdom, which would outlast them all. Nebuchadnezzar was deeply impressed. Daniel and his companions were richly rewarded, and the soothsayers spared.

Left and right: *Nebuchadnezzar listens intently to Daniel's interpretation of his dream, then falls at his feet in praise of God.*

583 Nebuchadnezzar orders worship of a golden image; Shadrach, Meshach, and Abed-nego refuse but are miraculously preserved.

1: In the third year of the reign of Jehoiakim king of Judah came Nebuchadnezzar king of Babylon unto Jerusalem, and besieged it.
2: And the Lord gave Jehoiakim king of Judah into his hand, with part of the vessels of the house of God: which he carried into the land of Shinar to the house of his god; and he brought the vessels into the treasure house of his god. 3: And the king spake unto Ashpenaz the master of his eunuchs, that he should bring certain of the children of Israel, and of the king's seed, and of the princes;
4: Children in whom was no blemish, but well favoured, and skilful in all wisdom, and cunning in knowledge, and understanding science, and such as had ability in them to stand in the king's palace, and whom they might teach the learning and the tongue of the Chaldeans. 5: And the king appointed them a daily provision of the king's meat, and of the wine which he drank: so nourishing them three years, that at the end thereof they might stand before the king. 6: Now among these were of the children of Judah, Daniel, Hananiah, Mishael, and Azariah: 7: Unto whom the prince of the eunuchs gave names: for he gave unto Daniel the name of Belteshazzar; and to Hananiah, of Shadrach; and to Mishael, of Meshach; and to Azariah, of Abed-nego. *— Daniel 1: 1–7*

examples of disobedience and brought before the king. Intransigent, they were duly sentenced, and the fiery furnace was heated especially high. Tightly bound, they were cast into the flames, where they were joined by an angel. But the fire did not consume them, and they emerged without even having their clothes singed. King Nebuchadnezzar, astounded, decreed that any person speaking ill of the exiles' God would be cut into little pieces.

Another dream subsequently troubled Nebuchadnezzar's nights. It was of a great beautiful tree, so high it reached to the heavens, its branches laden with fruit, with the beasts of the Earth dwelling in its shade and birds nesting above. Then he heard a message from Heaven commanding that the tree be cut down, so that all that was left would be the stump and roots. The king would live with the mind of an animal, eating grass like cattle.

Daniel once more consulted God to interpret the dream. The tree represented the king, strong, with dominion over far and wide; but he would be driven from his

Some while later, Nebuchadnezzar decided to set up a new idol for worship, a statue of gold of great height, which he set in the plain of Dura. The people were to fall down and worship this upon summons by music played on a variety of instruments, and it was dedicated in a splendid ceremony. Failure to worship, the king ordained, would be met with death by fire in a blazing furnace.

The people did as they were bid; but not so the Jews. When this was noted, Shadrach, Meshach, and Abed-nego were singled out as

Above: *Nebuchadnezzar's golden idol.*

Right: *The fiery furnace.*

people to live with the animals, eating grass, and feeling the dew on his back, until after an allotted time he acknowledged that God is the sovereign over the kingdom of men. Only then would he be restored to his high position. He must renounce his sins, embrace the Lord and show compassion for all men.

A year later it happened – Nebuchadnezzar went mad. And at the end of the specified time, his sanity was restored, he praised God and returned to his throne.

572 Nebuchadnezzar's dream of calamity (lycanthropy) interpreted by Daniel; as he foretells, Nebuchadnezzar is insane for seven years; on recovery he worships the God of the Jews.

> 24: This is the interpretation, O king, and this is the decree of the most High, which is come upon my lord the king: 25: That they shall drive thee from men, and thy dwelling shall be with the beasts of the field, and they shall make thee to eat grass as oxen, and they shall wet thee with the dew of heaven, and seven times shall pass over thee, till thou know that the most High ruleth in the kingdom of men, and giveth it to whomsoever he will. 26: And whereas they commanded to leave the stump of the tree roots; thy kingdom shall be sure unto thee, after that thou shalt have known that the heavens do rule. 27: Wherefore, O king, let my counsel be acceptable unto thee, and break off thy sins by righteousness, and thine iniquities by shewing mercy to the poor; if it may be a lengthening of thy tranquillity. 28: All this came upon the king Nebuchadnezzar. — *Daniel 4:24–28*

Above and left: *Nebuchadnezzar's dream, his suffering as an animal, and his acceptance of God.*

Some time after the death of Nebuchadnezzar, there sat on the throne of Babylon a king called Nabonidus, who made his son Belshazzar co-ruler and retired to the country. By now the Babylonian monarchs had forgotten the lessons that Nebuchadnezzar had learned and gave themselves over to debauchery and impiety. One night Belshazzar threw a particularly lavish feast, and used the gold goblets looted from the Temple in Jerusalem for the wine. As they were eating and drinking, there suddenly appeared a hand, mysteriously writing on the wall. This apparition terrified the king, who called upon his magicians and soothsayers to explain what it meant. They could not, but the queen remembered Daniel's interpretation of Nebuchadnezzar's dreams, and he was called for.

Now an old man, Daniel examined the writing and explained its meaning. The words were about numbers, essentially "number," "weigh," and "divide." They meant that the king's days were numbered – he had ignored the lessons of his ancestor, had not honored God and had desecrated the sacred objects from the Temple. And that very night the Persian Cyrus captured Babylon with great slaughter.

Left: *Daniel interprets the writing on the wall. "Mene" meant "number," or "mina," a unit of currency; "Tekel" "weighed," or a shekel; Peres "divided," or half a shekel, or "Persia."*

Right: *Daniel in the den of lions.*

> 24: Then was the part of the hand sent from him; and this writing was written. 25: And this is the writing that was written, MENE, MENE, TEKEL, UPHARSIN. 26: This is the interpretation of the thing: MENE; God hath numbered thy kingdom, and finished it. 27: TEKEL; Thou art weighed in the balances, and art found wanting. 28: PERES; Thy kingdom is divided, and given to the Medes and Persians. 29: Then commanded Belshazzar, and they clothed Daniel with scarlet, and put a chain of gold about his neck, and made a proclamation concerning him, that he should be the third ruler in the kingdom. 30: In that night was Belshazzar the king of the Chaldeans slain. — *Daniel 5:24–30*

Daniel survived the end of the Babylonian Empire. Indeed, the Persian conquerors evidently saw in Daniel a man of competence, and he rose further in the administration. But this provoked sharp jealousy among his Chaldean colleagues and rivals, who sought charges to bring against him. They could find nothing of corruption or negligence: so they chose instead a religious device to bring him down. A royal edict was promulgated forbidding worship of any god except the king for thirty days. Daniel ignored this, was reported and brought to trial. The penalty was to be confined in a den of lions. But no harm came to him, for God protected his servant. Next morning the king was astonished and penitent: the false accusers were rounded up, with their wives and children, and consigned to the lions' den, where they were appropriately consumed by the hungry beasts. The king meanwhile issued a new edict that the God of Daniel should receive his due reverence.

During the remainder of his days, Daniel received a number of visions, most forecasting what was to come, the struggle for power in the world and the eventual triumph of God.

560 Upon the death of Nebuchadnezzar, his successor, Amel-Marduk (Evil-merodach), releases Jehoiachin.
555 Belshazzar becomes king of Babylon.
541 Cyrus of Persia besieges Babylon.
539/8 Belshazzar's feast and Cyrus the Great's conquest of Babylon. The Persian Empire replaces that of Babylon, as prophesied.
Daniel's vision of the 70 weeks.
537 Daniel cast into a den of lions.

19: Then the king arose very early in the morning, and went in haste unto the den of lions. 20: And when he came to the den, he cried with a lamentable voice unto Daniel: and the king spake and said to Daniel, O Daniel, servant of the living God, is thy God, whom thou servest continually, able to deliver thee from the lions? 21: Then said Daniel unto the king, O king, live for ever. 22: My God hath sent his angel, and hath shut the lions' mouths, that they have not hurt me: forasmuch as before him innocency was found in me; and also before thee, O king, have I done no hurt. 23: Then was the king exceeding glad for him, and commanded that they should take Daniel up out of the den ... 25: Then king Darius wrote unto all people, nations, and languages, that dwell in all the earth; Peace be multiplied unto you. 26: I make a decree, That in every dominion of my kingdom men tremble and fear before the God of Daniel: for he is the living God, and stedfast for ever, and his kingdom that which shall not be destroyed, and his dominion shall be even unto the end. 27: He delivereth and rescueth, and he worketh signs and wonders in heaven and in earth, who hath delivered Daniel from the power of the lions. 28: So this Daniel prospered in the reign of Darius, and in the reign of Cyrus the Persian. — *Daniel 6:16–28*

The demise of the Babylonian Empire brought great changes to the way the imperial administration functioned. More autonomy was afforded the subject nations (it was cheaper and more efficient), and they were allowed to resume worshipping their own gods – Cyrus began sending back the idols and effigies that had been taken to Babylon by the previous conquerors. This applied also to the Jews, and the exiles were now offered the freedom to return to their homeland. Fewer chose to return than those who stayed in Babylonia; but in 538 a large party set off for Jerusalem led by Zerubbabel, a grandson of King Joiachim, who was appointed Governor of the region. He was also encouraged to rebuild the city and the Temple, and Cyrus even gave back the sacred objects plundered from the Temple by Nebuchadnezzar. At Zerubbabel's side went Jeshua (Joshua), the High Priest.

Left: *The exiles rejoice that they can at last return to the home of their ancestors.*

Above: *But desolation awaits them at the site of Jerusalem.*

During the period of exile, the Jews had inevitably built up a memory of an idealized city: the Jerusalem they found was disheartening in the extreme – a ruined wasteland (just as Ezekiel had foretold) and unoccupied for half a century. But they made a start, setting up an altar on the site of the original and making sacrifice, and within two years the Temple foundations had been laid.

But now a conflict became apparent between "the children of the captivity" and "the people of the land," those left behind, who had intermarried with other peoples and included the Samaritans. Their attachment to the God of Israel was abhorrent to the Jews, who refused them any part in the reconstruction. Resentments and distrust of the people from Babylon who presumed to take over the area led the Samaritans and others to make representations to the Persian court for the reconstruction work to be stopped. At first they succeeded, until court records in the imperial capital indicated that the reconstruction had indeed been permitted. But these delays, added to a certain indifference and apathy among some of the returnees, slowed progress to a halt.

Among the first to return was Haggai, whose role it was to preach encouragement to the Jews. Born in Babylon, he longed, like the others, to see the Temple rebuilt. This he saw as essential to maintain Israel's religious purity; and the Temple would be the first sign of a new beginning. His message to his fellows was always of encouragement and an exhortation to get on with this vital task. True, the returnees found life hard, with shortages of food and provisions. And naturally their immediate concerns were for their own wellbeing and safety. But Haggai upbraided them for getting their priorities wrong. They should not concentrate upon their own homes while that of God lay in ruin. They were being selfish, neglecting him. (And punishment duly came in the form of a drought.)

> 3: Then came the word of the Lord by Haggai the prophet, saying, 4: Is it time for you, O ye, to dwell in your cieled houses, and this house lie waste? 5: Now therefore thus saith the Lord of hosts; Consider your ways. 6: Ye have sown much, and bring in little; ye eat, but ye have not enough; ye drink, but ye are not filled with drink; ye clothe you, but there is none warm; and he that earneth wages earneth wages to put it into a bag with holes. 7: Thus saith the Lord of hosts; Consider your ways. 8: Go up to the mountain, and bring wood, and build the house; and I will take pleasure in it, and I will be glorified, saith the Lord. *— Haggai 1:3–8*

536 End of the 70 years of captivity. Cyrus, king of Persia, reverses the Babylonian policy of deportation: he releases the captive Jews and encourages them to rebuild Jerusalem and the Temple. The returnees, most of whom are exiles from Judah, are led by Zerubbabel.

535 Jews arrive in Jerusalem, observe their feasts and begin rebuilding.

534 Foundations of the new Temple laid; Daniel's last vision.

530 Death of Cyrus the Great; Cambyses king of Persia (–522).

525 Egypt becomes part of the Persian Empire.

522 Darius I king of Persia (–486). He builds the cities of Susa and Persepolis.

521 Samaritans, many of who are of mixed Jewish marriage, offer help but this is spurned, for God had decreed no intermarriage with foreigners. So the Samaritans obtain a Persian decree forbidding further work on rebuilding the Temple.

520 Prophets Haggai and Zechariah inspire Zerubbabel and Jeshua to rebuild the Temple.

***Above:** Cyrus tells the Jews they are free to take back the sacred objects for the Temple.*

Zechariah was Haggai's companion prophet, a man of priestly descent and, like Haggai, with a message of hope and recovery. Past guilt could be atoned for; Zerubbabel and Jeshua would indeed complete the Temple and the kingdom be restored. Like Daniel and Ezekiel, he was a visionary, and his visions signified the final restoration of Jerusalem and the establishment of God's kingdom on Earth. It was a message of hope and fulfilment – and doom to Israel's neighbors.

Zechariah's visions pointed to God's mercy on Jerusalem and his people; one vision was of Jerusalem surrounded by a wall of fire, this being God protecting the city and people. A vision of four horsemen in a myrtle-grove was interpreted by an angel, for these were messengers from God. Then the angel asked: when will he

1: Then I turned, and lifted up mine eyes, and looked, and behold a flying roll. 2: And he said unto me, What seest thou? And I answered, I see a flying roll; the length thereof is twenty cubits, and the breadth thereof ten cubits. 3: Then said he unto me, This is the curse that goeth forth over the face of the whole earth: for every one that stealeth shall be cut off as on this side according to it; and every one that sweareth shall be cut off as on that side according to it. 4: I will bring it forth, saith the Lord of hosts, and it shall enter into the house of the thief, and into the house of him that sweareth falsely by my name: and it shall remain in the midst of his house, and shall consume it with the timber thereof and the stones thereof. —*Zechariah 5:1–4*

Above left: *Zerubbabel directs the reconstruction of the Temple.*

Above: *The Temple, finally finished, despite much opposition, is dedicated in 515 BC.*

show mercy to Jerusalem and Judah? God replied that he had now returned to Jerusalem; he had used other nations to execute judgment on his people; now those other nations would themselves be judged, and God would comfort his own. His final vision was of a great war of the nations against Jerusalem, God appearing with his angels to triumph and make the whole Earth his kingdom, so that all would worship him.

In 515 the Temple was at last finished and dedicated, but much remained to be done in the still very empty city.

In 458 another band of Jews arrived, this time led by Ezra, who was to play a vital part in steering the restoration in the right spiritual direction. Of priestly Zadokite descent, he was an austere and commanding character, who came intent on infusing the community with new zeal and accelerating progress toward making Jerusalem once again the true spiritual capital of the Jews.

Arrival in Jerusalem revealed clearly why so many Jews preferred to remain in Mesopotamia. There they had established themselves – it was a century and a half since their ancestors had been carried off. Many now owned property, while some had risen to positions of seniority and authority within the imperial bureaucracy. In contrast, Ezra found the inhabitants of Judaea in poverty, struggling to cope and with Jerusalem far from rebuilt.

More important to Ezra, however, was the poor moral and spiritual state of affairs. Over the years, the Jews had mingled freely with the other races, including the colonists sent by the Babylonians, and intermarrying, which was expressly forbidden by the Mosaic Law. This was an impurity that needed to be cleansed, so Ezra set up a special divorce court (over which he himself presided) and Jews began setting aside their foreign wives.

518 Further Samaritan attempts to stop rebuilding work are frustrated when King Darius of Persia consults the records and decides that the work is authorized.
517 Revolt in Babylon; city walls pulled down.
The prophet Haggai foretells that the new Temple shall be more glorious even than its predecessor.
515 Temple completed and dedicated. Like its predecessor, it features cedar wood from Lebanon. Passover is celebrated.
500/499–494/3 Persia crushes the Ionian revolt.
490 Persian invasion of Greece defeated at Battle of Marathon.
486 Xerxes king of Persia (–465).
480–79 Persian King Xerxes launches a massive expedition into Greece, which fails at Battles of Salamis and Plataea.
478 Persian king Xerxes destroys the temple of Bel at Babylon.
465/4 Artaxerxes I king of Persia (–424/3).
458 Jewess Esther becomes queen of Artaxerxes (named Ahasuerus in the Bible).
458 A priest, Ezra, is sent by Artaxerxes as Governor of Jerusalem; this begins Daniel's "70 weeks."
456 Ezra arrives in Jerusalem with Levite priests and much treasure; he separates the Jews from their heathen wives (the prohibition being not racial but against risk of idolatry).
452 Queen Esther defeats Haman's plan to destroy the Jews in exile at Babylon.

***Left:** Esther at the royal palace of Susa.*

***Below:** Haman shares his outrage at Mordecai's lack of obeisance and plans his vengeance – not just on Mordecai but upon all his compatriots.*

5: Now in Shushan the palace there was a certain Jew, whose name was Mordecai, the son of Jair, the son of Shimei, the son of Kish, a Benjamite; 6: Who had been carried away from Jerusalem with the captivity which had been carried away with Jeconiah king of Judah, whom Nebuchadnezzar the king of Babylon had carried away. 7: And he brought up Hadassah, that is, Esther, his uncle's daughter: for she had neither father nor mother, and the maid was fair and beautiful; whom Mordecai, when her father and mother were dead, took for his own daughter. —*Esther 2:5–7*

The story of Esther is a great romance of the captivity. Esther was a beautiful Benjamite girl among the exiles in Babylonia, an orphan raised by her cousin Mordecai, who was a minor official at the king's palace. When King Artaxerxes' queen, Vashti, was deemed to have disgraced herself by disobeying her husband, she was put aside; Esther was brought to the attention of the king at his winter palace of Susa, and he made her his new queen.

Trouble began when Mordecai offended the court favorite, Haman, who, upon discovering that Mordecai was a Jew, determined upon an evil plan. He would take revenge upon the insulting Jew by petitioning the king to sign a decree for the slaughter of all the Jews in Babylon, whom he accused of plotting rebellion – with the

Mordecai and the falsehoods behind his petition. Revealing that she was a Jew was dangerous in itself; but the king at once understood. The edict could not be stopped – once an edict bore the seal of the king's ring it could not be revoked. Instead he issued a second decree permitting the Jews to fight back. Meanwhile Haman was arraigned before the king and sentenced to death, together with his ten sons, while Esther was granted his lands and property, and the honors and promotion Haman had recommended to the king for himself were heaped upon Mordecai. The Jewish exiles, prepared for the onslaught, destroyed Haman's attackers, saved by the cunning and courage of Queen Esther. The celebration of this event gave rise to the feast of Purim.

added incentive of seizing their money and property. This he achieved – but there was a constitutional delay before the edict would be put into effect, which gave time for Mordecai to learn what was in store.

He spoke with Esther, who determined on a scheme to thwart Haman. She invited both the king and her enemy to two banquets on successive nights. After the first banquet, the king asked to see the royal records and discovered that Mordecai had rendered conspicuous service to the throne – he had prevented an assassination attempt upon the king. But he had never been rewarded for this, so Artaxerxes consulted his court favorite. But the conceited and egotistical Haman quite misunderstood the king, thinking he meant himself, so he recommended high honors.

At the banquet the following day Esther courageously spoke to the king, revealing that she was herself of Jewish origin and telling Artaxerxes about Haman's ill intent toward

Above left: *Esther confesses her origin and tells the king about Haman's plot.*

Below: *The king grants Esther's plea.*

To complement this spiritual work, there arrived in 445/4 a man who would take in hand the physical completion of the restoration. This was Nehemiah (Sheshbazzar), a Jewish prince who had risen to be the king's cup-bearer, a position of great prominence at the court in Susa. Hearing reports of the poor state of affairs yet prevailing in Jerusalem, he obtained permission from King Artaxerxes to go there for a term as Governor. On arrival he spent several days clandestinely investigating how matters stood before revealing his identity and beginning work.

Above: *Nehemiah, told by his brother of the parlous situation of the Jews in Jerusalem, asks permission of the Persian king to take leave of absence and go as Governor to the city.*

Right: *Under armed guard, the walls of Jerusalem rise up again.*

A practical man with a sense of purpose, Nehemiah set about the reconstruction of the city walls as a matter of priority, in the face of considerable opposition and hostility – he was even moved to mount guards against interference from malcontents. The walls were completed in just two months and dedicated in a splendid ceremony.

With Ezra, he now embarked upon the completion of the religious and social reform necessary to establish a strong state. Ezra read the Book of the Law in solemn assembly, investing it with a sanctity and significance it had not known for centuries. The Covenant was renewed, and observation of the Sabbath instituted, while Nehemiah made provision for a reliable source of revenue for the Temple. In any such period of confusion and change, there are those who seek to profit from the weakness of others. Rich men had been charging interest; profiteers were at work, and there were even slave traders. These Nehemiah sought out and punished, and measures for debt relief were put in place.

After a dozen or so years of dynamic leadership, Nehemiah returned to Susa; but he later came back to Jerusalem to halt yet again the slide into the old abuses and corruption. His work, and that of Ezra, ended with the Jews back in their Promised Land, their Temple, faith and city re-established on a sure foundation.

> 4: Remember ye the law of Moses my servant, which I commanded unto him in Horeb for all Israel, with the statutes and judgments. 5: Behold, I will send you Elijah the prophet before the coming of the great and dreadful day of the Lord: 6: And he shall turn the heart of the fathers to the children, and the heart of the children to their fathers, lest I come and smite the earth with a curse.
>
> *— Malachi 4:4 – 6*

***Right:** Ezra reads the Mosaic Law to the people in Jerusalem.*

445 Nehemiah sent by Artaxerxes as Governor to Jerusalem, with commission to rebuild the city walls and revive the fortunes, civic and religious, of the city. The Persian king's Chief Butler (a very senior position), he has been advised by his brother Hanani about the poor state of affairs in Jerusalem. He is an inspirational leader and rebuilds the city walls, dedicating them in a splendid ceremony.

432 or later After a brief absence in the Persian court, Nehemiah returns to Jerusalem to discover much corruption, including the sale of Jewish slaves to foreigners, which he takes measures to resolve, including the banishment of Eliashib, the grandson of the High Priest.

The Covenant is renewed, and the people pledge that they will henceforth abide by all of God's Laws.

During the time of Nehemiah, Ezra prepares a correct edition of the scriptures and reads the Law to the people, provoking a national outpouring of repentance.

424/3 Darius II king of Persia (–404).

420 Prophecy of Malachi, last of the Old Testament prophets.

HERE ENDS THE RECORD OF THE OLD TESTAMENT.

Left: Alexander the Great in battle with Darius, king of Persia.

424/3(–404) Darius II king of Persia.
404(–338) Artaxerxes II king of Persia.
404 End of the Peloponnesian War.
400/399 Sparta and Persia at War.
386 Treaty between Sparta and Persia.
358(–338) Artaxerxes III king of Persia.
348 Artaxerxes III makes further deportations of Jews from Jerusalem.
343/2 Egypt reconquered by Persia.
338(–336) Arses king of Persia.
336(–330) Darius III king of Persia.
334–323 Conquests of Alexander the Great.
332 Alexander conquers Palestine and Egypt.
330 Death of Darius III and end of the Persian Empire.
323 Death of Alexander the Great.
323 Era of the Diadochi (successors to Alexander) begins. Ptolemy attains control of Egypt, founding Ptolemaic dynasty (to 31); by **301** the eastern part of Alexander's empire is under the control of the Seleucid dynasty. The area of Palestine and Syria is disputed between Egypt and the Seleucids in a series of wars to 199, when the latter secures control.

Left: Seleucid King Antiochus IV Epiphanes, whose Hellenizing culminated in the proscription of Jewish worship – and resulted in revolt.

176/5(–164) Antiochus IV Epiphanes. Hellenism flourishes, and foreign religious sects enter Jerusalem.
175 He deposes the High Priest, Onian III, and appoints High Priests who bring Greek elements into the Temple. Rivalry over the appointment of High Priests leads to conflict, massacres, the destruction of Jerusalem's walls and the construction of a Syrian-occupied fortified area within the city. In **168** Antiochus finally proscribes Jewish worship, which leads to passive resistance and then outright revolt.

Left: Judas Maccabeus used guerrilla tactics to defeat the Seleucids and gain independence for Jerusalem in a war that began as a religious revolt and became a fight for political independence.

167/6 Maccabean revolt against the Seleucids and Greeks, led by Mattathias the Hasmonean and his five sons, Judas, Jonathan, Simon, John, and Eleazar.
166–37 Hasmonean dynasty.
164 Judas wins control of Jerusalem, ejects idols from the Temple and rededicates it. This is subsequently celebrated by Jews as the festival of Hanukkah.
152/150–143/2 Judas attains independence from the Seleucids and is acknowledged as High Priest.
150 or earlier, the Essenes, Pharisees and Sadducees develop in Jerusalem.
140–76 Internecine conflict between successive members of the Hasmonean dynasty, ending with the reign of Queen Alexandra Salome (76–67), who ushers in a period of stability.
134 Seleucid King Antiochus VII besieges Jerusalem.
94 Pharisees revolt against Alexander Janneus.
67 Civil war between Hyrcanus and

Left: Pompey the Great, one of the greatest Roman warlords in the 1st century BC; it was he who brought Jerusalem into the Roman sphere.

Left: Pharisees in conference.

PHARISEES AND SADDUCEES

These rival religious parties, which developed during the period between the two Testaments, were at the forefront of opposition to Jesus, who encountered criticism and hostility from them for his teachings and for such actions as healing the sick or plucking grain on the Sabbath.

Pharisees were flexible in allowing a wider interpretation of the Mosaic Law and regarded the oral traditions as of equal importance to the written Law. Jesus would denounce their self-righteousness, and purely external observance of the Law.

Sadducees represented the interests of the priestly aristocracy, claiming descent from Zadok, High Priest under David and Solomon. They rejected the oral traditions and accepted only the written Law; they did not believe in resurrection of the body and denied the existence of angels and spirits.

Aristobulus, sons of Alexandra Salome, both sides appealing to Rome for aid.

64/63 Pompeius Magnus (Pompey the Great) conquers Syria in the name of Rome; end of the Seleucid dynasty.

63 Pompey besieges and captures Jerusalem, renaming it Judaea. He enters the Holy of Holies. Hyrcanus becomes High Priest and Rome's client king.

57 Rome divides the area of Jerusalem into five independent districts ruled by the Governor of Syria.

49–45 Roman Civil War. Hyrcanus' adviser Antipater becomes administrator of Judaea.

48–47 Julius Caesar's Alexandrine War.

47 Caesar in Egypt, Syria, and Asia.

47 Hyrcanus confirmed as High Priest and declared Ethnarch. Antipater is procurator of Judaea.

46 Antipater makes his sons Phasael and Herod commanders in Judaea and Galilee.

46 Rome introduces the Julian calendar.

44 Assassination of Julius Caesar.

43 Assassination of Antipater.

42 Julius Caesar included among the gods of the state, forerunner of the religious cult of the emperor, which will clash with Judaism.

42(–31) Antony ruler of the eastern half of the Roman Empire.

42 Antony declares Phasael and Herod tetrarchs.

40 Parthians invade Palestine and take Jerusalem. Phasael commits suicide; Herod flees to Rome, where he is formally made king of Judaea.

40(–37) Antigonus II king and High Priest.

39–37 Herod reconquers Judaea.

37(–4) Herod the Great king of Judaea. He exterminates the line of the Hasmoneans and separates the functions of High Priest and secular ruler.

34 Jericho and Palestine coastal cities ceded to Egypt, which is ruled by Queen Cleopatra.

Left: Antony and Cleopatra at the Battle of Actium.

31 Battle of Actium: defeat of Antony and Cleopatra. Death of Cleopatra, last queen of Egypt, the following year.

31 Earthquake in Judaea.

Right: King Herod the Great renovated the Temple in Jerusalem after the depradations of Greeks and Romans.

30 Jericho, Gadara, Samaria and Gaza taken into Herod's kingdom.

30 – AD 10 Consolidation of Pharisaic rabbinical Judaism by the theologian Hillel.

27 Herod rebuilds Samaria.

24 Herod builds palace in Jerusalem.

20/19 Herod begins rebuilding the Temple.

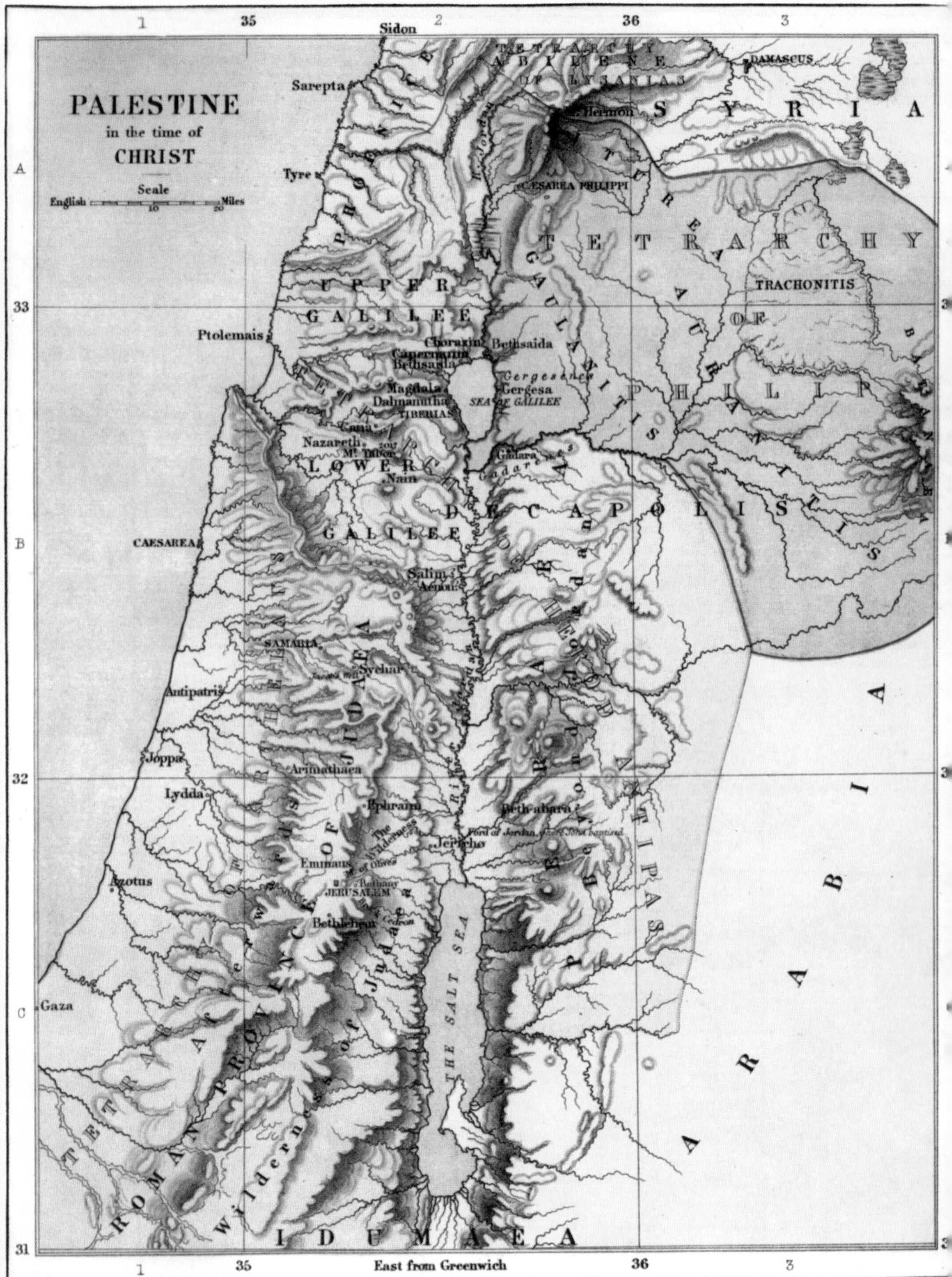
PALESTINE
in the time of
CHRIST
Scale
English Miles
10 20
Sidon
Sarepta
Tyre
Ptolemais
CAESAREA
Antipatris
Joppa
Lydda
Azotus
Gaza
DAMASCUS
Hermon
SYRIA
CESAREA PHILIPPI
TETRARCHY
TRACHONITIS
OF
PHILIP
UPPER
GALILEE
Chorazin
Bethsaida
Capernaum
Bethsaida
Magdala
Dalmanutha
TIBERIAS
Gergesenes
Gergesa
SEA OF GALILEE
Cana
Nazareth
Mt. Tabor
LOWER
Nain
GALILEE
Gadara
Gadarenes
DECAPOLIS
Salim
Aenon
SAMARIA
Sychar
Arimathaea
Ephraim
The Wilderness
Jericho
Beth-abara
Ford of Jordan, where John baptised
Emmaus
Bethany
JERUSALEM
Bethlehem
Cedron
THE SALT SEA
ARABIA
IDUMAEA
Wilderness of Judaea
ROMAN PROVINCE OF JUDAEA
1
2
3
35
36
A
B
C
33
32
31
East from Greenwich

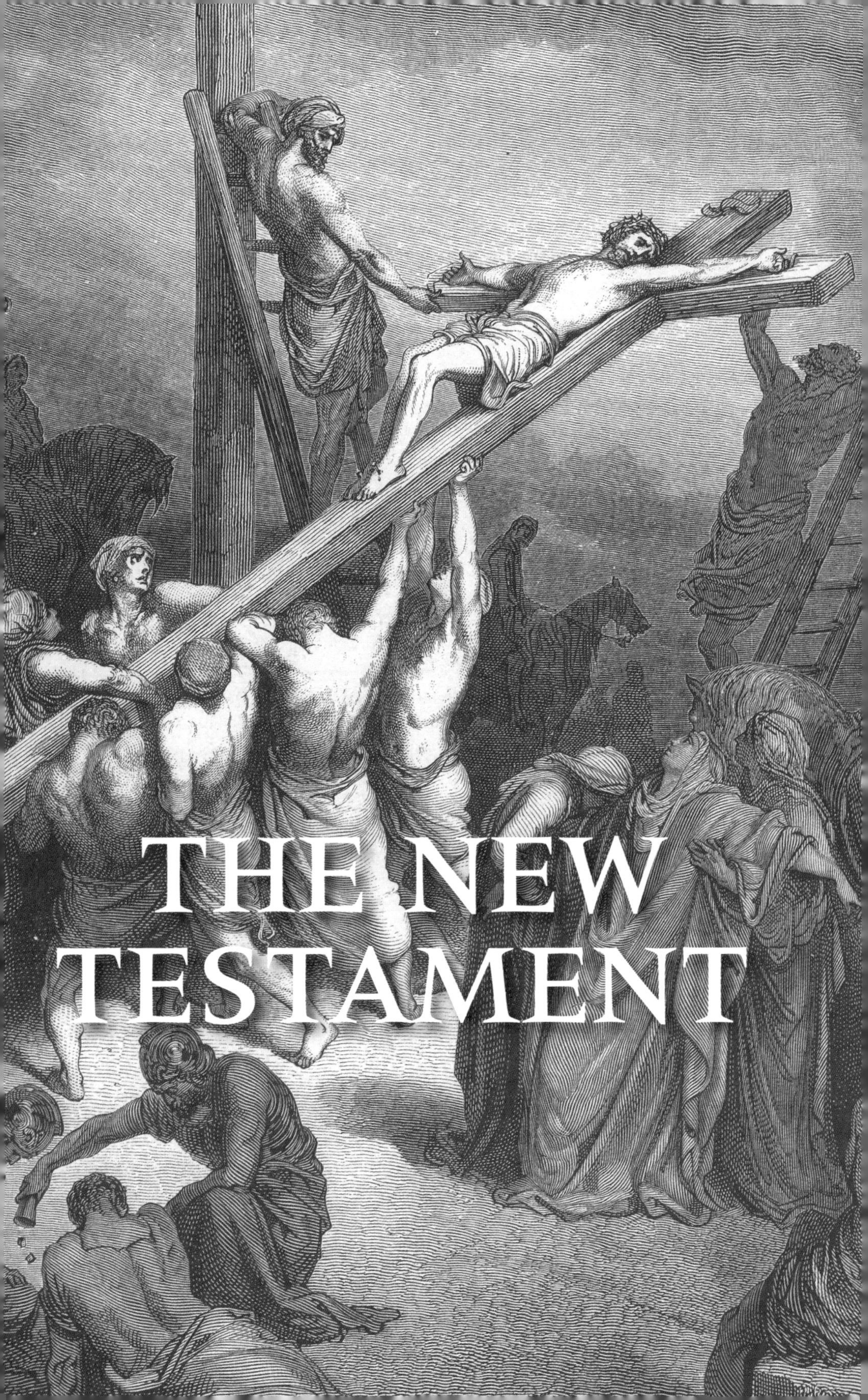
THE NEW
TESTAMENT

God chose Mary, a virgin betrothed to a carpenter in Nazareth, to bear his son. When the archangel Gabriel appeared to her and announced this astounding news, Mary went to share it with her kinswoman, Elizabeth, who was married to a priest called Zacharias. Elizabeth too was with child and would give birth to John the Baptist.

It was at the time Mary's son was due, that the Romans decreed a census of the land they ruled, and for this every citizen was directed to return to their own native town to be counted.

Left: *The annunciation – Mary learns from the archangel Gabriel that she will bear the Son of God.*

Below right: *No room at the inn. A heavily pregnant and exhausted Mary droops in the saddle as Joseph fails to find accommodation in Bethlehem.*

39: And Mary arose in those days, and went into the hill country with haste, into a city of Juda; 40:
And entered into the house of Zacharias, and saluted Elisabeth. 41: And it came to pass, that, when
Elisabeth heard the salutation of Mary, the babe leaped in her womb; and Elisabeth was filled with
the Holy Ghost: 42: And she spake out with a loud voice, and said, Blessed art thou among women,
and blessed is the fruit of thy womb ... 46: And Mary said, My
soul doth magnify the Lord, 47: And my spirit hath rejoiced in
God my Saviour. 48: For he hath regarded the low estate of his
handmaiden: for, behold, from henceforth all generations shall
call me blessed. 49: For he that is mighty hath done to me great
things; and holy is his name. 50: And his mercy is on them that
fear him from generation to generation. 51: He hath shewed
strength with his arm; he hath scattered the proud in the imagination of their hearts. 52: He hath put down the mighty from
their seats, and exalted them of low degree. 53: He hath filled
the hungry with good things; and the rich he hath sent empty
away. 54: He hath holpen his servant Israel, in remembrance of
his mercy; 55: As he spake to our fathers, to Abraham, and to
his seed for ever. 56: And Mary abode with her about three
months, and returned to her own house. 57: Now Elisabeth's
full time came that she should be delivered; and she brought
forth a son. *— Luke 1:39–57*

So Joseph and Mary set off for Bethlehem, but when they arrived they found accommodation difficult to find, for the town was swollen with people returning from the countryside to register. The inns being full, the family were forced to accept the only lodging available, in a stable, where a manger stood in for a crib.

6 BC An angel appears to the priest Zacharias.
5 BC Birth of John the Baptist, six months before the birth of Jesus.
4 BC Annunciation of the incarnation of the Son of God, to the Virgin Mary.
Roman tax census requires Jews to return to their place of birth: Joseph and Mary journey from Nazareth to Bethlehem.

26: And in the sixth month the angel Gabriel was sent from God unto a city of Galilee, named Nazareth, 27: To a virgin espoused to a man whose name was Joseph, of the house of David; and the virgin's name was Mary. 28: And the angel came in unto her, and said, Hail, thou that art highly favoured, the Lord is with thee: blessed art thou among women. 29: And when she saw him, she was troubled at his saying, and cast in her mind what manner of salutation this should be. 30: And the angel said unto her, Fear not, Mary: for thou hast found favour with God. 31: And, behold, thou shalt conceive in thy womb, and bring forth a son, and shalt call his name JESUS. 32: He shall be great, and shall be called the Son of the Highest: and the Lord God shall give unto him the throne of his father David: 33: And he shall reign over the house of Jacob for ever; and of his kingdom there shall be no end. 34: Then said Mary unto the angel, How shall this be, seeing I know not a man? 35: And the angel answered and said unto her, The Holy Ghost shall come upon thee, and the power of the Highest shall overshadow thee: therefore also that holy thing which shall be born of thee shall be called the Son of God. 36: And, behold, thy cousin Elisabeth, she hath also conceived a son in her old age: and this is the sixth month with her, who was called barren. 37: For with God nothing shall be impossible. 38: And Mary said, Behold the handmaid of the Lord; be it unto me according to thy word. And the angel departed from her.

—Luke 1: 26–38

1: And it came to pass in those days, that there went out a decree from Caesar Augustus, that all the world should be taxed. 2: (And this taxing was first made when Cyrenius was governor of Syria.) 3: And all went to be taxed, every one into his own city. 4: And Joseph also went up from Galilee, out of the city of Nazareth, into Judaea, unto the city of David, which is called Bethlehem; (because he was of the house and lineage of David:) 5: To be taxed with Mary his espoused wife, being great with child. 6: And so it was, that, while they were there, the days were accomplished that she should be delivered. 7: And she brought forth her firstborn son, and wrapped him in swaddling clothes, and laid him in a manger; because there was no room for them in the inn.

—Luke 2: 1–7

Left: *The shepherds in the fields are the first to be told about the miraculous birth.*

4 BC Birth of Jesus Christ, December 25.

8: And there were in the same country shepherds abiding in the field, keeping watch over their flock by night. 9: And, lo, the angel of the Lord came upon them, and the glory of the Lord shone round about them: and they were sore afraid. 10: And the angel said unto them, Fear not: for, behold, I bring you good tidings of great joy, which shall be to all people. 11: For unto you is born this day in the city of David a Saviour, which is Christ the Lord. 12: And this shall be a sign unto you; Ye shall find the babe wrapped in swaddling clothes, lying in a manger. 13: And suddenly there was with the angel a multitude of the heavenly host praising God, and saying, 14: Glory to God in the highest, and on earth peace, good will toward men. 15: And it came to pass, as the angels were gone away from them into heaven, the shepherds said one to another, Let us now go even unto Bethlehem, and see this thing which is come to pass, which the Lord hath made known unto us. 16: And they came with haste, and found Mary, and Joseph, and the babe lying in a manger. 17: And when they had seen it, they made known abroad the saying which was told them concerning this child. 18: And all they that heard it wondered at those things which were told them by the shepherds. 19: But Mary kept all these things, and pondered them in her heart. 20: And the shepherds returned, glorifying and praising God for all the things that they had heard and seen, as it was told unto them. —*Luke 2:8-20*

Right: *The shepherds find, as directed by the angel, the baby in a manger.*

21: And when eight days were accomplished for the circumcising of the child, his name was called JESUS, which was so named of the angel before he was conceived in the womb. 22: And when the days of her purification according to the law of Moses were accomplished, they brought him to Jerusalem, to present him to the Lord ... 25: And, behold, there was a man in Jerusalem, whose name was Simeon; and the same man was just and devout, waiting for the consolation of Israel: and the Holy Ghost was upon him. 26: And it was revealed unto him by the Holy Ghost, that he should not see death, before he had seen the Lord's Christ. 27: And he came by the Spirit into the temple: and when the parents brought in the child Jesus, to do for him after the custom of the law, 28: Then took he him up in his arms, and blessed God, and said, 29: Lord, now lettest thou thy servant depart in peace, according to thy word: 30: For mine eyes have seen thy salvation ...

—*Luke 2:21–30*

Left: *The three wise men follow the star in search of the King of the Jews.*

Below: *Arriving at Bethlehem, they ask the inhabitants where the child may be found.*

Far to the east, wise men had been told of a new King of the Jews, to whom they should pay obeisance. A star would guide them to him, and when they arrived in Judaea, news of their arrival sped through the streets of Jerusalem, reaching the ears of the king. Herod was instantly suspicious, recognizing the potential threat to his throne, and called the three visitors to his presence, where he interrogated them, then sent them on their way with instructions to report back when they had found the child. And the celestial messenger duly led the wise men to the stable.

Circumcision of Jesus.
Wise men come to worship Jesus.
Purification of the Virgin Mary.
Jesus presented in the Temple.

Right: *Gold, frankincense, and myrrh, gifts for a royal child.*

1: Now when Jesus was born in Bethlehem of Judaea in the days of Herod the king, behold, there came wise men from the east to Jerusalem, 2: Saying, Where is he that is born King of the Jews? for we have seen his star in the east, and are come to worship him. 3: When Herod the king had heard these things, he was troubled, and all Jerusalem with him. 4: And when he had gathered all the chief priests and scribes of the people together, he demanded of them where Christ should be born. 5: And they said unto him, In Bethlehem of Judaea: for thus it is written by the prophet, 6: And thou Bethlehem, in the land of Juda, art not the least among the princes of Juda: for out of thee shall come a Governor, that shall rule my people Israel. 7: Then Herod, when he had privily called the wise men, inquired of them diligently what time the star appeared. 8: And he sent them to Bethlehem, and said, Go and search diligently for the young child; and when ye have found him, bring me word again, that I may come and worship him also. 9: When they had heard the king, they departed; and, lo, the star, which they saw in the east, went before them, till it came and stood over where the young child was. 10: When they saw the star, they rejoiced with exceeding great joy. 11: And when they were come into the house, they saw the young child with Mary his mother, and fell down, and worshipped him: and when they had opened their treasures, they presented unto him gifts; gold, and frankincense, and myrrh.

— *Matthew 2:1–11*

Left: *King Herod's massacre of the innocents.*

Right: *Joseph leads Mary, with the newborn babe in her arms, to safety in Egypt.*

Below right: *The family return to Nazareth.*

12: And being warned of God in a dream that they should not return to Herod, [the wise men] departed into their own country another way. 13: And when they were departed, behold, the angel of the Lord appeareth to Joseph in a dream, saying, Arise, and take the young child and his mother, and flee into Egypt, and be thou there until I bring thee word: for Herod will seek the young child to destroy him. 14: When he arose, he took the young child and his mother by night, and departed into Egypt ... 19: But when Herod was dead, behold, an angel of the Lord appeareth in a dream to Joseph in Egypt, 20: Saying, Arise, and take the young child and his mother, and go into the land of Israel: for they are dead which sought the young child's life. 21: And he arose, and took the young child and his mother, and came into the land of Israel. —*Matthew 2: 12–21*

3 BC Flight into Egypt and massacre of the innocents at Bethlehem.
Death of Herod the Great; his kingdom divided as a tetrarchy between Herod Antipas (– AD 39), Galilee, and Peraea; Herod Archelaus (– AD 6), Judaea, Idumaea, and Samaria; Philip (– AD 34), Batanaea, Trachonitis, and Auranitis.
2 BC Jewish revolt put down by Varus.
Joseph, Mary, and Jesus return from Egypt and go to live in Nazareth.
AD 9 Jesus Christ, at twelve years of age, visits the Temple in Jerusalem, and is there for three days, unknown to his parents.

The wise men did not report back to Herod, however. Warned in a dream of the consequences of such an action, they quietly departed to their lands in the east, leaving an infuriated Herod unable to locate what he saw as a potential usurper. His reaction was infamous. He decreed that all children in the Bethlehem area under two years of age be slaughtered. This massacre of the innocents was foreseen by God, of course, who sent a message to Joseph in a dream, that he should take his wife and the child to Egypt until it was safe. So they slipped out of Bethlehem by night and made the journey beyond Sinai, and there, in the land of the Pharaohs, the infant Jesus was weaned.

Upon the death of King Herod, Judaea was split into three, and the threat of a usurping King of the Jews was forgotten. An angel told Joseph that they could return, and they made their way home to Nazareth.

Jesus grew up living the life of a normal boy of his time but showing also a precocious knowledge of scripture. As childhood gave way to youthful manhood, he began working in his father's workshop, learning the trade of carpentry. In later life, he would be spoken of as the carpenter from Nazareth.

Meanwhile his kinsman, John, was abroad in the country, gathering large crowds to his meetings at which he preached the word of God and told the people that they should make themselves ready for the Messiah, whose arrival was imminent. Those who accepted his message he baptized, a symbolic cleansing of their lives, in the River Jordan.

40: And the child grew, and waxed strong in spirit, filled with wisdom: and the grace of God was upon him. 41: Now his parents went to Jerusalem every year at the feast of the passover. 42: And when he was twelve years old, they went up to Jerusalem after the custom of the feast. 43: And when they had fulfilled the days, as they returned, the child Jesus tarried behind in Jerusalem; and Joseph and his mother knew not of it. 44: But they, supposing him to have been in the company, went a day's journey; and they sought him among their kinsfolk and acquaintance. 45: And when they found him not, they turned back again to Jerusalem, seeking him. 46: And it came to pass, that after three days they found him in the temple, sitting in the midst of the doctors, both hearing them, and asking them questions. 47: And all that heard him were astonished at his understanding and answers. 48: And when they saw him, they were amazed: and his mother said unto him, Son, why hast thou thus dealt with us? behold, thy father and I have sought thee sorrowing. 49: And he said unto them, How is it that ye sought me? wist ye not that I must be about my Father's business? 50: And they understood not the saying which he spake unto them. 51: And he went down with them, and came to Nazareth, and was subject unto them: but his mother kept all these sayings in her heart. 52: And Jesus increased in wisdom and stature, and in favour with God and man.

—Luke 2:40–52

Above left: *Jesus in the Temple.*

Above right: *The boyhood of Jesus.*

Right: *John the Baptist begins preaching.*

1: In those days came John the Baptist, preaching in the wilderness of Judaea, 2: And saying, Repent ye: for the kingdom of heaven is at hand. 3: For this is he that was spoken of by the prophet Esaias, saying, The voice of one crying in the wilderness, Prepare ye the way of the Lord, make his paths straight. 4: And the same John had his raiment of camel's hair, and a leathern girdle about his loins; and his meat was locusts and wild honey. 5: Then went out to him Jerusalem, and all Judaea, and all the region round about Jordan, 6: And were baptized of him in Jordan, confessing their sins.

— *Matthew 3:1–6*

Now grown to full adulthood, Jesus was ready to embark upon his momentous ministry. He sought out John by the banks of the Jordan, where he was baptized. His mission on earth was about to begin, but not before he spent a soul-searching forty days and nights in the dry, stony wilderness, in total solitude. During this time the devil tempted him to misuse his divine powers, but each time Jesus sent him away.

***Left:** The baptism of Jesus.*

***Right:** Jesus sets off to spend 40 days and nights in the wilderness.*

13: Then cometh Jesus from Galilee to Jordan unto John, to be baptized of him. 14: But John forbad him, saying, I have need to be baptized of thee, and comest thou to me? 15: And Jesus answering said unto him, Suffer it to be so now: for thus it becometh us to fulfill all righteousness. Then he suffered him. 16: And Jesus, when he was baptized, went up straightway out of the water: and, lo, the heavens were opened unto him, and he saw the Spirit of God descending like a dove, and lighting upon him: 17: And lo a voice from heaven, saying, This is my beloved Son, in whom I am well pleased.

— Matthew 3:13–17

14 Death of Roman Emperor Augustus; Tiberius succeeds him.
23 Eleazar, son of Annas, is made High Priest instead of Ismael.
25 Simon, son of Camith, is made High Priest in the place of Eleazar.
26 Joseph, surnamed Caiaphas, the son of Annas, is made High Priest instead of Simon.
28 Pilate sent as Governor to Judaea.
29 John the Baptist begins to preach.
30 Jesus Christ baptized by John.
Jesus goes into the Wilderness and after forty days, Jesus returns to John.

1: Then was Jesus led up of the Spirit into the wilderness to be tempted of the devil. 2: And when
he had fasted forty days and forty nights, he was afterward an hungred. 3: And when the tempter
came to him, he said, If thou be the Son of God, command that these stones be made bread. 4: But
he answered and said, It is written, Man shall not live by bread alone, but by every word that pro-
ceedeth out of the mouth of God. 5:
Then the devil taketh him up into
the holy city, and setteth him on a
pinnacle of the temple, 6: And
saith unto him, If thou be the Son
of God, cast thyself down: for it is
written, He shall give his angels
charge concerning thee: and in
their hands they shall bear thee up,
lest at any time thou dash thy foot
against a stone. 7: Jesus said unto
him, It is written again, Thou shalt
not empt the Lord thy God. 8:
Again, the devil taketh him up into
an exceeding high mountain, and
sheweth him all the kingdoms of
the world, and the glory of them; 9:
And saith unto him, All these
things will I give thee, if thou wilt
fall down and worship me. 10: Then
saith Jesus unto him, Get thee
hence, Satan: for it is written,
Thou shalt worship the Lord thy
God, and him only shalt thou serve.
11: Then the devil leaveth him,
and, behold, angels came and min-
istered unto him.

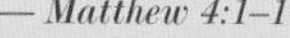

— *Matthew 4:1–11*

Much of Jesus' ministry – his teaching and healing work – was to be spent in the northern province of Galilee, especially about the shores of the Sea of Galilee. Here he encountered men who would become the first of his followers, or disciples – Andrew and his brother Simon Peter, James and John (sons of Zebedee), all fishermen; and Philip and Nathanael. The first to recognize him was Andrew, a follower of John the Baptist, for John was now directing his followers to Jesus, whom he named "the Lamb of God."

Jesus' first miracle was at Cana, not far from Nazareth, where he was born. With his mother and several of his followers, he had been invited to a wedding there, and as the festivities wore on the wine ran out. Mary was worried and came to Jesus: and reluctantly he told the servants to fill six stone water jars with water, then to serve the guests from these. When they did so, the water had turned into wine, so impressing the bridegroom that he complimented the host on saving the best for last.

However, Jesus' teaching work had not yet begun, and with his new companions he went south to Jerusalem for the feast of the Passover. When he entered the Temple there he beheld a sordid scene not in

***Top left:** The Wedding at Cana.*

***Left:** Jesus angrily expels the moneychangers and merchants from the courtyard of the Temple at Jerusalem.*

***Right:** The visit of the Pharisee Nicodemus.*

keeping with the high religious purpose of the building, for there were moneychangers and traders everywhere, selling cattle, sheep, and doves. Fashioning a whip from some cords, he overturned the counting tables and chased them out, crying, "Make not my Father's house an house of merchandise!" (*John 2: 16*) This caused a stir in the city, and many were intrigued, including a priest named Nicodemus, a Pharisee. One night, he came to Jesus to find out more, and Jesus told him that, even at his age, he must be 'born again'. A member of the Sanhedrin, Nicodemus was to become a believer in Jesus and to lend Joseph of Arimathea help after the crucifixion.

30 The Wedding at Cana.
Jesus visits Jerusalem for the Passover.
He cleanses the Temple.
He is visited by Nicodemus.

1: There was a man of the Pharisees, named Nicodemus, a ruler of the Jews: 2: The same came to Jesus by night, and said unto him, Rabbi, we know that thou art a teacher come from God: for no man can do these miracles that thou doest, except God be with him. 3: Jesus answered and said unto him, Verily, verily, I say unto thee, Except a man be born again, he cannot see the kingdom of God. 4: Nicodemus saith unto him, How can a man be born when he is old? can he enter the second time into his mother's womb, and be born? 5: Jesus answered, Verily, verily, I say unto thee, Except a man be born of water and of the Spirit, he cannot enter into the kingdom of God. 6: That which is born of the flesh is flesh; and that which is born of the Spirit is spirit. 7: Marvel not that I said unto thee, Ye must be born again. 8: The wind bloweth where it listeth, and thou hearest the sound thereof, but canst not tell whence it cometh, and whither it goeth: so is every one that is born of the Spirit. *—John 3:1–8*

***Left:** Speaking with the woman by the well at Sychar.*

***Below:** The royal officer returns home to find that his son has recovered from his fatal illness.*

***Right:** Jesus healing the sick, watched by an ever-growing crowd of people.*

Returning to Galilee via Samaria, Jesus and his companions one day stopped by Jacob's Well, at Sychar, and the disciples went to find food. When a local woman approached the well, Jesus asked her for water, and they fell into conversation. He was able to tell her something of her past, which so impressed her that she realized he was a prophet and told her friends. The returning disciples were astonished at the conversation, for the Jews and the Samaritans maintained a long-held mutual antagonism. And indeed, on a later visit, Jesus found himself without a welcome there.

When they got to Cana, a royal officer sought him out, a measure perhaps of his spreading reputation. His son, he said, was in Capernaum and dying; could Jesus save him? Jesus told him that when he went home he would find the child healed, and the officer set off. On the road he encountered his servants bringing the good news that the boy was better; and the officer discovered that he had recovered at the exact moment Jesus had spoken to him.

At Nazareth, Jesus entered the local tabernacle on the Sabbath and read from the book of Isaiah: "The Spirit of the Lord is upon me, because he hath anointed me to preach the gospel to the poor; he hath sent me to heal the brokenhearted, to preach deliverance to the captives, and recovering of sight to the blind, to set at liberty them that are bruised, to preach the acceptable year of the Lord" (*Luke 4:18–19*) and told them that the scripture was now fulfilled. The priests were astonished, and outraged when Jesus implied their own shortcomings – "Physician, heal thyself" – and that because of their disbelief the gospel would be offered to non-Jews. But, Jesus said, "No prophet is accepted in his own country" (*Luke 4:24*), and they ran him out of town.

30 Jesus speaks with the woman of Samaria.
At Cana he cures the son of an officer of Herod's army.
He is rejected in his home town.

Above: Jesus speaks to the crowds from Simon Peter's boat by the shore.

But his fame among the ordinary folk was beginning to draw crowds. At Capernaum, on the northern coast of the Sea of Galilee, Jesus addressed the people on shore from Simon Peter's boat. When he had finished speaking, he heard Peter and Andrew complaining about their lack of success with the fish, so he guided them to a particular place and told them to cast their nets. Such was the prodigious catch that Andrew and Peter called to their partners, James and John, for help in landing the fish. Later, ashore, Jesus turned to Andrew and Peter and said: "Come ye after me, and I will make you to become fishers of men." At once they laid down their nets and were soon joined by James and John.

30 Jesus calls his first disciples.

Left: *The great catch of fish.*

Above: *The call to become "fishers of men."*

18: And Jesus, walking by the sea of Galilee, saw two brethren, Simon called Peter, and Andrew his brother, casting a net into the sea: for they were fishers. 19: And he saith unto them, Follow me, and I will make you fishers of men. 20: And they straightway left their nets, and followed him. 21: And going on from thence, he saw other two brethren, James the son of Zebedee, and John his brother, in a ship with Zebedee their father, mending their nets; and he called them. 22: And they immediately left the ship and their father, and followed him. —*Matthew 4:18–22*

Most potent in spreading the fame of Jesus were the miraculous healings he performed, visible and impressive proof of his powers. At the synagogue in Capernaum, he cast unclean spirits from a man; he cured Peter's mother-in-law of a fever; he cured a paralytic; and a leper. Wherever he stayed, word spread of this sensational healer, and the sick came or were brought to him, such that it began to impede his progress.

Meanwhile John the Baptist, continuing his work, had publicly criticized the ruler of Galilee, the tetrarch Herod, for setting aside his wife in order to marry Herodias, the wife of his half-brother, which was contrary to the Law of Moses. For this he had been cast into prison but not executed – he had become a familiar and popular figure in the countryside.

Left: John the Baptist in the royal prison.

Above: Jesus cures a leper in Capernaum.

Left: A man sick of palsy is lowered through the roof where Jesus is performing miracles, to avoid the press of the crowd.

30 John the Baptist criticizes Herod Antipas and is imprisoned.
30 Jesus teaching and healing in Galilee.

22: And, behold, there cometh one of the rulers of the synagogue, Jairus by name; and when he saw him, he fell at his feet, 23: And besought him greatly, saying, My little daughter lieth at the point of death: I pray thee, come and lay thy hands on her, that she may be healed; and she shall live. 24: And Jesus went with him; and much people followed him, and thronged him. 25: And a certain woman, which had an issue of blood twelve years, 26: And had suffered many things of many physicians, and had spent all that she had, and was nothing bettered, but rather grew worse, 27: When she had heard of Jesus, came in the press behind, and touched his garment. 28: For she said, If I may touch but his clothes, I shall be whole. 29: And straightway the fountain of her blood was dried up; and she felt in her body that she was healed of that plague. 30: And Jesus, immediately knowing in himself that virtue had gone out of him, turned him about in the press, and said, Who touched my clothes? 31: And his disciples said unto him, Thou seest the multitude thronging thee, and sayest thou, Who touched me? 32: And he looked round about to see her that had done this thing. 33: But the woman fearing and trembling, knowing what was done in her, came and fell down before him, and told him all the truth. 34: And he said unto her, Daughter, thy faith hath made thee whole; go in peace, and be whole of thy plague.

— *Mark 5:22–34*

***Left:** Jesus calls the tax-collector Matthew to follow him.*

***Right:** At the Pool of Bethesda.*

***Far right:** His disciples violate the Sabbath by plucking ears of corn.*

It was about this time that Jesus recruited another disciple, Matthew. He was a "publican," a tax-collector, a profession despised throughout the ages. When Jesus dined with Matthew and other tax-collectors (whom the priests regarded as sinners), the Pharisees were scandalized that one who purported to be a man of God should keep such company. As for Matthew, taking up Jesus' call was a courageous step, for as a relatively wealthy man he would lose everything.

When Jesus went to Jerusalem again for the next Passover, he visited a place called the Pool of Bethesda, where the sick and disabled came because the waters were said to have restoring properties. There he treated a man who had been crippled for years and had nobody to help him into the healing waters – "Rise, take up thy bed, and walk." (*John 5:12*) But that day was the Sabbath, which the priests alleged he had broken. Several other such accusations were made after the disciples were seen eating ears of corn in a field on the Sabbath; and when Jesus healed a man's withered hand on the Sabbath. To these petty restrictions imposed by officious priests, Jesus replied, "I come in my Father's name and ye receive me not ... The Sabbath was made for man, and not man for the Sabbath: therefore the Son of Man is Lord also of the Sabbath." (*Mark 2:27–28*) Was it lawful on the Sabbath to do good or to do evil; to save life or to destroy it? The priests now conspired to destroy him, for they could not succeed in arguing with him. Seeing this, Jesus took his disciples back north to continue healing and teaching.

Jesus calls Matthew.
He cures a cripple at the Pool of Bethesda and invokes the wrath of the priests for doing this on the Sabbath.
Jesus preaches the Sermon on the Mount.

32: And they bring unto him one that was deaf, and had an impediment in his speech; and they beseech him to put his hand upon him. 33: And he took him aside from the multitude, and put his fingers into his ears, and he spit, and touched his tongue; 34: And looking up to heaven, he sighed, and saith unto him, Ephphatha, that is, Be opened. 35: And straightway his ears were opened, and the string of his tongue was loosed, and he spake plain. 36: And he charged them that they should tell no man: but the more he charged them, so much the more a great deal they published it; 37: And were beyond measure astonished, saying, He hath done all things well: he maketh both the deaf to hear, and the dumb to speak. — *Mark 7:32–37*

One day Jesus ascended a mountain to spend the night in prayer, and at daybreak he called and ordained twelve disciples whom he would send forth to preach, heal sickness, and cast out devils. He then came down to the lower slopes, where a multitude of people had gathered to witness healing and to hear him speak. There followed one of his most significant lessons, which is now known as the Sermon on the Mount. In this he set out his fundamental message in a wide-ranging discourse that all could understand, emphasizing the moral and spiritual aspects of the Law, the love of God, and how people should behave to one another.

God's blessing, he told them, would be manifested to those who lived their lives free from selfishness and greed. In nine simple sayings, which have become known as the Beatitudes, he set out the basic essentials of good living.

THE BEATITUDES

Blessed are the poor in spirit: for theirs is the kingdom of heaven.

Blessed are they that mourn: for they shall be comforted.

Blessed are the meek: for they shall inherit the earth.

Blessed are they which do hunger and thirst after righteousness: for they shall be filled.

Blessed are the merciful: for they shall obtain mercy.

Blessed are the pure in heart: for they shall see God.

Blessed are the peacemakers: for they shall be called the children of God.

Blessed are they which are persecuted for righteousness' sake: for theirs is the kingdom of heaven.

Blessed are ye, when men shall revile you, and persecute you, and shall say all manner of evil against you falsely, for my sake. Rejoice, and be exceeding glad: for great is your reward in heaven ...

(Matthew 5:3–12)

13: And he goeth up into a mountain, and calleth unto him whom he would: and they came unto him. 14: And he ordained twelve, that they should be with him, and that he might send them forth to preach, 15: And to have power to heal sicknesses, and to cast out devils: 16: And Simon he surnamed Peter; 17: And James the son of Zebedee, and John the brother of James; and he surnamed them Boanerges, which is, The sons of thunder: 18: And Andrew, and Philip, and Bartholomew, and Matthew, and Thomas, and James the son of Alphaeus, and Thaddaeus, and Simon the Canaanite, 19: And Judas Iscariot, which also betrayed him ... —*Mark 3:13–19*

He went on to discuss the Law and the testimony of the Prophets, consistently stressing their authority, but interpreting them in a practical and easily comprehensible manner. He warned against the hypocrisy of superficial piety ostentatiously displayed in prayer, fasting, and giving to charity but without spiritual substance. Purity of the heart would receive its own reward; happiness lay not in material things but was available to those who put their trust in God.

He explained a number of specific issues to which all could relate as examples of how the Law should be applied. Looking at a woman lustfully, he said, was already committing adultery in one's heart; divorce was acceptable only in cases of marital unfaithfulness; and where oaths were concerned, one should let "yes" and "no" be absolute. Concerning retaliation, he replaced the old "eye for an eye" with "turn the other cheek," and instead of hating them, love your enemies and pray for those who persecute you. Fasting and giving to the poor should not be done in an ostentatious way; nor should one be hasty to judge others, "lest ye be judged yourself." And he warned against false prophets.

When he had finished this momentous address, he came farther down the hillside among the people, curing a leper, and the crowd gradually dispersed, their heads full of this new and inspiring teaching.

Right: *The Sermon on the Mount.*

The Golden Rule Therefore all things whatsoever ye would that men should do to you, do ye even so to them: for this is the law and the prophets. — *Matthew 7:12*

47: Whosoever cometh to me, and heareth my sayings, and doeth them, I will shew you to whom he is like: 48: He is like a man which built an house, and digged deep, and laid the foundation on a rock: and when the flood arose, the stream beat vehemently upon that house, and could not shake it: for it was founded upon a rock. 49: But he that heareth, and doeth not, is like a man that without a foundation built an house upon the earth; against which the stream did beat vehemently, and immediately it fell; and the ruin of that house was great.

— Luke 6:47–49

Jesus continued traveling through the cities and villages, preaching and performing miraculous cures, but still the priests rejected him and now sought a sign from him. On one occasion the crowd was so dense that his mother and the disciples could not get near him; when they were pointed out to him, Jesus said, "Who is my mother? and who are my brethren?" And he stretched forth his hand toward his disciples, and said, "Behold my mother and my brethren! For whosoever shall do the will of my Father which is in heaven, the same is my brother, and sister, and mother. (*Matthew 12:48–50*)

Jesus continued using parables to teach, placing questions of spiritual and moral behavior in real-life situations that all could understand.

11: And it came to pass the day after, that he went into a city called Nain; and many of his disciples went with him, and much people. 12: Now when he came nigh to the gate of the city, behold, there was a dead man carried out, the only son of his mother, and she was a widow: and much people of the city was with her. 13: And when the Lord saw her, he had compassion on her, and said unto her, Weep not. 14: And he came and touched the bier: and they that bare him stood still. And he said, Young man, I say unto thee, Arise. 15: And he that was dead sat up, and began to speak. And he delivered him to his mother. 16: And there came a fear on all: and they glorified God, saying, That a great prophet is risen up among us; and, That God hath visited his people. 17: And this rumour of him went forth throughout all Judaea, and throughout all the region round about. *—Luke 7:11–17*

3: And he spake many things unto them in parables, saying, Behold, a sower went forth to sow; 4: And when he sowed, some seeds fell by the way side, and the fowls came and devoured them up: 5: Some fell upon stony places, where they had not much earth: and forthwith they sprung up, because they had no deepness of earth: 6: And when the sun was up, they were scorched; and because they had no root, they withered away. 7: And some fell among thorns; and the thorns sprung up, and choked them: 8: But other fell into good ground, and brought forth fruit, some an hundredfold, some sixtyfold, some thirtyfold. 9: Who hath ears to hear, let him hear.

— *Matthew 13:3–9*

24: Another parable put he forth unto them, saying, The kingdom of heaven is likened unto a man which sowed good seed in his field: 25: But while men slept, his enemy came and sowed tares among the wheat, and went his way. 26: But when the blade was sprung up, and brought forth fruit, then appeared the tares also. 27: So the servants of the householder came and said unto him, Sir, didst not thou sow good seed in thy field? from whence then hath it tares? 28: He said unto them, An enemy hath done this. The servants said unto him, Wilt thou then that we go and gather them up? 29: But he said, Nay; lest while ye gather up the tares, ye root up also the wheat with them. 30: Let both grow together until the harvest: and in the time of harvest I will say to the reapers, Gather ye together first the tares, and bind them in bundles to burn them: but gather the wheat into my barn.

— *Matthew 13:24–30*

John the Baptist, in prison, had become puzzled by what must have been conflicting reports brought to him by his friends to his prison cell. Jesus sent him messages of reassurance that he was indeed who John thought he was.

One evening, after speaking before crowds by the shore of the Sea of Galilee, he took ship with his disciples for the other shore. As they crossed, a great storm blew up, imperiling the boat as Jesus slept in the stern. The disciples, in fear for their lives at the severity of the weather, woke him and he reassured them: "Why are ye fearful, O ye of little faith?" – then told the wind and sea to be still, and the waters became calm again.

By now Jesus was attracting large crowds, and he saw that he could not speak to them all himself – "The harvest truly is plenteous, but the labourers are few" – so he sent out his disciples in pairs, empowered to cure disease and cast out devils, preaching that the Kingdom of Heaven was at hand. But he warned them: "Behold, I send you forth as sheep in the midst of wolves: be ye therefore wise as serpents and harmless as doves. But beware ... He that receiveth you receiveth me ..." *(Matthew 10:1,40)*

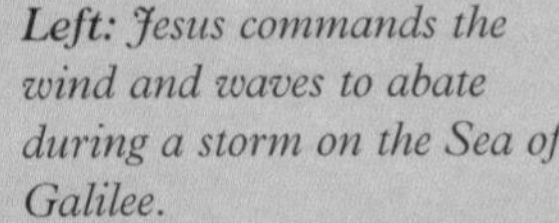

***Left:** Jesus commands the wind and waves to abate during a storm on the Sea of Galilee.*

***Above:** The disciples go forth to heal and teach.*

***Right:** With just five loaves and two fish (inset), Jesus feeds 5,000 people gathered to hear and see him.*

Meanwhile John the Baptist languished in Herod's prison. The king's wife, Herodias, was determined to have him killed and manipulated Herod with her degenerate daughter Salome. John was beheaded and his body buried by his followers, who hastened to tell Jesus.

When the disciples returned, Jesus took them out to a quiet place to rest, near Bethsaida, but news of their presence attracted attention, and soon a great crowd had gathered. So Jesus spoke and healed, but as the day progressed on the disciples began to worry that in this wilderness there was nothing for the people to eat. All they could bring to hand was a boy who had five barley loaves and two small fish. So Jesus blessed the food and told the multitude to sit in groups on the grass, and from those loaves and fish the whole crowd of 5,000 were miraculously fed, with twelve basketfuls left over. Some of the people were so excited by this that thy tried to take hold of him and proclaim him King, but Jesus and his followers made a quick departure.

31 John the Baptist inquires about Jesus.
Jesus calms a storm on the Sea of Galilee.
His disciples are sent out to teach and heal.
Death of John the Baptist.
Jesus miraculously feeds 5,000 people with five loaves and two fish.

That evening the disciples took ship and the wind again rose, so that the rowers found themselves making little progress. Suddenly they were struck with fear as they saw a figure coming up beside them, then realized that it was Jesus, walking upon the water. They cried out, and Peter asked Jesus if he too could walk on the sea. But after a few steps, his confidence failed and he began to sink until Jesus – "O thou of little faith, wherefore didst thou doubt?" – helped him back into the boat and the wind ceased. When they made land at Gennesaret, a host of people came to meet them, bringing their sick to be healed.

At Capernaum, Jesus expounded upon the miracle of the loaves and fishes in allegorical language: "I am that bread of life." But many could not understand and took his words about sacrificing his flesh and blood for their eternal life literally. Many turned away. But a short time later he repeated the miraculous feeding of a crowd, this time of some 4,000, with just seven loaves and a few small fish.

21: From that time forth began Jesus to shew unto his disciples, how that he must go unto Jerusalem, and suffer many things of the elders and chief priests and scribes, and be killed, and be raised again the third day. 22: Then Peter took him, and began to rebuke him, saying, Be it far from thee, Lord: this shall not be unto thee. 23: But he turned, and said unto Peter, Get thee behind me, Satan: thou art an offence unto me: for thou savourest not the things that be of God, but those that be of men. 24: Then said Jesus unto his disciples, If any man will come after me, let him deny himself, and take up his cross, and follow me. 25: For whosoever will save his life shall lose it: and whosoever will lose his life for my sake shall find it. 26: For what is a man profited, if he shall gain the whole world, and lose his own soul? or what shall a man give in exchange for his soul? 27: For the Son of man shall come in the glory of his Father with his angels; and then he shall reward every man according to his works. 28: Verily I say unto you, There be some standing here, which shall not taste of death, till they see the Son of man coming in his kingdom. — *Matthew 16:22–28*

Despite these big crowds, many had stopped following him, while the priests still refused to accept him and demanded a sign, which exasperated him. But his disciples remained firm. Jesus questioned them about how the people saw him. Some, they said, thought he was John the Baptist; others Elias, or Jeremiah or another of the prophets of old risen again. But, he asked them: who did they think he was? It was Peter who spoke up: "Thou art the Christ,* the Son of the living God." Jesus blessed him and told him that he was Peter (which means "rock") and that upon this rock would he build his Church; and he should have the keys to the Kingdom of Heaven.

Jesus now broke the news to his disciples that he was destined to go to Jerusalem,

* Christ, from the Greek, Christ, meaning "one anointed," specifically appointed and empowered by God through his own spirit to become the savior of his people.

suffer and be rejected by the priests, be killed and rise again on the third day. Surely not, responded Peter, but Jesus rebuked him. (*Matthew 16:22–28*)

A week later Jesus took Peter, James and John up a mountainside to pray by night, and there they witnessed his Transfiguration – his face and body shining in glory as a dazzling bright light, while he spoke with two figures about his death. These were Moses and Elias (Elijah), come to give him strength. Then a bright cloud enveloped them all and a voice spoke to them: "This is my beloved son, in whom I am well pleased: hear ye him." The vision cleared and Jesus told them they must say nothing of what they had seen until after he had risen from the dead.

One day the question arose as to whether Jesus should pay the Temple tax, or tribute, which was at that time set at two drachmas per head. Jesus replied obliquely but told Peter that to avoid offending the priests they should pay. He told him to cast a line in the sea and open the mouth of the first fish he caught: he did, and found there a four-drachma coin, enough to pay for both their taxes.

32 Jesus miraculously walks on the waters of the Sea of Galilee.
Simon Peter avows that Jesus is the Christ.
The Transfiguration.
The miracle of the coin in the fish's mouth.

Far left: *The disciples are amazed as Jesus catches them up halfway across the Sea of Galilee.*

Below: *The Transfiguration of Jesus. He talks with Moses and Elijah.*

Above: *The seventy go forth.*

Left: *In the Temple Jesus encounters a woman condemned for adultery.*

In Judaea, Jesus heard that there were threats to his life, so he returned to Galilee and appointed seventy of his followers to go out, again in pairs, to the cities and villages he could not himself visit. Shortly after, he ventured to Jerusalem for the Feast of Tabernacles, independently of the disciples, and took the possibly risky step of speaking in the Temple. But he was not arrested. When the priests' officers approached him, he convinced them and they went back to the priests empty-handed. When the Pharisees reacted angrily, Nicodemus (both a priest and a secret follower of Jesus) told them that they must not find a man guilty before they had judged him.

While Jesus was in Jerusalem, a woman was brought to the Temple accused of adultery. According to the Mosaic Law, she should be stoned to death – which Jesus invited them to do: "He that is without sin, let him first cast a stone at her." Abashed, they left, and Jesus asked her who had accused her. No one, she replied. "Neither do I condemn thee," said Jesus, "go, and sin no more."

More discourse and debate with the hostile priests followed, ending almost in violence, for they would not understand who he was. Jesus then returned to Galilee to receive the seventy disciples he had sent out, and they greeted him with joy at their evident success, heartening Jesus himself.

Again he received criticism for curing people on the Sabbath – first a woman who for some eighteen years had suffered such an ailment in her back that she was bent nearly double; Jesus straightened her, then cured a case of dropsy. He spoke of humility – a man invited to a wedding should sit in the lowest place so that the host might bring him to sit higher up – "For whosoever exalteth himself shall be abased; and he that humbleth himself shall be exalted."

32 Mission of the seventy disciples.
Jesus goes to Jerusalem for the Feast of Tabernacles.
He saves a woman accused of adultery from being stoned to death.

Below: *Jesus heals a woman with a crippled back.*

1: Then drew near unto him all the publicans and sinners for to hear him. 2: And the Pharisees and scribes murmured, saying, This man receiveth sinners, and eateth with them. 3: And he spake this parable unto them, saying, 4: What man of you, having an hundred sheep, if he lose one of them, doth not leave the ninety and nine in the wilderness, and go after that which is lost, until he find it? 5: And when he hath found it, he layeth it on his shoulders, rejoicing. 6: And when he cometh home, he calleth together his friends and neighbours, saying unto them, Rejoice with me; for I have found my sheep which was lost. 7: I say unto you, that likewise joy shall be in heaven over one sinner that repenteth, more than over ninety and nine just persons, which need no repentance. — *Luke 15:1–7*

THE PARABLES RECORDED IN THE GOSPELS		
Parable	Source	Lesson
The barren fig tree	Luke 13:6	Unprofitableness under grace
The fig tree and all the trees	Matthew 24:32, Mark 13:28, Luke 21:29	Indications of Second Advent
The friend at midnight	Luke 11:5	Perseverance in prayer
The good Samaritan	Luke 10:30	Active benevolence
The great supper	Matthew 22:2, Luke 14:16	Universality of the divine call
The guests at the wedding feast	Luke 14:7	The humble shall be exalted
The hid treasure	Matthew 13:44	Value of the gospel
The house on rock and on sand	Matthew 7:24, Luke 6:47	Consistent and false profession
The householder	Matthew 13:52	Watchfulness
The labourers in the vineyard	Matthew 20:1	Precedence in service gives no claim for priority in reward
The lamp under the bushel	Matthew 5:15, Mark 4:21, Luke 8:16	Dissemination of truth
The leaven	Matthew 13:33, Luke 13:21	Pervading influence of religion
The lost piece of silver	Luke 15:8	Joy over penitence
The lost sheep	Matthew 18:12, Luke 15:4	Joy over penitent
The mustard seed	Matthew 13:31, Mark 4:31, Luke 13:19	Spread of the gospel
The net cast into the sea	Matthew 13:47	Visible Church a mixed body
New cloth on old	Matthew 9:16, Mark 2:21, Luke 5:36	New doctrine on old prejudices
New wine in old bottles	Matthew 9:17, Mark 2:22, Luke 5:37	New spirit in unregenerate heart
The pearl of great price	Matthew 13:45	Seeker finding salvation
The Pharisee and the publican	Luke 18:10	Self-righteousness and humility
The prodigal son	Luke 15:11	Fatherly love to returning sinner
The rich fool	Luke 12:16	Worldly mindedness
The rich man and Lazarus	Luke 16:19	Hopeless future of the unfaithful
The seed growing secretly	Mark 4:26	The law of growth in religion
The sheep and the goats	Matthew 25:33	Love the test of life
The sower	Matthew 13:3, Mark 4:3, Luke 8:5	Hearers divided into classes
The tares	Matthew 13:24	Good and evil in life and judgement
The ten talents	Matthew 25:14, Luke 19:11	Diligence rewarded, sloth punished
The ten virgins	Matthew 25:1	Watchful preparation and careless security
The two debtors	Luke 7:41	Gratitude for pardon
The two sons	Matthew 21:28	Insincerity and repentance
The unjust judge	Luke 18:2	Advantage of persevering prayer
The unjust steward	Luke 16:1	Faithfulness to trust
The unmerciful servant	Matthew 18:23	Duty of forgiveness
The unprofitable servants	Luke 17:7	God's claim on all our services
The wicked husbandmen	Matthew 21:33, Mark 12:1, Luke 20:9	Rejection of Jesus by the Jews

7: But when ye pray, use not vain repetitions, as the heathen do ... 9: After this manner therefore pray ye: Our Father which art in heaven, Hallowed be thy name. 10: Thy kingdom come. Thy will be done in earth, as it is in heaven. 11: Give us this day our daily bread. 12: And forgive us our debts, as we forgive our debtors. 13: And lead us not into temptation, but deliver us from evil: For thine is the kingdom, and the power, and the glory, for ever. Amen. *—Matthew 6:7–13*

18: And a certain ruler asked him, saying, Good Master, what shall I do to inherit eternal life? 19: And Jesus said unto him, Why callest thou me good? none is good, save one, that is, God. 20: Thou knowest the commandments, Do not commit adultery, Do not kill, Do not steal, Do not bear false witness, Honour thy father and thy mother. 21: And he said, All these have I kept from my youth up. 22: Now when Jesus heard these things, he said unto him, Yet lackest thou one thing: sell all that thou hast, and distribute unto the poor, and thou shalt have treasure in heaven: and come, follow me. 23: And when he heard this, he was very sorrowful: for he was very rich. 24: And when Jesus saw that he was very sorrowful, he said, How hardly shall they that have riches enter into the kingdom of God! 25: For it is easier for a camel to go through a needle's eye, than for a rich man to enter into the kingdom of God. *—Luke 18:18–25*

29: But he, willing to justify himself, said unto Jesus, And who is my neighbour? 30: And Jesus answering said, A certain man went down from Jerusalem to Jericho, and fell among thieves, which stripped him of his raiment, and wounded him, and departed, leaving him half dead. 31: And by chance there came down a certain priest that way: and when he saw him, he passed by on the other side. 32: And likewise a Levite, when he was at the place, came and looked on him, and passed by on the other side. 33: But a certain Samaritan, as he journeyed, came where he was: and when he saw him, he had compassion on him, 34: And went to him, and bound up his wounds, pouring in oil and wine, and set him on his own beast, and brought him to an inn, and took care of him. 35: And on the morrow when he departed, he took out two pence, and gave them to the host, and said unto him, Take care of him; and whatsoever thou spendest more, when I come again, I will repay thee. 36: Which now of these three, thinkest thou, was neighbour unto him that fell among the thieves? 37: And he said, He that shewed mercy on him. Then said Jesus unto him, Go, and do thou likewise.

—Luke 10:29–37

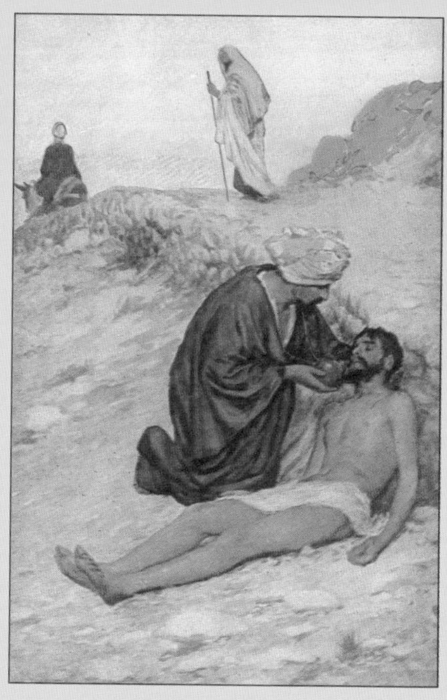

Poorly received in Samaria, Jesus entered a village and encountered ten lepers who approached him for help. So he cleansed them and all went away joyous except one, who turned back and thanked Jesus. "Arise, go thy way," replied Jesus,"thy faith hath made thee whole."

9: And he spake this parable unto certain which trusted in themselves that they were righteous, and despised others: 10: Two men went up into the temple to pray; the one a Pharisee, and the other a publican. 11: The Pharisee stood and prayed thus with himself, God, I thank thee, that I am not as other men are, extortioners, unjust, adulterers, or even as this publican. 12: I fast twice in the week, I give tithes of all that I possess. 13: And the publican, standing afar off, would not lift up so much as his eyes unto heaven, but smote upon his breast, saying, God be merciful to me a sinner. 14: I tell you, this man went down to his house justified rather than the other: for every one that exalteth himself shall be abased; and he that humbleth himself shall be exalted. —*Luke 18:9–14*

It was in Bethany, a short distance east of Jerusalem, that Jesus made a special friendship with two sisters, Mary and Martha, and their brother Lazarus. One day, Martha was busy about the house and complained to Jesus that her sister left her to do the work while she sat at Jesus' feet. "Martha, Martha," he replied, "thou art careful and troubled about many things: But one thing is needful: and Mary hath chosen that good part, which shall not be taken away from her." (*Luke 10:38–42*)

Left: *Jesus with Mary and Martha at their home in Bethany.*

Below left: *The man born blind healed at the Pool of Siloam.*

Finding a man blind from birth, the disciples asked Jesus whether the sin lay in the man or his parents that he had been born thus. Neither, replied Jesus, anointing the eyes of the blind man and sending him to the Pool of Siloam, to wash. Wiping off the clay, he opened his eyes and could see for the first time. Word of this miracle spread, and it perplexed the Pharisees, who could neither understand nor accept it and threw the man out of the Temple. Jesus told them that he was the "good shepherd: the good shepherd giveth his life for the sheep." His sheep, he said, knew him. But they, the priests, did not believe, for they were not his sheep. Angered, they sought to harm him, but he escaped beyond the Jordan, where John had baptized him.

10: Likewise, I say unto you, there is joy in the presence of the angels of God over one sinner that repenteth. 11: ... A certain man had two sons: 12: And the younger of them said to his father, Father, give me the portion of goods that falleth to me. And he divided unto them his living. 13: And not many days after the younger son gathered all together, and took his journey into a far country, and there wasted his substance with riotous living. 14: And when he had spent all, there arose a mighty famine in that land; and he began to be in want. 15: And he went and joined himself to a citizen of that country; and he sent him into his fields to feed swine. 16: And he would fain have filled his belly with the husks that the swine did eat: and no man gave unto him ... 20: And he arose, and came to his father. But when he was yet a great way off, his father saw him, and had compassion, and ran, and fell on his neck, and kissed him. 21: And the son said unto him, Father, I have sinned against heaven, and in thy sight, and am no more worthy to be called thy son. 22: But the father said to his servants, Bring forth the best robe, and put it on him; and put a ring on his hand, and shoes on his feet: 23: And bring hither the fatted calf, and kill it; and let us eat, and be merry: 24: For this my son was dead, and is alive again; he was lost, and is found. And they began to be merry. 25: Now his elder son ... heard musick and dancing ... 28: And he was angry, and would not go in: therefore came his father out, and intreated him. 29: And he answering said to his father, Lo, these many years do I serve thee, neither transgressed I at any time thy commandment: and yet thou never gavest me a kid, that I might make merry with my friends: 30: But as soon as this thy son was come, which hath devoured thy living with harlots, thou hast killed for him the fatted calf. 31: And he said unto him, Son, thou art ever with me, and all that I have is thine. 32: It was meet that we should make merry, and be glad: for this thy brother was dead, and is alive again; and was lost, and is found. *— Luke 15:10–32*

A message now arrived from Jesus' friends in Bethany – Lazarus was desperately ill. Martha came to meet him and told him Lazarus had been dead these four days: but this Jesus already knew. If he had been there, he would not have died, said Martha; though she knew he would rise again at the last day. But Jesus said, "I am the resurrection and the life: he that believeth in me, though he were dead, yet shall he live: and whosoever liveth and believeth in me shall never die." Mary joined them, in tears, and Jesus asked them to lead him to the tomb. He cried out, "Lazarus, come forth," and the brother appeared, still wrapped in the grave clothes, but alive. This miraculous raising of the dead had serious consequences, for it made sensational news that reached the ears of the High Priest in Jerusalem. The threat the priests perceived from a man credited with such a miracle (especially after previous reports of his miracles) was

***Right:** Jesus calls forth the dead Lazarus.*

15: And they brought unto him also infants, that he would touch them: but when his disciples saw it, they rebuked them. 16: But Jesus called them unto him, and said, Suffer little children to come unto me, and forbid them not: for of such is the kingdom of God. 17: Verily I say unto you, Whosoever shall not receive the kingdom of God as a little child shall in no wise enter therein.

— Luke 18:15–17

confronting them, and they determined that they should find a way to put him to death.

And once more Jesus told his disciples about his sufferings to come, but once again they were unable fully to appreciate the importance of what he was saying and what would transpire in the coming days.

33 Lazarus raised from the dead.
Jesus sets out for Jerusalem to celebrate the Passover and for what will become known as Passion Week.

The Miracles Recorded in the Gospels	
Water turned into wine at Cana	John 2:1
A leper made clean	Matthew 8:1, Mark 1:40, Luke 5:12
Healing a centurion's servant	Matthew 8:5, Luke 7:1
Peter's mother-in-law cured of fever	Matthew 8:14, Mark 1:29, Luke 4:38
A storm at sea calmed	Matthew 8:23, Mark 4:35, Luke 8:22
A man possessed of devils at Gadara healed	Matthew 8:28, Mark 5:1, Luke 8:26
A man healed of palsy	Matthew 9:2, Mark 2:4, Luke 5:18
A haemorrhaging woman cured	Matthew 9:20, Mark 5:25, Luke 8:43
Jairus' daughter raised	Matthew 9:23, Mark 5:22, Luke 8:41
Sight restored to two blind men	Matthew 9:27
A dumb man possessed by the devil cured	Matthew 9:32
A man's withered hand restored	Matthew 12:10, Mark 3:1, Luke 6:6
Feeding of the five thousand	Matthew 14:15, Mark 6:35, Luke 9:12, John 6:1
Walking on the waters	Matthew 14:22, Mark 6:47, John 6:16
Casting the devil from a Syrophoenician girl	Matthew 15:21, Mark 7:25
Many dumb, lame, maimed or blind cured	Matthew 15:29, Mark, 7:32
Feeding of the four thousand	Matthew 15:32, Mark 8:1
Devils cast out of a boy	Matthew 17:14, Mark 9:17, Luke 9:38
Restoring sight to two blind men	Matthew 20:30
A man with an unclean spirit cleansed	Mark 1:23, Luke 4:33
Healing a blind man at Bethsaida	Mark 8:22
Blind Bartimaeus healed at Jericho	Mark 10:46, Luke 18:35
The miraculous catch of fish	Luke 5:4, John 21:1
A widow's son raised from dead	Luke 7:12
A woman crippled eighteen years made straight	Luke 13:11
A man with dropsy cured	Luke 14:2
Ten lepers healed	Luke 17:12
Malchus' ear healed	Luke 22:50
A nobleman's son healed of fever	John 4:46
An infirm man at the pool at Bethesda healed	John 5:1
Sight given to a man blind from birth	John 9:1, Matthew 20:29, Mark 10:46, Luke 18:35
Lazarus raised from the dead	John 11:1–44

Jesus had declared his intention of celebrating the Passover in Jerusalem but chose not to attempt finding a place to stay in the city, which would be crowded with the faithful. Instead he stayed with his friends Martha, Mary, and Lazarus at Bethany, no more than a two-mile walk from Jerusalem. Jesus and the disciples arrived there on the Friday, six days before the Passover, and that night they dined at the house of Simon the leper. While they were eating, Mary went out and fetched an alabaster box containing fragrant ointment, with which she anointed Jesus' head and feet, wiping his feet with her hair. But some of the disciples, led by Judas, were indignant at such apparent waste of a very precious fragrance: a more fitting action

***Left:** Mary anoints Jesus with fragrant ointment, to the indignation of the disciples.*

***Right:** Jesus begins his triumphant entry to Jerusalem.*

would have been to sell the ointment and donate the proceeds to the poor. Jesus rebuked them: the poor, he said, "are always with you, and you may do good to them"; but he would not always be there.

On the Sunday, Jesus and the disciples set out for Jerusalem. His presence at Bethany had already attracted great public attention, for his fame as a teacher and healer had spread far and wide, especially after the raising of Lazarus. As they drew near to the city, the crowds came out to welcome him, and Jesus sent two of his companions to a nearby village to find a donkey and a colt, so that when he entered the city gates he fulfilled Zechariah's centuries-old prophecy.

The crowds thronged about him as he rode the donkey, lining the route and crying "Hosannah, Blessed is the King of Israel that cometh in the name of the Lord" and throwing down their cloaks and palm-tree branches in his path. (But, as he rode in triumph through the noisy multitude, Jesus wept for Jerusalem, knowing the disaster that would befall this city in the years to come.)

Friday: Jesus comes to Bethany and dines with his friends.
Saturday is the Sabbath.
Sunday: Jesus makes his triumphant entry to Jerusalem.

6: And the disciples went, and did as Jesus commanded them, 7: And brought the ass, and the colt, and put on them their clothes, and they set him thereon. 8: And a very great multitude spread their garments in the way; others cut down branches from the trees, and strawed them in the way. 9: And the multitudes that went before, and that followed, cried, saying, Hosanna to the Son of David: Blessed is he that cometh in the name of the Lord; Hosanna in the highest. 10: And when he was come into Jerusalem, all the city was moved, saying, Who is this? 11: And the multitude said, This is Jesus the prophet of Nazareth of Galilee. — *Matthew 21: 6–11*

While the entry to Jerusalem was joyous and passionate, it further increased the concern of the priests. Jerusalem was tense: relations between the people and the Roman garrison were still very uneasy following outbreaks of rioting not long before. They feared that this young prophet could stir up more unrest leading to bloodshed. At the Temple, his actions did little to calm their apprehension: overturning the tables of the moneychangers and vendors of sacrificial birds, he accused the traders of desecrating the Temple – "You have made it a den of robbers!"

After spending much of the day receiving the sick and the lame who came to be healed, Jesus returned to Bethany for the night and came back into Jerusalem next day. In the Temple, the priests and scribes questioned him closely; among them were some who already believed in him but would not admit it in public. The more outspoken questioned his authority, and he replied with parables, effectively questioning their own authority and contrasting their lack of belief in him with the belief of the people. The priests, he implied, were not worthy of their responsibilities as guardians of the faith.

Sunday to Wednesday: Jesus heals at the Temple and discourses with the people and the priests.

> 34: The people answered him, We have heard out of the law that Christ abideth for ever: and how sayest thou, The Son of man must be lifted up? who is this Son of man? 35: Then Jesus said unto them, Yet a little while is the light with you. Walk while ye have the light, lest darkness come upon you: for he that walketh in darkness knoweth not whither he goeth. 36: While ye have light, believe in the light, that ye may be the children of light. These things spake Jesus, and departed, and did hide himself from them. — *John 12:34–36*

The Pharisees then attempted to snare him with their questions. Was it lawful to give tribute to the Roman emperor? The implication of a negative answer would be tantamount to treason: but Jesus simply asked them to produce a coin. Whose image was on it? Caesar's, they replied. Then, said Jesus, render to Caesar the things which are Caesar's and to God the things that are God's. Another question was about the Resurrection: if a man had been married several times in his lifetime, which of his women would be his wife when they rose from the dead? Again Jesus replied simply: that God was the God of the living, not of the dead.

Opposite page: *Jesus condemns those who carry merchandise through the Temple building, contrary to the Law, then heals the sick.*

Above and right: *The priests question Jesus and attempt to trick him with a question about tax.*

The Parable of the Wise and Foolish Virgins 1: Then shall the kingdom of heaven be likened unto ten virgins, which took their lamps, and went forth to meet the bridegroom. 2: And five of them were wise, and five were foolish. 3: They that were foolish took their lamps, and took no oil with them: 4: But the wise took oil in their vessels with their lamps. 5: While the bridegroom tarried, they all slumbered and slept. 6: And at midnight there was a cry made, Behold, the bridegroom cometh; go ye out to meet him. 7: Then all those virgins arose, and trimmed their lamps. 8: And the foolish said unto the wise, Give us of your oil; for our lamps are gone out. 9: But the wise answered, saying, Not so; lest there be not enough for us and you: but go ye rather to them that sell, and buy for yourselves. 10: And while they went to buy, the bridegroom came; and they that were ready went in with him to the marriage: and the door was shut. 11: Afterward came also the other virgins, saying, Lord, Lord, open to us. 12: But he answered and said, Verily I say unto you, I know you not. 13: Watch therefore, for ye know neither the day nor the hour wherein the Son of man cometh. *—Matthew 25:1–13*

Left: *"The wise and foolish virgins."*

One of the Pharisees was a lawyer. He asked Jesus which was the greatest Commandment. The first and the second, Jesus replied; which silenced the priests. Then Jesus spoke to all the crowd. The teachers of the Law and Pharisees sat in Moses' seat, he said; while they told the people what to do, they did not practice what they preached. They were hypocrites, snakes, a brood of vipers.

34: But when the Pharisees had heard that he had put the Sadducees to silence, they were gathered together. 35: Then one of them, which was a lawyer, asked him a question, tempting him, and saying, 36: Master, which is the great commandment in the law? 37: Jesus said unto him, Thou shalt love the Lord thy God with all thy heart, and with all thy soul, and with all thy mind. 38: This is the first and great commandment. 39: And the second is like unto it, Thou shalt love thy neighbour as thyself. 40: On these two commandments hang all the law and the prophets. *— Matthew 22:34–40*

The Parable of the Two Sons 25: The baptism of John, whence was it? from heaven, or of men? And they reasoned with themselves, saying, If we shall say, From heaven; he will say unto us, Why did ye not then believe him? 26: But if we shall say, Of men; we fear the people; for all hold John as a prophet. 27: And they answered Jesus, and said, We cannot tell. And he said unto them, Neither tell I you by what authority I do these things. 28: But what think ye? A certain man had two sons; and he came to the first, and said, Son, go work to day in my vineyard. 29: He answered and said, I will not: but afterward he repented, and went. 30: And he came to the second, and said likewise. And he answered and said, I go, sir: and went not. 31: Whether of them twain did the will of his father? They say unto him, The first. Jesus saith unto them, Verily I say unto you, That the publicans and the harlots go into the kingdom of God before you. 32: For John came unto you in the way of righteousness, and ye believed him not: but the publicans and the harlots believed him: and ye, when ye had seen it, repented not afterward, that ye might believe him. *—Matthew 21:25–32*

The Widow's Mite 41: And Jesus sat over against the treasury, and beheld how the people cast money into the treasury: and many that were rich cast in much. 42: And there came a certain poor widow, and she threw in two mites, which make a farthing. 43: And he called unto him his disciples, and saith unto them, Verily I say unto you, That this poor widow hath cast more in, than all they which have cast into the treasury: 44: For all they did cast in of their abundance; but she of her want did cast in all that she had, even all her living. *—Mark 12:41–44*

As he left the Temple, Jesus pointed to the building and forecast its destruction. It would be the end of an age, he told his disciples, and gave them an apocalyptic vision of an ending that could come at any time. Therefore, he said, keep watch, because you do not know the day or the hour. He spoke in parables – of the wise and foolish virgins, of the two sons, the ten talents, and the tenants – in explanation. On the Last Day, he said, God would divide the nations and the people as sheep from goats, sending them to eternal life or to everlasting punishment.

18: Now in the morning as he returned into the city, he hungered. 19: And when he saw a fig tree in the way, he came to it, and found nothing thereon, but leaves only, and said unto it, Let no fruit grow on thee henceforward for ever. And presently the fig tree withered away. 20: And when the disciples saw it, they marvelled, saying, How soon is the fig tree withered away! 21: Jesus answered and said unto them, Verily I say unto you, If ye have faith, and doubt not, ye shall not only do this which is done to the fig tree, but also if ye shall say unto this mountain, Be thou removed, and be thou cast into the sea; it shall be done. 22: And all things, whatsoever ye shall ask in prayer, believing, ye shall receive.

—Matthew 21:18–22

The Parable of the Ten Talents 14: For the kingdom of heaven is as a man travelling into a far country, who called his own servants, and delivered unto them his goods. 15: And unto one he gave five talents, to another two, and to another one; to every man according to his several ability; and straightway took his journey. 16: Then he that had received the five talents went and traded with the same, and made them other five talents. 17: And likewise he that had received two, he also gained other two. 18: But he that had received one went and digged in the earth, and hid his lord's money. 19: After a long time the lord of those servants cometh, and reckoneth with them. 20: And so he that had received five talents came and brought other five talents, saying, Lord, thou deliveredst unto me five talents: behold, I have gained beside them five talents more. 21: His lord said unto him, Well done, thou good and faithful servant: thou hast been faithful over a few things, I will make thee ruler over many things: enter thou into the joy of thy lord. 22: He also that had received two talents came and said, Lord, thou deliveredst unto me two talents: behold, I have gained two other talents beside them. 23: His lord said unto him, Well done, good and faithful servant; thou hast been faithful over a few things, I will make thee ruler over many things: enter thou into the joy of thy lord. 24: Then he which had received the one talent came and said, Lord, I knew thee that thou art an hard man, reaping where thou hast not sown, and gathering where thou hast not strawed: 25: And I was afraid, and went and hid thy talent in the earth: lo, there thou hast that is thine. 26: His lord answered and said unto him, Thou wicked and slothful servant, thou knewest that I reap where I sowed not, and gather where I have not strawed: 27: Thou oughtest therefore to have put my money to the exchangers, and then at my coming I should have received mine own with usury. 28: Take therefore the talent from him, and give it unto him which hath ten talents. 29: For unto every one that hath shall be given, and he shall have abundance: but from him that hath not shall be taken away even that which he hath. 30: And cast ye the unprofitable servant into outer darkness: there shall be weeping and gnashing of teeth.

—Matthew 25:14–30

1: I am the true vine, and my Father is the husbandman. 2: Every branch in me that beareth not fruit he taketh away: and every branch that beareth fruit, he purgeth it, that it may bring forth more fruit. 3: Now ye are clean through the word which I have spoken unto you. 4: Abide in me, and I in you. As the branch cannot bear fruit of itself, except it abide in the vine; no more can ye, except ye abide in me. 5: I am the vine, ye are the branches: He that abideth in me, and I in him, the same bringeth forth much fruit: for without me ye can do nothing. 6: If a man abide not in me, he is cast forth as a branch, and is withered; and men gather them, and cast them into the fire, and they are burned. 7: If ye abide in me, and my words abide in you, ye shall ask what ye will, and it shall be done unto you. 8: Herein is my Father glorified, that ye bear much fruit; so shall ye be my disciples. 9: As the Father hath loved me, so have I loved you: continue ye in my love.

—John 15:1–9

The Parable of the Tenants 33: Hear another parable: There was a certain householder, which planted a vineyard, and hedged it round about, and digged a winepress in it, and built a tower, and let it out to husbandmen, and went into a far country: 34: And when the time of the fruit drew near, he sent his servants to the husbandmen, that they might receive the fruits of it. 35: And the husbandmen took his servants, and beat one, and killed another, and stoned another. 36: Again, he sent other servants more than the first: and they did unto them likewise. 37: But last of all he sent unto them his son, saying, They will reverence my son. 38: But when the husbandmen saw the son, they said among themselves, This is the heir; come, let us kill him, and let us seize on his inheritance. 39: And they caught him, and cast him out of the vineyard, and slew him. 40: When the lord therefore of the vineyard cometh, what will he do unto those husbandmen? 41: They say unto him, He will miserably destroy those wicked men, and will let out his vineyard unto other husbandmen, which shall render him the fruits in their seasons. 42: Jesus saith unto them, Did ye never read in the scriptures, The stone which the builders rejected, the same is become the head of the corner: this is the Lord's doing, and it is marvellous in our eyes? 43: Therefore say I unto you, The kingdom of God shall be taken from you, and given to a nation bringing forth the fruits thereof. 44: And whosoever shall fall on this stone shall be broken: but on whomsoever it shall fall, it will grind him to powder. 45: And when the chief priests and Pharisees had heard his parables, they perceived that he spake of them. 46: But when they sought to lay hands on him, they feared the multitude, because they took him for a prophet. *—Matthew 21: 33–46*

> 31: When the Son of man shall come in his glory, and all the holy angels with him, then shall he sit upon the throne of his glory: 32: And before him shall be gathered all nations: and he shall separate them one from another, as a shepherd divideth his sheep from the goats: 33: And he shall set the sheep on his right hand, but the goats on the left. 34: Then shall the King say unto them on his right hand, Come, ye blessed of my Father, inherit the kingdom prepared for you from the foundation of the world: 35: For I was an hungred, and ye gave me meat: I was thirsty, and ye gave me drink: I was a stranger, and ye took me in: 36: Naked, and ye clothed me: I was sick, and ye visited me: I was in prison, and ye came unto me. 37: Then shall the righteous answer him, saying, Lord, when saw we thee an hungred, and fed thee? or thirsty, and gave thee drink? 38: When saw we thee a stranger, and took thee in? or naked, and clothed thee? 39: Or when saw we thee sick, or in prison, and came unto thee? 40: And the King shall answer and say unto them, Verily I say unto you, Inasmuch as ye have done it unto one of the least of these my brethren, ye have done it unto me. 41: Then shall he say also unto them on the left hand, Depart from me, ye cursed, into everlasting fire, prepared for the devil and his angels: 42: For I was an hungred, and ye gave me no meat: I was thirsty, and ye gave me no drink: 43: I was a stranger, and ye took me not in: naked, and ye clothed me not: sick, and in prison, and ye visited me not. 44: Then shall they also answer him, saying, Lord, when saw we thee an hungred, or athirst, or a stranger, or naked, or sick, or in prison, and did not minister unto thee? 45: Then shall he answer them, saying, Verily I say unto you, Inasmuch as ye did it not to one of the least of these, ye did it not to me. 46: And these shall go away into everlasting punishment: but the righteous into life eternal. — *Matthew 25:31–46*

To his disciples Jesus again foretold his betrayal and crucifixion. Meanwhile, Caiaphas, the High Priest, was gathering the chief priests, scribes, and elders to discuss what they should do about Jesus. They could not kill him on the feast day, but Judas Iscariot, one of Jesus' disciples, now made the way for them. They struck a shameful bargain – for thirty pieces of silver, Judas would betray him.

On Wednesday night, Jesus did not return to Bethany but slept on the Mount of Olives, outside the city walls to the east. Next day was the feast of the unleavened

Above: *The perplexed priests meet to decide how they will deal with Jesus. Not only did they see him as a threat to law and order; he was challenging their own positions as priests.*

bread, and the disciples came to him to ask where they would eat for Passover. So he sent Peter and John to a certain house in the city, where an upper room would be made ready. Assembled there that evening, Jesus and his twelve disciples sat down to what has become known as the Last Supper.

When they had eaten, Jesus rose, took a towel, filled a basin with water and began to wash the astonished disciples' feet. It was Peter who

Above: *Two disciples are sent ahead by Jesus to be guided by a man carrying a pitcher of water to the guest chamber, made ready for Jesus and the others.*

Right: *Jesus gives the disciples a lesson in humility by washing their feet.*

objected first: surely this was not right, that his master should wash his servants' feet? Jesus completed his task then told them the significance of what he had done. "The servant is not greater than his lord; neither is he that is sent greater than he that sent him. If ye know these things, happy are ye if ye do them." (*John 13:16–17*)

Thursday: The Last Supper. Jesus washes the disciples' feet and discourses on many subjects.

1: Let not your heart be troubled: ye believe in God, believe also in me. 2: In my Father's house are many mansions: if it were not so, I would have told you. I go to prepare a place for you ... 4: And whither I go ye know, and the way ye know. 5: Thomas saith unto him, Lord, we know not whither thou goest; and how can we know the way? 6: Jesus saith unto him, I am the way, the truth, and the life: no man cometh unto the Father, but by me. —*John 14:1–7*

11: Believe me that I am in the Father, and the Father in me ... 12: Verily, verily, I say unto you, He that believeth on me, the works that I do shall he do also; and greater works than these shall he do; because I go unto my Father. 13: And whatsoever ye shall ask in my name, that will I do, that the Father may be glorified in the Son. —*John 14: 14:11–13*

27: Peace I leave with you, my peace I give unto you: not as the world giveth, give I unto you. Let not your heart be troubled, neither let it be afraid. 28: Ye have heard how I said unto you, I go away, and come again unto you. If ye loved me, ye would rejoice, because I said, I go unto the Father: for my Father is greater than I. —*John 14:27–28*

1: I am the true vine, and my Father is the husbandman. 2: Every branch in me that beareth not fruit he taketh away: and every branch that beareth fruit, he purgeth it, that it may bring forth more fruit ... 4: Abide in me, and I in you. As the branch cannot bear fruit of itself, except it abide in the vine; no more can ye, except ye abide in me. 5: I am the vine, ye are the branches: He that abideth in me, and I in him, the same bringeth forth much fruit: for without me ye can do nothing. 6: If a man abide not in me, he is cast forth as a branch, and is withered; and men gather them, and cast them into the fire, and they are burned. 7: If ye abide in me, and my words abide in you, ye shall ask what ye will, and it shall be done unto you. 8: Herein is my Father glorified, that ye bear much fruit; so shall ye be my disciples. —*John 15:1–8*

12: This is my commandment, That ye love one another, as I have loved you. 13: Greater love hath no man than this, that a man lay down his life for his friends. 14: Ye are my friends, if ye do whatsoever I command you. —*John 15:12–14*

23: ...Verily, verily, I say unto you, Whatsoever ye shall ask the Father in my name, he will give it you. 24: Hitherto have ye asked nothing in my name: ask, and ye shall receive, that your joy may be full. 25: These things have I spoken unto you in proverbs: but the time cometh, when I shall no more speak unto you in proverbs, but I shall shew you plainly of the Father ... 27: For the Father himself loveth you, because ye have loved me, and have believed that I came out from God. 28: I came forth from the Father, and am come into the world: again, I leave the world, and go to the Father. —*John 16:23–28*

As they went on talking, Jesus again shocked them by telling them that one of their number, sitting at this very table, would betray him. They were horrified. Peter whispered to know whom he meant, and Jesus replied by offering a sop to Judas, who soon rose from the table and went out. Much troubled, the remaining disciples sought to know what was about to happen, and he told them that he was going where

Right: *"And as they were eating, Jesus took bread, and blessed it, and brake it, and gave it to the disciples, and said, Take, eat; this is my body. And he took the cup, and gave thanks, and gave it to them, saying, Drink ye all of it; For this is my blood of the new testament, which is shed for many for the remission of sins. But I say unto you, I will not drink henceforth of this fruit of the vine, until that day when I drink it new with you in my Father's kingdom." (Matthew 26:26–29)*

Inset: *Judas leaves the room, having been identified as the one who would betray Jesus.*

they could not follow. Peter pleaded that he would follow even to death and would gladly lay down his life for Jesus. But Jesus told him that before cockcrow he would deny Jesus three times. In vain, Peter protested. Now the perplexed disciples clamored to know what would happen when he left them, and in a lengthy discourse he sought to comfort and reassure them.

Then he led them out into the night, beyond the city walls and across the valley of the Kidron (Cedron), to the Garden of Gethsemane on the western slopes of the Mount of Olives, where they had often gone before. There, leaving all but Peter and John behind, he went a little way off to pray, asking the two disciples to keep watch. Alone, he prayed that God would relent: "if it be possible, and all things are possible unto thee, take away this cup from me..." After a while he returned to find Peter and John fast asleep; waking them, he gently chided them – "the spirit is willing, but the flesh is weak" – then returned to his prayers. A second time he came back to find them asleep, and prayed again. This time an angel came to him, to give him strength, and he prayed earnestly. At last he returned to the slumbering disciples, and they rejoined the others.

Thursday: Jesus prays in the Garden of Gethsemane.

> 41: And he was withdrawn from them about a stone's cast, and kneeled down, and prayed, 42: Saying, Father, if thou be willing, remove this cup from me: nevertheless not my will, but thine, be done. 43: And there appeared an angel unto him from heaven, strengthening him. 44: And being in an agony he prayed more earnestly: and his sweat was as it were great drops of blood falling down to the ground. — *Luke 22:41–44*

Left and right: *In the Garden of Gethsemane, Jesus prays while Peter and John fail to stay awake.*

Soon the tranquillity of the hillside grove was broken by the sound of voices and a tumult of men armed with swords and staves, their way lit by torches and lanterns. It was a band of the priests' men, with many followers, come to arrest Jesus. They asked for him by name, and he identified himself; whereupon Judas kissed him, the agreed signal that this was indeed the man they sought. As they went to seize him, Peter drew his sword and struck out, severing the right ear of Malchus, the High Priest's own servant. Jesus told him to put up his sword – did he not realize, Jesus admonished him, that if he prayed to God he could muster twelve legions of angels to protect himself? But how then would the scriptures be fulfilled? And he touched Malchus' ear, healing it. The disciples fled, leaving the officers of the priests to bind Jesus and lead him back into the city.

Thursday: Jesus is arrested at Gethsemane.

42: Rise up, let us go; lo, he that betrayeth me is at hand. 43: And immediately, while he yet spake, cometh Judas, one of the twelve, and with him a great multitude with swords and staves, from the chief priests and the scribes and the elders. 44: And he that betrayed him had given them a token, saying, Whomsoever I shall kiss, that same is he; take him, and lead him away safely. 45: And as soon as he was come, he goeth straightway to him, and saith, Master, master; and kissed him. 46: And they laid their hands on him, and took him. *— Mark 14:43–46*

Left: *The priests' men issue forth from Jerusalem to Gethsemane.*

Below center: *Judas kisses Jesus as a sign for the arresting officers.*

Below: *Peter cuts off Malchus' ear.*

Jesus was taken first to Annas, father-in-law of the High Priest, then to Caiaphas himself, who had assembled the Sanhedrin, a council of the chief priests, elders, and scribes. Here, in the middle of the night, they sought to arraign Jesus and condemn him to death. They began questioning him, one of the officers hitting him, but they

could neither intimidate him nor force a confession of guilt. Then they produced a stream of false witnesses, but these contradicted each other in many details. At last Caiaphas ran out of patience and took the floor himself, asking Jesus directly if he were indeed Christ, the Son of God. Jesus' answer angered the priest, and the assembly erupted in vehement outrage, spitting at the prisoner, blindfolding him and hitting him.

All this was witnessed by Peter, who had followed from a distance and managed to gain entry to the assembly hall. There he was recognized by a maid as one of Jesus' disciples, but he denied it. The same thing happened again, and finally he was spotted by a kinsman of Malchus, whose ear he had cleaved in Gethsemane. For a third time, Peter denied having anything to do with Jesus; and as he spoke these words the cock crew. Looking up, he saw Jesus looking back at him as they led him away.

Jesus is taken before the priests.

62: And the high priest arose, and said unto him, Answerest thou nothing? what is it which these witness against thee? 63: But Jesus held his peace. And the high priest answered and said unto him, I adjure thee by the living God, that thou tell us whether thou be the Christ, the Son of God. 64: Jesus saith unto him, Thou hast said: nevertheless I say unto you, Hereafter shall ye see the Son of man sitting on the right hand of power, and coming in the clouds of heaven. 65: Then the high priest rent his clothes, saying, He hath spoken blasphemy; what further need have we of witnesses? behold, now ye have heard his blasphemy. 66: What think ye? They answered and said, He is guilty of death. — *Matthew 26:62–66*

Left: Jesus before the council of priests as they angrily throw questions at him.

Right: Peter denies Jesus a third time: "And after a while came unto him they that stood by, and said to Peter, Surely thou also art one of them; for thy speech bewrayeth thee. Then began he to curse and to swear, saying, I know not the man. And immediately the cock crew. And Peter remembered ... And he went out, and wept bitterly." (Matthew 26:73–75)

Later they brought Jesus before a full meeting of the Sanhedrin, which attempted to question him further and then condemned him. But a death sentence could only be carried out by the Romans, not by the Jews. So Jesus was taken before Pontius Pilate, Governor of Jerusalem. The overriding concern of this senior Roman officer was for the maintenance of law and order; he had already had to contend with too many riots and bloodshed in this city. So his approach was circumspect: to execute Jesus or spare him might equally stir up passions that could get out of control. Pilate questioned Jesus and could find no fault in him. But the crowd of priests insisted that Jesus had been going about fomenting trouble, inciting the people to rebel from Galilee to Jerusalem. At the mention of Galilee, Pilate saw a potential escape from his dilemma, for justice in the north of the province was the responsibility of Herod, Tetrarch of Galilee.

For his part, Herod, in Jerusalem for the Passover, was interested to meet Jesus, of whom he had heard much and hoped to see a miracle. But Herod's interrogation achieved nothing, for Jesus would not answer despite the continual mockery and accusations hurled at him by the priestly mob. Bored, Herod sent him back to Pilate, this time wrapped in a costly robe to show his contempt for the man called "the King of the Jews."

Left: Pilate questions Jesus.

***Right:** After Jesus had been questioned by Herod, he is stripped of his own clothes and mockingly clad in a fine robe as "King of the Jews."*

Jesus is brought before Pilate and then Herod.

33: Then Pilate entered into the judgment hall again, and called Jesus, and said unto him, Art thou the King of the Jews? 34: Jesus answered him, Sayest thou this thing of thyself, or did others tell it thee of me? 35: Pilate answered, Am I a Jew? Thine own nation and the chief priests have delivered thee unto me: what hast thou done? 36: Jesus answered, My kingdom is not of this world: if my kingdom were of this world, then would my servants fight, that I should not be delivered to the Jews: but now is my kingdom not from hence. 37: Pilate therefore said unto him, Art thou a king then? Jesus answered, Thou sayest that I am a king. To this end was I born, and for this cause came I into the world, that I should bear witness unto the truth. Every one that is of the truth heareth my voice. 38: Pilate saith unto him, What is truth? And when he had said this, he went out again unto the Jews, and saith unto them, I find in him no fault at all. — *John 18:33–38*

A weary Pilate told the priests that a death sentence was excessive; he would punish him and let him go. It was customary at the time of the Passover for the Romans to free a prisoner at the choice of the people, so Pilate offered this option to the crowd. They would have none of it and instead chose another prisoner, an infamous bandit named Barabbas, with much blood on his hands. Pilate was in a difficult position; his instinct to release Jesus reinforced by a message from his

Above: *Pilate's wife sends him a message.*

Left: *Pilate examines Jesus again, but can still find no fault in him. He sends him for punishment.*

wife, who had seen in a dream that Jesus was indeed a just man.

But the crowd were insistent and would not quieten until they had their way, shouting "Crucify him!" Pilate saw there was no choice. Symbolically, he washed his hands, released Barabbas and sent Jesus for punishment. The soldiers were merciless in scourging him, and in mocking him as "King of the Jews" they set a crown of thorns upon his head and jeered as they bowed before him.

Pilate is warned by his wife that Jesus is a just man.
Barabbas is chosen by the people to be freed at Passover.
Jesus is sent to be scourged.

Right: *"Then released he Barabbas unto them: and when he had scourged Jesus, he delivered him to be crucified. Then the soldiers of the Governor took Jesus into the common hall, and gathered unto him the whole band of soldiers. And they stripped him, and put on him a scarlet robe. And when they had platted a crown of thorns, they put it upon his head, and a reed in his right hand: and they bowed the knee before." (Matthew 27:26–29)*

Bloodied and with the plaited crown still upon his head, Jesus was once more brought before the mob. "Behold the man!" announced Pilate; but they grew ever louder in their calls for execution, now crying out that this was a rebel against Rome. At the judgment seat, called Gabbatha, Pilate delivered Jesus to be crucified that day.

While this was happening, the wretched Judas saw the evil he had set in motion and regretted his treachery. He returned to the Temple and threw down the thirty pieces of silver, crying out that he had betrayed an innocent man. The priests were unmoved: they had what they wanted. And Judas slunk away to hang himself.

Pilate is finally constrained to condemn Jesus to death.
Judas repents and hangs himself.

3: Then Judas, which had betrayed him, when he saw that he was condemned, repented himself, and brought again the thirty pieces of silver to the chief priests and elders, 4: Saying, I have sinned in that I have betrayed the innocent blood. And they said, What is that to us? see thou to that. 5: And he cast down the pieces of silver in the temple, and departed, and went and hanged himself. 6: And the chief priests took the silver pieces, and said, It is not lawful for to put them into the treasury, because it is the price of blood. 7: And they took counsel, and bought with them the potter's field, to bury strangers in. 8: Wherefore that field was called, The field of blood, unto this day. 9: Then was fulfilled that which was spoken by Jeremy the prophet, saying, And they took the thirty pieces of silver, the price of him that was valued, whom they of the children of Israel did value; 10: And gave them for the potter's field, as the Lord appointed me.

— *Matthew 27:3–10*

Above: *Pilate presents Jesus to the mob one last time, but they call for him to be crucified and Barabbas released.*

Right: *At the place called the Pavement, or Gabbatha, Pilate finally sentences Jesus to be crucified.*

Five days earlier, Jesus had entered Jerusalem in triumph, his way strewn with branches in joyous welcome. Now he left the city in a dreadful procession, dragging a heavy wooden cross through streets lined by a jeering mob. It was a long, slow journey, made with two criminals also condemned to crucifixion. Exhausted by the beating and scourging of the night and morning, Jesus collapsed more than once under the great weight of the cross, until eventually the soldiers dragged a man from the crowd, named Simon from Cyrene, and forced him to bear it.

The procession to Calvary and crucifixion. Simon of Cyrene forced to carry the cross.

Left: *Jesus is forced to carry the cross upon which he will die.*

Below left: *He falls for the first time.*

Right: *Eventually the soldiers pick upon a bystander, Simon of Cyrene, to carry Jesus' burden.*

At the hill of Golgotha, Jesus was stripped, laid on the cross and nailed to it by his hands and feet. They offered him wine mixed with gall, but he would not drink, and then the three crosses were erected, Jesus between the two criminals. On his cross they had nailed a board, at Pilate's command, inscribed in Aramaic, Greek, and Roman: THIS IS THE KING OF THE JEWS (despite the objections of the priests). As was the custom, the soldiers divided his garments and cast lots for his coat. Bystanders, joined by the priests, jeered and mocked Jesus – if he were indeed the king of the Jews, they said, why did he not save himself? One of his fellows in crucifixion joined in – could he not save all three? – but the other man, a thief, rebuked him. We deserve our punishment for our deeds, he said; but this man has done nothing.

> 39: And one of the malefactors which were hanged railed on him, saying, If thou be Christ, save thyself and us. 40: But the other answering rebuked him, saying, Dost not thou fear God, seeing thou art in the same condemnation? 41: And we indeed justly; for we receive the due reward of our deeds: but this man hath done nothing amiss. 42: And he said unto Jesus, Lord, remember me when thou comest into thy kingdom. 43: And Jesus said unto him, Verily I say unto thee, To day shalt thou be with me in paradise. *— Luke 23:39–43*

> 33: And when they were come to the place, which is called Calvary, there they crucified him, and the malefactors, one on the right hand, and the other on the left. 34: Then said Jesus, Father, forgive them; for they know not what they do. And they parted his raiment, and cast lots. 35: And the people stood beholding. And the rulers also with them derided him, saying, He saved others; let him save himself, if he be Christ, the chosen of God. 36: And the soldiers also mocked him, coming to him, and offering him vinegar, 37: And saying, If thou be the king of the Jews, save thyself. 38: And a superscription also was written over him in letters of Greek, and Latin, and Hebrew, THIS IS THE KING OF THE JEWS.
>
> *— Luke 23:33–38*

Above left: *Jesus is nailed to the cross, and the soldiers cast lots for his clothes.*

Above: *"Now there stood by the cross of Jesus his mother, and his mother's sister, Mary the wife of Cleophas, and Mary Magdalene. When Jesus therefore saw his mother, and the disciple standing by, whom he loved, he saith unto his mother, Woman, behold thy son! Then saith he to the disciple, Behold thy mother! And from that hour that disciple took her unto his own home." (John 19:25–27)*

45: Now from the sixth hour there was darkness over all the land unto the ninth hour. 46: And about the ninth hour Jesus cried with a loud voice, saying, Eli, Eli, lama sabachthani? that is to say, My God, my God, why hast thou forsaken me? 47: Some of them that stood there, when they heard that, said, This man calleth for Elias. *— Matthew 27:45–47*

28: After this, Jesus knowing that all things were now accomplished, that the scripture might be fulfilled, saith, I thirst. 29: Now there was set a vessel full of vinegar: and they filled a spunge with vinegar, and put it upon hyssop, and put it to his mouth. 30: When Jesus therefore had received the vinegar, he said, It is finished ... *— John 19:28–30*

46: And when Jesus had cried with a loud voice, he said, Father, into thy hands I commend my spirit: and having said thus, he gave up the ghost. *— Luke 23:46*

Far left: At the foot of the cross.

Left: A darkness came upon the land.

51: And, behold, the veil of the
temple was rent in twain from the
top to the bottom; and the earth
did quake, and the rocks rent; 52:
And the graves were opened; and
many bodies of the saints which
slept arose, 53: And came out of
the graves after his resurrection,
and went into the holy city, and
appeared unto many. 54: Now
when the centurion, and they that
were with him, watching Jesus,
saw the earthquake, and those
things that were done, they feared
greatly, saying, Truly this was the
Son of God. — *Matthew 27:51–54*

The hours of agony continued, an unnatural darkness fell, and Jesus cried out to God. When he gave up the ghost, the earth shook, rocks cracked asunder and the veil in the Temple dividing the sanctuary was torn apart. Graves opened and the spirits of the dead were seen floating in the city. Awestruck, the centurion on Golgotha proclaimed, "Truly this was the Son of God."

Crucifixion could often take days to kill a man, but it was forbidden to let the bodies of executed men hang there after sunset on the Sabbath, which was the following day. So, to hasten the death of the victims, the soldiers went to break their legs. But when they came to Jesus they perceived that he was already dead; instead one of them pierced Jesus' side.

Joseph, a wealthy man from Arimathaea, and a secret follower of Jesus, had meanwhile obtained permission from Pilate to take possession of Jesus' body. Now, with another secret follower, the Pharisee Nicodemus, he had the body anointed with oils and perfumes, and then wrapped in a linen shroud. They made their way to a nearby rock-hewn sepulcher, which Joseph had prepared, and within, watched by Mary and Mary Magdalen, they placed the body, sealing the tomb with a great stone door.

On the Sabbath, the priests set a watch upon the tomb, fearing that the body of Jesus might be carried away and pretense made of his having risen from the dead. They were joined there at sunrise on the following day by Mary Magdalen and Mary, the mother of James, bringing oils to anoint the body again. As they approached, the earth shook and an angel descended, rolling back the stone door. The guards fled, and the women cautiously entered the tomb. There sat an angel clad all in white. Jesus, he told them, had risen from the dead; they should go quickly and tell the disciples.

They returned soon with Peter and John, who examined the empty sepulcher. All that remained were the linen wrappings of the body. When the two disciples departed to tell the others, Mary Magdalen remained, in tears, outside the tomb, overwhelmed by grief. She was the first to see the risen Jesus, whom she first mistook for the gardener. But when she told the disciples, they did not believe her.

Left: *On the first day of the week the women arrive to find the tomb empty.*

Right: *"Mary stood without at the sepulchre weeping: and as she wept, she stooped down, and looked into the sepulchre ... And when she had thus said, she turned herself back, and saw Jesus standing, and knew not that it was Jesus ... Jesus saith unto her, Woman, why weepest thou? whom seekest thou? She, supposing him to be the gardener, saith unto him, Sir, if thou have borne him hence, tell me where thou hast laid him, and I will take him away. Jesus saith unto her, Mary. She turned herself, and saith unto him, Rabboni; which is to say, Master. Jesus saith unto her, Touch me not; for I am not yet ascended to my Father: but go to my brethren, and say unto them, I ascend unto my Father, and your Father; and to my God, and your God." (John 20:11–17*

The women and disciples find the tomb empty.
Mary Magdalen is the first to see the risen Jesus.

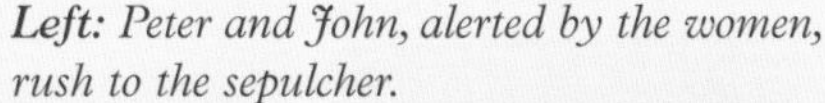

Left: *Peter and John, alerted by the women, rush to the sepulcher.*

Emmaus was a village not far from Jerusalem, and later that day two of Jesus' followers were walking, discussing the amazing events they had witnessed, when they were joined by another man. When he fell in with them, Jesus was not recognized; nor during their walk, as he discussed and explained the scriptures to them. Only when they invited him to dine with them and he broke and blessed the bread did they realize who this was; and in a moment Jesus vanished. The two hastened to Jerusalem to tell the disciples what they had seen and heard.

That evening ten of the disciples assembled discretely, behind closed doors, not knowing whether the priests might continue their persecution. Suddenly in their midst stood Jesus, terrifying them and showing them his pierced hands, feet, and side so that they were sure it was truly their master. When they told all this to Thomas, the missing disciple, that night, he doubted their account and was only persuaded eight days later when Jesus appeared and invited him to touch his wounds.

The third time Jesus appeared to them was in Galilee, where several of them were fishing on the Sea of Tiberias. They had worked through the night but had nothing to show for their efforts. In the morning, they beheld a figure on the shore, who directed them to where the fish were in abundance. They recognized him and came ashore with a goodly catch, then dined with him.

The final meeting of the disciples with Jesus was in Jerusalem. He led them out to Bethany, telling them that they must go forth and preach and assuring them of the divine support that would strengthen their endeavors. Then they saw him no more: he blessed them and ascended to heaven, and the disciples returned to the city, joyful and full of hope in the expectation for what they would do.

24: But Thomas, one of the twelve, called Didymus, was not with them when Jesus came. 25: The other disciples therefore said unto him, We have seen the Lord. But he said unto them, Except I shall see in his hands the print of the nails, and put my finger into the print of the nails, and thrust my hand into his side, I will not believe. 26: And after eight days again his disciples were within, and Thomas with them: then came Jesus, the doors being shut, and stood in the midst, and said, Peace be unto you. 27: Then saith he to Thomas, reach hither thy finger, and behold my hands; and reach hither thy hand, and thrust it into my side: and be not faithless, but believing. 28: And Thomas answered and said unto him, My Lord and my God. 29: Jesus saith unto him, Thomas, because thou hast seen me, thou hast believed: blessed are they that have not seen, and yet have believed. — *John 20:24–29*

Jesus appears to followers in Emmaus.
He appears several times to his disciples.
He appears on the shore of the Sea of Tiberias.
Finally, at Bethany, he ascends to heaven.

Above left: *Two followers encounter the resurrected Jesus but do not recognize him.*

Above: *The encounter on the Sea of Tiberias in Galilee.*

Right: *"And he led them out as far as to Bethany, and he lifted up his hands, and blessed them. And it came to pass, while he blessed them, he was parted from them, and carried up into heaven. And they worshipped him, and returned to Jerusalem with great joy: And were continually in the temple, praising and blessing God ... (Luke 24:50–53)*

Following Jesus' Ascension, it fell to the eleven remaining apostles to carry on his work and to spread the word of the Kingdom of Heaven and the way of the Lord. They held a meeting with more than a hundred other followers and decided upon a replacement for Judas in order to bring their number back up to twelve (symbolic of the twelve tribes). They cast lots and the choice fell upon a long-time believer, Matthias, who had been one of the seventy disciples Jesus sent out during his ministry.

Fifty days after the feast of the Passover, the Jews celebrated the feast of Pentecost, or First Fruits. When the apostles and followers assembled, a great wind blew through the room they were in, and tongues of flame descended upon the heads of the

***Above:** Pentecost – the Holy Ghost descends upon the apostles as tongues of fire.*

The Apostles

Peter Originally named Simon Peter, brother of Andrew. Impulsive, often the mouthpiece of the apostles. One of the inner circle of disciples; after Ascension takes leading role in the apostolate. Opens the way to Gentiles. In tradition, crucified in Rome during Nero's persecutions.
Andrew Former disciple of John the Baptist. Preaches in Jerusalem after the Ascension. In tradition martyred by crucifixion on an X-shaped cross.
James Son of Zebedee and Salome (traditionally sister of Virgin Mary), older brother of John. Father has house in Jerusalem and maintains friendly relationship with High Priest Caiaphas. One of inner circle of disciples; first apostle to be martyred.
John From Bethsaida, Galilee, youngest disciple, known as the disciple whom Jesus loves, and one of the inner circle. Takes care of Jesus' mother after crucifixion. In tradition, settles in Ephesus, but is exiled for a time to Patmos. Only apostle to escape violent death and lives a long life, dying at the age of *c.*100.
Philip From Bethsaida. Generally paired with Nathanael as preaching companion and dies a martyr at Hieropolis.
Bartholomew Sometimes identified with Nathanael. Two stories of his death are traditionally told: crucified in India or flayed alive in Albanopolis, Armenia.
Thomas ("Doubting Thomas") Best-known as disciple who doubts accounts of the other disciples about Jesus' resurrection; when he does see risen Lord, becomes first to express Jesus' divinity: "My Lord and my God." In tradition, evangelizes Parthians, possibly preaches in India, meeting his death in India.
Matthew Former tax-collector in Capernaum, becoming a prominent apostle and traditionally author of the first Gospel. Killed in Nadabah with halberd.
James the Lesser (or the Younger) In tradition formerly a tax-gatherer, like Matthew. His mother is one of the women at the foot of the cross and at the empty tomb. Dies in Jerusalem, stoned and clubbed to death.
Thaddeus or Judas, brother of James. Writes that love is the secret of obedience and obedience is the secret of blessedness. Crucified at Edessa.
Simon the Zealot or Simon the Lesser Belongs to nationalistic Zealot sect. Travels widely; is traditionally linked with Jude. Martyred in Persia.
Judas Iscariot Only non-Galilean apostle; treasurer for the disciples. Betrays Jesus, after which he repents and hangs himself – "it had been good for that man if he had not been born." *(Matthew 26:24)*
Matthias Chosen by lot to replace Judas; follower of Jesus from the beginning of his ministry. Traditionally one of the seventy. In tradition, he travels to Ethiopia, where he is martyred.

twelve. The Holy Ghost had entered them, empowering them to heal, teach the way of the Lord – and at the same time the curse of Babel was reversed, for all who heard them speak, no matter their native tongue, could understand them. Peter addressed those present, telling them that Jesus, the Messiah, had risen from the dead; and that day alone some 3,000 people were converted.

The apostles began healing and preaching just as Jesus had done, but teaching also the resurrection. One of the first to be healed was a crippled beggar, a familiar face at the Temple gate, whom Peter healed. Arising, he went into the Temple, where all who knew him were filled with wonder.

Now there was not just one man performing miracles but twelve. And they were not only teaching the resurrection but openly blaming the Sanhedrin for the death of Jesus. The priests reacted by persecuting them, starting with Peter and John, who spent a night in jail before appearing before Annas, Caiaphas, and the Sanhedrin. They were threatened and released this time, but it was not long before the apostles were again imprisoned. This time, at dead of night, an angel descended and opened the locked doors, freeing them – next morning the priests beheld the apostles at work as usual, at Solomon's Porch, and were astounded. Brought before the council yet again, they were sentenced to be scourged and released with more warnings – this after an intervention by the law teacher Gamaliel. His argument was simple: if this were a movement springing from human origins, it would surely fail; if not, they were fighting God himself.

***Above right:** Peter and John heal a beggar outside the Temple.*

***Right:** They stand before the Sanhedrin.*

33 Matthias chosen as the twelfth apostle.
33 Apostles receive the Holy Ghost.
Apostles continue Jesus' work of healing and preaching.

And so the apostles continued their work, news of their activities bringing in the sick and lame from far and wide. This active, empowered fellowship of believers shared their possessions and pooled their resources, supported also by donations made by the faithful. Many sold property and gave the proceeds to the community. One such was Joseph, a Levite, whom the apostles named Barnabas. By contrast, a couple named Ananias and Sapphira sold land and gave only half of the received moneys; this met with stern condemnation by Peter, who called it deception and lying to the Lord. Both husband and wife fell down dead, which sent a frisson of fear through the church.

One of the believers elected as a deacon, or administrator, was Stephen, who was destined to become the first Christian martyr. Arrested for blasphemy, and condemned by the testimony of false witnesses, he made a strong speech to the Sanhedrin – to no avail. Their fury boiled over: they dragged him outside, stoned him to death and embarked with much greater ferocity in persecuting the followers of Jesus. The Greek speakers among the faithful were particularly singled out, so they scattered to the countryside, leaving the nucleus of the apostles in Jerusalem.

Samaria was Philip's destination, and here he found a receptive audience. Indeed, the enthusiasm of those who heard him led Philip to call Peter and John, who also met with great success, baptizing and dispensing the Holy Spirit. Among those who came to them was a magician of much repute named Simon, who was baptized and then offered Peter money if he would grant him the Holy Spirit. "May your money perish with you!" retorted Peter – the gift of God could not be bought. Meanwhile Philip directed his attention toward Gaza, and on the road encountered an Ethiopian eunuch, treasurer of the Queen of Cush, who had been to Jerusalem to worship. The traveler was reading from

1: And in those days, when the number of the disciples was multiplied, there arose a murmuring of the Grecians against the Hebrews, because their widows were neglected in the daily ministration. 2: Then the twelve called the multitude of the disciples unto them, and said, It is not reason that we should leave the word of God, and serve tables. 3: Wherefore, brethren, look ye out among you seven men of honest report, full of the Holy Ghost and wisdom, whom we may appoint over this business. 4: But we will give ourselves continually to prayer, and to the ministry of the word. 5: And the saying pleased the whole multitude: and they chose Stephen, a man full of faith and of the Holy Ghost, and Philip, and Prochorus, and Nicanor, and Timon, and Parmenas, and Nicolas a proselyte of Antioch: 6: Whom they set before the apostles: and when they had prayed, they laid their hands on them. 7: And the word of God increased; and the number of the disciples multiplied in Jerusalem greatly; and a great company of the priests were obedient to the faith. —*Acts 6:1–7*

the Book of Isaiah, and he asked Philip to explain it. They fell into conversation which ended in the Ethiopian being baptized.

Foremost among the persecutors in Jerusalem was a man called Paul*. Born in Tarsus of a well-to-do family, he was a Benjamite Pharisee who brought the enthusiasm of a zealous bigot to his work. After hunting out the followers of the way of the Lord in Jerusalem – he was there at the stoning of Stephen – he obtained letters of introduction to the synagogues of Damascus and departed for that city intending to put new vigor into the persecutions there. On the road to Damascus, he experienced one of the most momentous conversions in history – a great flash of light blinded him, and as he lay terrified in the road Jesus spoke to him. He was to become one of the two greatest proponents of the new faith and would make the way of the Lord an international movement.

Left: *The stoning of Stephen. "Then they ... cast him out of the city, and stoned him: and the witnesses laid down their clothes at a young man's feet, whose name was Saul. And they stoned Stephen, calling upon God, and saying, Lord Jesus, receive my spirit." (Acts 7:57–59)*

Right: *The conversion of Paul. "And as he journeyed, he came near Damascus: and suddenly there shined round about him a light from heaven: And he fell to the earth, and heard a voice saying unto him, Saul, Saul, why persecutest thou me? And he said, Who art thou, Lord? And the Lord said, I am Jesus whom thou persecutest ... And he trembling and astonished said, Lord, what wilt thou have me to do? And the Lord said unto him, Arise, and go into the city, and it shall be told thee what thou must do." (Acts 9:3–6)*

* Saul was his Jewish name; Paul (the name by which he is more generally known) was part of his Roman name.

Peter and John seized and imprisoned.
34 Deacons elected to administer the fellowship of the way.
34 Stephen stoned to death.
34 Philip, Peter, and John in Samaria.
35 Conversion of Paul.

3: And as he journeyed, he came near Damascus: and suddenly there shined round about him a light from heaven: 4: And he fell to the earth, and heard a voice saying unto him, Saul, Saul, why persecutest thou me? 5: And he said, Who art thou, Lord? And the Lord said, I am Jesus whom thou persecutest: it is hard for thee to kick against the pricks. 6: And he trembling and astonished said, Lord, what wilt thou have me to do? And the Lord said unto him, Arise, and go into the city, and it shall be told thee what thou must do. 7: And the men which journeyed with him stood speechless, hearing a voice, but seeing no man. 8: And Saul arose from the earth; and when his eyes were opened, he saw no man: but they led him by the hand, and brought him into Damascus. —*Acts 9:3–8*

First, Paul was led to Damascus, and one of the disciples, directed to him by God, healed his eyes. For some days Paul remained there and confounded the priests by beginning to preach the very faith he had come to condemn. Soon the priests conspired to kill him, but Paul escaped over the city walls and made his way back to Jerusalem, where he made contact with the apostles. Naturally, they were extremely wary of this former enemy, but Barnabas spoke up for him, and they began to believe in his conversion. His presence in Jerusalem, and the story of his incredible change of attitude soon reached the authorities, and the brethren got him out of Jerusalem to Caesarea, where he took ship for his home city. In time, however, the fury of persecution in Jerusalem gradually diminished, affording the disciples more freedom to spread the word.

Peter, meanwhile, experienced a vision that was just as momentous in its consequences as Paul's conversion. He had been active along the coast of the Mediterranean: at Lydda, he healed a paralytic; and at Joppa he even raised from the dead one of the female disciples there, Tabitha (or Dorcas). Then on the way to Caesarea, where he had been summoned by a Roman centurion, he had a strange vision, which took him some while to interpret. He realized eventually that God was telling him that everyone could be welcomed into the way of the Lord, Gentiles and the uncircumcised as well as Jews. They must not call any man clean or unclean – baptism must be available to all. The centurion, already a believer, was baptized together with his friends and family, the first non-Jewish converts. When Peter returned to Jerusalem he faced criticism from his fellow apostles, but he

told them of his vision and its evident meaning. It was controversial, but the apostles accepted this; among the wider following, there was more circumspection.

After the period of relative peace, a new wave of persecution began, led by Herod Agrippa I (grandson of Herod the Great), who began making arrests, including James, brother of John, whom he put to the sword. Seeing that this pleased the priests, he seized Peter just before the Passover and threw him into prison, where he was chained and heavily guarded. But the angel of the Lord came to his rescue by night, waking him and leading him from the building, as if in a dream, past the jailers. When he turned up at the house of Mary, mother of John, the apostles gathered there were astonished to see him. And shortly afterwards, Herod Agrippa died.

Meanwhile Antioch, an important city in northern Syria, had become the focus of the faith in that area, having attracted a number of followers fleeing the earlier persecutions in Jerusalem. A strong community of believers grew there, and Barnabus was sent from Jerusalem to meet them. He than brought Paul from Tarsus to preach; and it was from this city that they would begin their missionary journeys.

Cyprus was their first destination, where they converted the Roman Proconsul, Sergius Paulus, despite the opposition of his attendant, Bar-Jesus, or Elymas, whom Paul blinded; and then Asia Minor, where in Pamphylia their reception was mixed. At Pisidian Antioch and Iconium, they met opposition from the Jews – but not from the Gentiles, whom they embraced. They withdrew to Lystra, but here they were mistaken for gods and then the local Jews had them stoned, leaving Paul for dead outside the city walls. Via Derbe, they returned to Antioch in Syria.

35 Peter's vision and first baptism of Gentiles.
44 Herod Agrippa I executes James. Peter imprisoned for the second time. Barnabas and Paul in Antioch.
45 Paul's first missionary journey.

Far left: *Paul escapes from Damascus by being let down in a basket from the walls of the city.*

Left: *Peter rescued from prison by an angel.*

Above: *The citizens of Lystra mistake Paul and Barnabas for gods.*

Over the following years the implications of Peter's great vision and the activities of Paul and Barnabas became a source of discontent among some of the faithful. Was Christianity (a term first used for the new faith in Antioch) to be for the Jews alone or for the uncircumcised Gentiles too? A delegation from Jerusalem came to Antioch, and a sharp debate ensued, with the result that Paul and Barnabas led a party to Jerusalem to settle the matter – all of their future work depended upon the resolution of this question. At a meeting that marked a turning point in the movement, the fundamentalist Jewish Christians insisted that Gentiles accepting the way of the Lord must be circumcised, while Peter spoke of his vision and Paul and Barnabas told them of their successes among the Gentiles of the north. After much debate, a potential, damaging schism in the movement was averted: two of the faithful, Silas and Judas Barsabas, were sent to Antioch with a letter asking simply that the Gentiles accommodate Jewish Christians by respecting their food laws. There was no mention of circumcision. Now all was clear, and the task of taking the message to the Gentiles could proceed in earnest.

> 23: And they wrote letters by them after this manner; The apostles and elders and brethren send greeting unto the brethren which are of the Gentiles in Antioch and Syria and Cilicia: 24: Forasmuch as we have heard, that certain which went out from us have troubled you with words, subverting your souls, saying, Ye must be circumcised, and keep the law: to whom we gave no such commandment: 25: It seemed good unto us, being assembled with one accord, to send chosen men unto you with our beloved Barnabas and Paul, 26: Men that have hazarded their lives for the name of our Lord Jesus Christ. 27: We have sent therefore Judas and Silas, who shall also tell you the same things by mouth. 28: For it seemed good to the Holy Ghost, and to us, to lay upon you no greater burden than these necessary things; 29: That ye abstain from meats offered to idols, and from blood, and from things strangled, and from fornication: from which if ye keep yourselves, ye shall do well. Fare ye well.
> —*Acts 15:23–29*

> 47: For so hath the Lord commanded us, saying, I have set thee to be a light of the Gentiles, that thou shouldest be for salvation unto the ends of the earth. 48: And when the Gentiles heard this, they were glad, and glorified the word of the Lord: and as many as were ordained to eternal life believed. —*Acts 13:47–48*

Paul set off on his second missionary journey, taking with him Timotheus and Silas. They traveled through Phrygia and Galatia in Asia Minor and then crossed the Hellespont to the continent of Europe. At Philippi, an important city in Macedonia, Paul established a community of believers but, as so often, encountered resistance too.

***Left:** Paul baptizes Lydia, a dealer in purple cloth, and they stay at her house in Philippi.*

Trouble was sparked by a slave-girl employed as a fortune-teller, who recognized Paul and Silas as servants of God. When she persisted in following them and calling out, Paul turned and cast out the devil within her, but now her psychic abilities were no longer of value to her owner. A riot resulted, and the apostles were imprisoned, this time chained to heavy blocks of wood. That night an earthquake shook the city, the doors of the jail flew open, and their chains were loosened. When the jailer discovered that they had not taken the opportunity to escape, he threw himself at their feet and was baptized. Shortly after, the authorities released Paul and Silas, but Paul upbraided them for so treating a citizen of Rome, whom they had no right to imprison.

From Philippi, the apostles traveled along the great Roman road, the Egnatian Way, to Thessalonica, and then went south to Athens, where they engaged in debate with scholars of the Epicurean and Stoic schools of philosophy. At Corinth they made an extended stop, but after a while ran into trouble again and were seized. However, the local Roman Governor, Gallio, refused to become involved and emptied the court when the local authorities attempted to bring them to trial.

Above right: *At Philippi, the jailer falls at Paul's feet and asks what he must do to be saved.*

Right: *"After these things Paul departed from Athens, and came to Corinth; And found a certain Jew named Aquila, born in Pontus, lately come from Italy, with his wife Priscilla; (because that Claudius had commanded all Jews to depart from Rome:) and came unto them. And because he was of the same craft, he abode with them, and wrought: for by their occupation they were tentmakers. And he reasoned in the synagogue every sabbath, and persuaded the Jews and the Greeks. (Acts 18:1–4)*

48 Jerusalem conference concerning the baptism of Gentiles.
48–51 Paul's second missionary journey.
53–58 Paul's third missionary journey.

They returned to Asia Minor and at Ephesus encountered an Alexandrian named Apollos, one of a number who had been baptized by John the Baptist. They now baptized them in the name of Jesus Christ. They also came across a number of sorcerers attempting to effect healings, so they instructed them in the way of the Lord, and the sorcerers publicly burned their magic books.

Via Caesarea, Paul returned to Jerusalem but was soon back in Antioch planning his next mission. This took him back to Ephesus, where his success had caused a backlash. Ephesus was the site of one of the Seven Wonders of the World, the temple to Artemis, long since destroyed but still the focus for worshippers. The silversmiths there saw their trade in statuettes of the goddess threatened by the new religion, and a certain Demetrius raised a riot in protest during which the apostles were jostled but escaped. Their route lay toward Macedonia again. Paul was now revisiting established Christian communities, encouraging them and helping to keep them in touch with the expanding movement. At many meetings, he preached, sometimes at great length. On one occasion, he spoke for so long that a young man named Eutychus fell asleep tumbling from a window; the fall was thought to have killed him, but Paul revived him.

They crossed over to Macedonia again and made the circuit to Corinth, then back to Philippi, along the coast of Asia Minor, and back to Tyre and Jerusalem. During these long travels, they faced the usual hazards of non-believers, bigots, and Jews, but Paul reinvigorated the Christian communities everywhere with his formidable courage and passion. During these travels, he wrote letters (epistles) to various communities putting in writing many of the ideas and thoughts he must have imparted verbally at his many meetings, and these have become fundamental sources of Christian theology and philosophy.

His reception in Jerusalem was warm, but serious trouble lay ahead, as predicted by a prophet named Agabus in Caesarea, where he stayed for a few days with Philip. Paul was not deterred.

While he was away it had been put about that he was teaching that Jews living among the Gentiles should not have their children circumcised, thus contradicting the Mosaic Law. Sure enough, his enemies saw him in the Temple and seized hold of him, leading to uproar in the city. His fate was not sealed, however: as a Roman citizen, he was not flogged, and the Roman commander, Claudius Lysia, became cautious. Next day Claudius sent him before the Sanhedrin, where he stood, defiant, and told them that he was a Pharisee. This upset the priests completely, for Paul preached resurrection and believed in angels and spirits – as did the Sadducees, but not the Pharisees. In the chaos that followed, the Romans took him away for his own safety, and after a plot to kill him was betrayed they moved him by night to imprisonment in Caesarea.

Right: Paul writing an Epistle from Corinth.

Left: Paul in Athens.

37: And as Paul was to be led into the castle, he said unto the chief captain, May I speak unto thee? ... I am a man which am a Jew of Tarsus, a city in Cilicia, a citizen of no mean city ... 24: The chief captain commanded him to be brought into the castle, and bade that he should be examined by scourging; that he might know wherefore they cried so against him. 25: And as they bound him with thongs, Paul said unto the centurion that stood by, Is it lawful for you to scourge a man that is a Roman, and uncondemned? ... And Paul said, But I was free born. 29: Then straightway they departed from him which should have examined him: and the chief captain also was afraid, after he knew that he was a Roman, and because he had bound him.

— Acts 21:37–39, 22:24–29

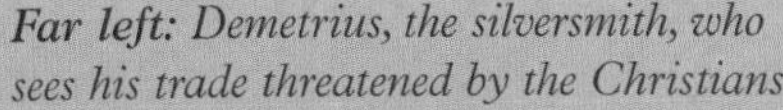

***Far left:** Demetrius, the silversmith, who sees his trade threatened by the Christians.*

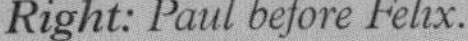

***Right:** Paul before Felix.*

Here the provincial Governor, Felix, found himself under pressure from the High Priest, who brought a lawyer called Tertullus to bring charges of trouble-making. Felix had heard about this new religion and talked privately with Paul, effectively keeping the priests at bay, but no conclusion was reached, and Paul waited in jail for some two years. Then Felix was replaced by a new Governor, Porcius Festus, which induced the priests and Jewish leaders to try again to bring him to trial. This time Paul, as a Roman citizen, lodged his right to appeal to the Emperor in Rome.

A few days later the Tetrarch, Herod Agrippa II, paid a courtesy visit to Porcius in Caesarea, and they spoke about the Christian prisoner. Herod Agrippa decided that he would see Paul himself, and the result – after Paul told him the story of his conversion – was that the King could find no fault in

Above left: *Paul before Herod Agrippa II.*

Left: *Paul's Italy-bound ship is assailed by a violent storm off Malta.*

Right: *Ashore on Malta, the shipwrecked travelers make a fire before moving inland. Paul's companions notice that, as he helps to make the fire, a viper bites him, but without ill effect.*

Far right: *Paul escorted to Rome along the Appian Way.*

him. However, his judgment to let Paul go free was complicated by the fact of his appeal to Caesar, and it was finally decided to send him to Rome.

The long journey across the Mediterranean was made in three stages, first to Myra, on the coast of Asia Minor, where they went aboard a large Alexandrian ship bound for Rome. The weather was bad, however, and after a difficult journey past Cyprus and Crete, they were shipwrecked on Malta (Melita), and forced to wait out the winter there.

Paul's relationship with his guards seems to have been relaxed, and indeed they stayed with Publius, the Governor of the island. When the Governor's father fell sick of dysentery, Paul cured him, and many other sick people were brought to him for healing. The final stage of the journey took them to Puteoli, where they were met by friends who accompanied them along the Appian Way to Rome.

There is no mention in the Bible of an audience with the Emperor, but Paul was held under house arrest for some two years, during which he spoke to local Jews and preached the message of the way of the Lord. Although not mentioned in the

58 Paul arrested in Jerusalem and imprisoned at Caesarea for two years.
60–61 Paul's voyage to Rome.

7: And when he was come, the Jews which came down from Jerusalem stood round about, and laid many and grievous complaints against Paul, which they could not prove. 8: While he answered for himself, Neither against the law of the Jews, neither against the temple, nor yet against Caesar, have I offended any thing at all. 9: But Festus, willing to do the Jews a pleasure, answered Paul, and said, Wilt thou go up to Jerusalem, and there be judged of these things before me? 10: Then said Paul, I stand at Caesar's judgment seat, where I ought to be judged: to the Jews have I done no wrong, as thou very well knowest. 11: For if I be an offender, or have committed any thing worthy of death, I refuse not to die: but if there be none of these things whereof these accuse me, no man may deliver me unto them. I appeal unto Caesar. 12: Then Festus, when he had conferred with the council, answered, Hast thou appealed unto Caesar? unto Caesar shalt thou go. —*Acts 25: 7–12*

64 Great fire in Rome; Christians become scapegoats and are persecuted.
65 Traditional date for the martyrdoms of Peter and Paul in Rome.
66–70 Jewish revolt: destruction of the Temple in Jerusalem.
69 The year of the four emperors. Vespasian establishes Flavian dynasty.
95 Gospel of John and Revelation written.
100 Death of the apostle John.

***Above:** The great fire of Rome in AD 64.*

***Above:** Paul imprisoned in Rome, shortly before his execution. "... I am now ready to be offered, and the time of my departure is at hand ... I have fought a good fight, I have finished my course, I have kept the faith: ..." (2 Timothy 4:6–8)*

Bible, it is thought possible that he was eventually released, and may have made his long-planned missionary journey to Spain.

The Bible tells us nothing about the ultimate fate of the apostles. All but John probably died violently, as martyrs. The traditional story is of Paul's execution by beheading in Rome, where Peter, after undocumented travels also met his fate, according to tradition crucified upside-down, having told his captors that he was unworthy to die in the same manner as Jesus. These executions probably took place about AD 64/65, following the great fire in Rome, when the Emperor Nero used the Christian community as a scapegoat. John, the last of the fellowship that had received the Holy Spirit in 33, lived longest, dying probably about the end of the first century.

***Above:** The vision of John. He hears a voice saying: "I am Alpha and Omega, the first and the last ..." (Revelation 1:11) and he sees the Son of Man amid seven candlesticks – "I am he that liveth, and was dead; and behold, I am alive for evermore, Amen; and have the keys of hell and of death." (Revelation 1:18)*